Metrics for Project Management

FORMALIZED APPROACHES

Metrics for Project Management

FORMALIZED APPROACHES

Parviz F. Rad

Ginger Levin

MANAGEMENTCONCEPTS

ᴦᴦᴦ
MANAGEMENTCONCEPTS

8230 Leesburg Pike, Suite 800
Vienna, VA 22182
(703) 790-9595
Fax: (703) 790-1371
www.managementconcepts.com

Printed in the United States of America

Library of Congress Cataloging-in-Publication Data

Rad, Parviz F., 1942–
    Metrics for project management: formalized approaches/Parviz F. Rad, Ginger Levin.
        p. cm.
    Includes bibliographical references and index.
    ISBN 1-56726-166-3 (pbk.)
    1. Project management—Quality control. 2. Performance standards. 3. Work measurement. I. Levin, Ginger. II. Title.

HD69.P75R334 2005
658.4'013—dc22

                                        2005049641

About the Authors

Parviz F. Rad, PhD, PE, CCE, PMP, is an independent project management consultant. He holds an MSc from Ohio State University and a PhD from Massachusetts Institute of Technology. He has over 35 years of professional experience, during which he has served in governmental, industrial, and academic capacities. He has participated in project management activities and in the development and enhancement of quantitative tools in project management in a multitude of disciplines, including software development, construction, and pharmaceutical research. He has authored and coauthored more than 60 publications in the areas of engineering and project management. Dr. Rad is the former Editor of the *Project Management Journal*.

Ginger Levin, DPA, is a senior consultant in project management with more than 30 years of experience. She is also an adjunct professor for the University of Wisconsin-Platteville in its Master of Science in Project Management program and serves as the university's program specialist in project management. Dr. Levin received her doctorate in public administration and information systems technology from The George Washington University (GWU), where she received the outstanding dissertation award for her research on large organizations. She also has an MSA, with a concentration in information systems technology, from GWU and a BBA from Wake Forest University.

Dr. Rad and Dr. Levin are also the authors of *The Advanced Project Management Office* and *Achieving Project Management Success Using Virtual Teams*.

To My Son
Darius

PFR

To My Husband
Morris

GL

Table of Contents

CHAPTER 3: PROJECT PEOPLE METRICS. 93

Instruments

CHAPTER 4: ENTERPRISE METRICS 279

Preface

Forward-looking organizations that are progressive in strategic planning will continually strive to improve performance by sustaining success in all business and operational areas, including project management. In organizations where upper management values improved efficiency, a metrics program will be an essential business practice, as metrics address the long-term implications of every project within the context of the long-term strategies of an organization. Typically, a metrics program is a natural fit within an organization's Project Management Office (PMO).

A metrics program can help guide an organization toward informed decisions, as it provides indicators regarding the quality, adequacy, and progress of projects, processes, and products. Metrics can help the enterprise recognize the sum of its collective capabilities, ensuring that plans for producing and delivering products and services are consistently realistic, achievable, and attainable. Metrics also can link the efforts of individual team members with the overall success of the project, and ultimately with the success of the organization. Consequently, properly designed metrics can indirectly promote teamwork and improve team morale.

Metrics for Project Management: Formalized Approaches describes a comprehensive set of project management metrics. Recognizing that project metrics can involve multiple dimensions, it presents metrics in the categories of "things," "people," and "enterprise."

Chapter 1 highlights the need for a methodical, logical approach to metrics, the various utilities of metrics, and their limitations. Chapter 2 describes tools that can be used to gauge the success of the project team in handling project issues such as cost, scope, duration, and performance. The chapter also highlights critical success factors.

Chapter 3 enumerates the instruments available for assessing the motivation, performance, and behavior of team members, based on the assumption that these attributes influence how team members perform their project-related functions. Chapter 4 discusses metrics that assess organizational capabilities and collective enterprise project management performance. Enterprise issues include project management maturity and project portfolio management. Chapter 4 also discusses the influence of the PMO on project performance.

Finally, Chapter 5 presents the considerations involved in establishing a metrics program. In particular, it describes a methodology for selecting the most appropriate suite of metrics and developing an implementation schedule.

Chapters 2 through 5 each closes with a unique set of instruments designed to help readers implement a metrics program within their own organization. These instruments are necessarily broad but are easily adaptable to any organization's unique needs.

Parviz F. Rad

Ginger Levin

Introduction

Organizations that follow a management-by-projects approach develop a performance-based style and continually grow in sophistication in the area of project management. Their project management philosophy is formalized, methodical, and dependent on practices that are objective and consistent. Project management metrics are key elements in this process, focusing on portfolio management, progress management, process improvement, and benchmarking. Organizational strategic objectives guide the selected focus of the metrics system, which in turn defines the structure of the measurement activities. In addition, metrics serve as historical benchmarks for purposes of future performance evaluation, with the expectation of facilitating continuous improvements.

Many organizations have used metrics for years, particularly in the areas of finance and manufacturing, but especially in those operations considered to be recurring in nature. These organizations know that metrics systems help improve the rate at which they achieve their business goals. Metrics also can identify important events and trends, helping guide these organizations toward informed decisions in all specialty areas, but particularly in project management.

Implementing a metrics system can help facilitate improvements in project success measures such as scope, quality, cost, schedule, and client satisfaction. Therefore, most project management professionals believe that enlightened organizations must implement a full complement of project life-cycle metrics in all branches of their organization where project accomplishment is part of the strategic mission.

In particular, sound metrics practices are essential to major project management activities such as project planning, monitoring, and control. Consistent tools and procedures, used by competent personnel, lead to lower overall project costs and increased corporate profits. Moreover, the span of the utility of metrics should go beyond scope-cost-schedule; metrics should be used in data collection as well as in predictive models. The scope-cost-schedule indices should always be addressed, however, as they represent the client's vantage point.

Benchmarking is rapidly becoming a popular mechanism for process improvement within enlightened organizations. However, effective benchmarking requires a system for gathering and refining data on all facets of the organization, particularly on projects. If upper management is focused on achieving improved efficiency, a metrics program becomes a necessary business practice.

A good metrics system is one that contributes to the right decisions in a timely manner based on fact rather than feeling (Augustine and Schroeder 1999). The most effective metrics programs are those in which the metrics are tailored to the organization's important issues and strategic objectives.

A well-planned set of metrics can help the enterprise recognize the level of sophistication of its collective capabilities, thus making organizational plans for producing and delivering products and services consistently realistic and achievable. It is paradoxical that the same financial considerations that might tempt organizations to abandon an extensive formalized metrics system are the very ones that help organizations realize cost-saving benefits through decreased expenses and increased profits.

Metrics can be collected and used throughout all phases and facets of project management. Metrics can measure the status, effectiveness, and progress of project activities to gauge the contribution of a project to the organization. Metrics also can serve as the basis for clear, objective communications with project stakeholders.

Ideally, and to offer more sophisticated capabilities for project tracking and control, project management tools should be integrated with business processes. In addition, metrics can promote teamwork and improve team morale by linking efforts of individual team members with the overall success of the project and, ultimately, the success of the organization.

Success in project management is contingent on an organization's capacity to assess project status realistically and predict performance accurately. Accurate performance forecasts can, in turn, be used to meet commitments relative to products and services. Metrics also can be used to determine the health of organizational processes affecting the successful conduct of projects.

Finally, some metrics can serve as barometers of organizational project management maturity. To that end, groups of metrics can be used to show where an organization stands in terms of the sophistication with which the collective project teams handle any of the project management knowledge areas.

ADVANTAGES OF METRICS-BASED PROJECT MANAGEMENT

To support all project management functions, such as project selection and project portfolio management, metrics need to be integrated into project life-cycle processes. A properly designed metrics program can ensure that the organization continues to pursue the right projects, even when organizational and environmental changes occur on a day-to-day basis during the life of these projects. Admittedly, some of these unplanned, unexpected changes present new opportunities for efficiency and success; however, positive unexpected events are rare.

Ideally, the underlying objective of a project metrics system is to provide accurate, verifiable information that can be used for improved performance of the enterprise's project management capability. One major advantage of a well-crafted, formalized metrics program is that its components provide unbiased testimony on the status of particular issues significant to the performance monitoring process. Such unbiased, objective data are necessary when dealing with divisional managers or clients who need to substantiate claims and requests. Probably the most significant advantage of a metrics system is that it makes explicit those items that are usually implicit in the decision-making process.

A good metrics system also can help formalize the rationale for making decisions by making available the expertise, knowledge, and wisdom of experienced project managers to all project management practitioners within the organization. This objective can be achieved through a metrics system that encompasses models and indices that, by design, provide accurate, unbiased information for project planning, execution, and monitoring. The availability of such data assists team members in minimizing project cost, shortening project duration, improving deliverable quality, and maximizing client satisfaction. Other goals of metrics system modules include refining the estimating processes for cost and duration, improving the project delivery process, handling unusual and unplanned project events better, enhancing communications, improving responsiveness, and achieving greater client satisfaction.

With the aid of an effective metrics system, each project can become an opportunity for learning that benefits the entire organization. Even failed projects hold potential for learning. There is no question that the cost of mistakes might be painfully high. However, if the circumstances and sequence of events are carefully documented, they constitute a rich data source of ways to avoid similar mistakes in future projects. Careful documentation also can provide insight into the current level of sophistication of the organization's project management processes.

A well-crafted metrics program can help identify areas where processes and procedures are exemplary and should continue to be followed. Likewise, this same metrics system can identify those processes in which improvement is needed. Finally, the metrics system can highlight those areas in which new processes are required.

With projects increasingly becoming a way of life for many enterprises, the organizational benefits of logical project management achieved through metrics-based project management methodologies, tools, and techniques are easily demonstrated. To assist in identifying a guiding example for such a self-appraisal, the company should look to other organizations that have already implemented a sophisticated, successful metrics system and borrow and adapt from its components.

As this new metrics system is being developed, or as it is becoming more sophisticated, it is possible to provide definitive answers to questions that executives in organizations often ask, such as:

• Does the organization normally achieve the results planned?

• Does the organization regularly achieve the desired return on investment?

• Are the projects selected for implementation aligned with the organization's strategic objectives?

• Do the selected projects support the organization's business needs and objectives?

• Are project objectives being met?

• Are client success criteria being met?

• Are projects considered strategic assets?

The answers to the questions not only respond to management inquiries but also warn of forthcoming problems. This warning mechanism enables the organization to avoid, or at least manage, emerging problems. Early diagnosis affords the organization the chance to turn the problem into an opportunity, at least some of the time.

The optimum solution to emerging project challenges lies in the use of a metrics system that supports timely dissemination of project information and improved communication (Lucero and Hall 2001). In turn, improved communication leads to better performance by project teams. Ultimately, improved performance translates to more successful projects.

Notably, metrics by themselves do not impart any value to the organization, because they do little, if anything, to resolve the issue being monitored. Metrics do not make decisions, people do; metrics simply provide the foundation and rationale for decisions. Thus, the return on investment of a metrics system derives from the actions that project professionals take to manage the issue at hand.

It is a somewhat common practice, albeit a short-sighted one, that organizations experiencing poor cash flows or low profits will minimize expenditures for things perceived to be luxuries. For functional organizations, two activities that might appear to be luxuries—although in reality they are excellent investments—are research and training. Similarly, some project-oriented organizations will tend to minimize and discourage detailed project planning and comprehensive project closeout in the face of difficult economic times.

Again, such cost-cutting measures are often counterproductive, as the short-term benefit of conducting these two activities is the success of individual projects. The long-term impact relates to the overall project management maturity of the organization.

Although some metrics might seem inappropriate or superfluous in less mature organizations, metrics can provide benefits to all organizations independent of their level of sophistication in project management. Some organizations use formalized, detailed metrics only for major projects, even though metrics allow the execution details of all projects to be predicted. Ideally, metrics should be applied across multiple projects, all organizational divisions, and the entire span of the project life cycle to benefit the organization's goals.

WHAT IS A METRIC?

In the context of project management activities, a suite of metrics can offer a glimpse into the full range of expectations of a particular deliverable item or the tasks that would produce that deliverable. Alternately, metrics can gauge the status of a deliverable item relative to expectations for scope, cost, and delivery date. In the latter case, metrics are aimed at small, measurable attributes that have a predictive or comparative capability.

The vast majority of project metrics focus on "things" attributes, which are quantitative and thus measurable. As "people" issues of projects move to the forefront of project management concerns, an increasing number of metrics deal with people attributes, which have behavioral characteristics such as morale, satisfaction, loyalty, trust, and leadership.

The assignment of ratings, numbers, and ranks for the latter category can be based on questionnaires or instruments that characterize and quantify selected attributes of team members, teams, or even the organization as a whole. Such quantification also can be based on the experience and judgment of a seasoned project manager entrusted to make such observations.

Metrics might measure particular attributes of the project team directly or indirectly. For example, a metric can measure Monday absenteeism, which, in turn, is an indirect metric for team morale (Neuendorf 2002).

When dealing with attributes that appear to defy measurement and ranking, it is important to use a binary metric for that attribute, one that signals the presence or absence of a project management feature or function. For example, one index of a metrics system could test the presence or absence of a formalized project estimating process using conceptual estimating techniques. Another index could measure the level of team participation in project review meetings, without attempting to explain or modify it.

Sometimes, a project metric is a numerical value that is computed from a collection of several pieces of data (e.g., earned value, percentage complete). In these cases, the resulting metric inherits the precision, accuracy, and validity of the primary indices that were used to derive it.

The individual indices and models that comprise a metrics system are sometimes cited independently, but usually they are presented in an integrated fashion, primarily because they are somewhat intertwined (Thamhain 1996). Almost always, multiple indices for project performance tend to produce synergistic results that can be used more reliably to make informed decisions about project direction, the program, the portfolio, and ultimately the organization's strategic direction.

Organizations can be classified as immature relative to project management if they have not yet transitioned to formal project management. Ordinarily, these organizations tend to view technical expertise in the project's subject matter as a fully sufficient skill for becoming a project manager. More than likely, these organizations have few, if any, procedures and metrics dealing with project management. If these organizations have any metrics at all, they tend to address project things, such as cost, schedule, and scope.

A slightly more sophisticated organization might have a full suite of procedures and metrics related to project things. These semi-sophisticated organizations generally accept that, if things issues are handled and measured properly, acceptable and reasonable success will be achieved. More mature organizations have metrics and procedures dealing with project people and project things, based on the assumption that people make projects happen. Thus, additional procedures and metrics might include human behavioral issues such as motivation, conflict management, professional responsibility, leadership, and trust (see Figure 1–1).

The final stage of sophistication is achieved when the project management processes and associated metrics also include issues that define the environment in which the project must operate, such as training, resource allocation, standard procedures, and overall organizational support.

Along this spectrum of maturity levels, all organizations use metrics that deal with the things aspects of the project such as cost, schedule, and scope. The difference in spectrum placement derives from the extent to which the things issues are supported, enhanced, and elevated by strengths in the areas of people and enterprise issues.

Figure 1-1
Project Management: Stages of Sophistication

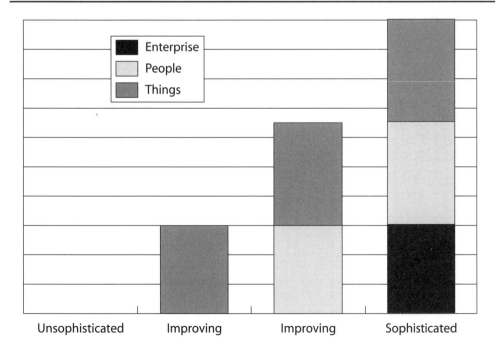

Projects will not thrive, and often will not survive, in organizations that are indifferent, or possibly hostile, to projects. Conversely, projects will achieve their highest level of success in organizations that are friendly toward, and supportive of, projects. Mature organizations will have metrics and procedures that define all three sets of issues that relate to projects (i.e., things, people, and enterprise).

Figure 1–2 presents brief descriptions of the project management maturity levels following a staged model. There is a distinct interrelationship, although not necessarily a linear one, between the levels of project management sophistication and traditional maturity levels (Rad and Levin 2002).

Figure 1–3 shows a stylized depiction of the relationship between maturity and the importance an organization places on people issues and organizational issues. Organizations that are at Level 1 (Initial) tend to support very few things-related metrics as part of their project management practices. In these organizations, proper handling of the technical content of the project is the primary project management concern. By contrast, Level 5 (Leader) organizations not only support competency in technical content but also value it in things, people, and enterprise issues.

The smallest component of a metrics system is an index, such as total cost or promised delivery date. A collection of indices, in a simple grouping or in a complex mathematical relationship, comprises a model. A model quantifies a multifaceted feature of a project, such as the components of a parametric estimating model or an earned value model. A full-scale metrics system contains many models and indices.

Figure 1-2
Project Management Maturity Level Descriptions

Level 5: Leader
• Quantitative data used to conduct continuous improvement

Level 4: Advanced
• Quantified performance data consistently captured

Level 3: Evolved
• Meaningful metrics implemented on most projects

Level 2: Developed
• Isolated implementation of metrics occurs in projects

Level 1: Initial
• Inconsistent procedures and ad hoc guidelines used by project teams

Figure 1-3
Maturity Level and Metrics Focus

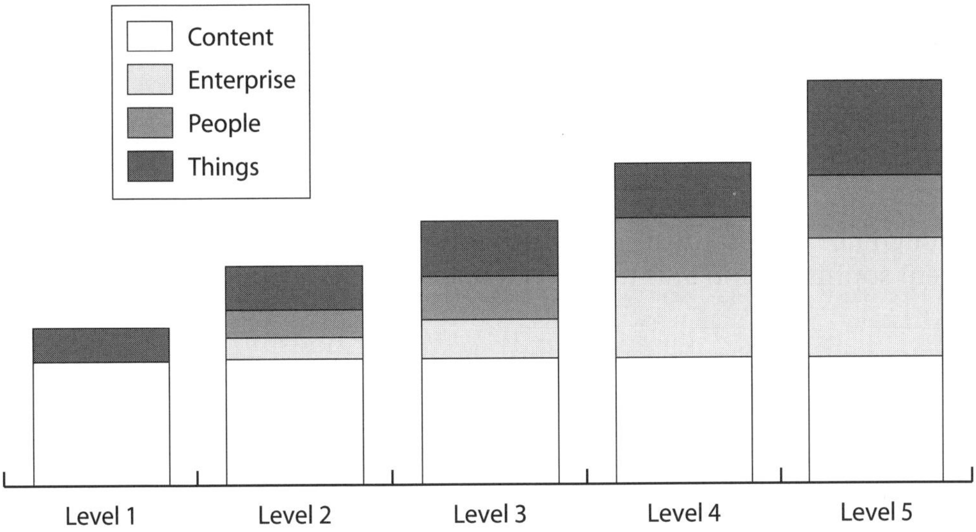

METRICS CATEGORIES

Discussing project metrics as things, people, and enterprise allows the various perspectives of the project, the project team, and the organization to be isolated, magnified, and elucidated. The metrics included in each category can be a blend of individual indices and models. The lines of demarcation between the categories are not precise, but the categorization allows the reader to visualize the concepts and areas in more detail, by virtue of being symbolically isolated as a distinct area.

Things attributes address the performance of the project team in tangible terms of efficiency, productivity, and deliverables. Things attributes include topics such as progress monitoring, procedure enhancement, historical data collection, and best practice development (see Figure 1–4). People attributes address team members' interrelationships with one another and focus on teamwork issues such as trust, collaboration, competency, communication, and conflict. Enterprise metrics address the environment in which the project team operates. These attributes describe an organization's friendliness toward projects, involvement of project teams in the organization's strategies, and recognition of the project management discipline by the organization.

The literature includes several other categorization patterns for project management metrics (Okkonen 2002), even though they involve the

Figure 1-4
Focus of Metrics

Enterprise
- Technical and business policy
- Investment decisions and analysis
- Organizational process improvement
- Project planning guidelines
- Normative performance baselines
- Performance-based guidelines
- Organizational norms and benchmarks

People
- Team formation
- Conflict management
- Collaboration
- Motivation
- Communication
- Diversity

Things
- Estimating and planning
- Performance tracking
- Tradeoff analysis
- Resource management

same universe of metrics. Ultimately, the decision how to categorize project management metrics in a particular organization should take into account the culture and operational practices of the individual organization in light of prevailing strategies and objectives.

Metrics bring consistency and formality to project management. With metrics, important project decisions can be made on an informed basis. In essence, metrics bring objectivity to the tools for monitoring project progress and help advance the organization by allowing uniformity, accuracy, and repeatability.

CHAPTER 2

Project Things Metrics

The quantitative facets of projects, also referred to as project "things," are the visible, tangible signs of the implementation—and eventual success—of the project. Until the 1990s, most project management metrics systems focused primarily on the "things" attributes of projects, particularly aspects involving schedule, cost, and resource utilization. This outlook still predominates in organizations that have not advanced beyond the first two levels of a staged maturity scale.

However, since the 1990s, many new, more comprehensive project management tools and techniques have evolved. In fact, project things now represent just one of three sets of project attributes that need to be quantitatively planned and monitored. The other attributes deal with people and the enterprise.

Generally speaking, project performance indices provide feedback on activities that lead to the project scope and, to the extent to which these activities are aligned with project objectives, client expectations and the organization's strategic objectives. It is fair to say that things metrics characterize tools that assess the progress and success of projects almost as if the project processes run by themselves without the intervention of people. However, to be accurate, the success of things issues reflects the success of project team members. Yet, when the focus of metrics is exclusively on things, the facets of the project measured are different. In essence, things metrics measure the health of a project. (Again, people and enterprise issues affect project health, but people and enterprise attributes are quantified separately.)

Things metrics quantify and measure cost, schedule, scope, quality, and the project's overall success in meeting client needs. If the organization already has one of several variations (Rad and Levin 2002) of a Project Management Office (PMO), the project functions of the PMO will directly benefit projects (see Figure 2–1). The enterprise functions of the PMO will directly benefit the enterprise, but they will indirectly benefit projects as well.

Figure 2-1
Functions of the Project Management Office

Project-Focused Functions
- Augment
  - Provide resources to support the project team if key areas of expertise are needed
- Mentor
  - Work side by side to assist team members
- Consult
  - Provide assistance upon request, including review of key data

Enterprise-Oriented Functions
- Promote
  - Advocate a project management culture by showing the tangible benefits of a corporate strategy
- Archive
  - Establish a knowledge repository or clearinghouse of project information
- Practice
  - Distribute project management best practices, procedures, and guidelines
- Train
  - Provide ongoing training in portfolio, program, and project management

---

The metrics relating to the project functions of the PMO, and even those relating to the enterprise functions of the PMO, have a major things component. Thus, most metrics that measure the sophistication or effectiveness of the project and enterprise categories of PMO functions also will quantify the success of project things issues.

CLIENT REQUIREMENTS

Requirements can be described as the articulation of a client's wishes, which often are expressed in terms of performance, such as speed, error rate, or processing rate. Requirements also can be defined in terms of deliverables such as software, hardware, machinery, or structures.

The project scope document represents the team's response to a client's wishes. This response is usually expressed in the details of deliverable attributes and through the means and modes of crafting the deliverable. Deliverable attributes can take the form of physical size, mechanical features, software modules, and test performance targets. (Instrument 2–A) Metrics can quantify the formality and sophistication of responding to a client's needs, as expressed in plans for managing cost, scope, quality, risk, communications, etc.

The description of project objectives should include attributes and characteristics of the deliverable, such as physical size, capacity, length, height, or strength. The objectives also should specify an identified level of performance, a prescribed level of quantified reliability, a critical speed to be attained, a quantified level of system availability, the ability to handle a given number of transactions within a defined period of time, or the ability to provide a certain level of quantified client satisfaction.

Other deliverables and objectives could include physical tolerance, physical speed, software tolerance limit, software processing speed, and software processing accuracy. Additional deliverable attributes could include indicators of surface texture, quantified robustness features, software error frequency, quantified measures of user friendliness of the software, and quantified personnel skills.

Usually, the information describing project requirements includes, and sometimes overlaps, the business case of the project and the scope definition of the project's deliverable. Although requirements are client wishes that dictate scope and quality of the deliverable, requirements and scope are not synonymous.

The project manager must draw a clear distinction between the project's business case and the description of the project's deliverables (see Figure 2–2). Because there should be a close and distinct correlation between the project plan and the requirements, the project manager must be vigilant in removing any real or perceived inconsistencies between client requirements and the project plan. Then, the project manager must carry this a step further by distinguishing among deliverables, constraints, and assumptions. (Instrument 2–B)

During the life of a project, requirements will change for a variety of reasons. Accordingly, it is necessary to track differences between planned and developed requirements by assessing the status of each component of the

Figure 2-2
Continuum from Strategic Vision to Project Deliverable

- Strategic vision
- Business needs
- Performance requirements
- Required functions
- Project objectives
- Scope of deliverable
- Quality of deliverable
- Specifications for the deliverable

deliverable as it moves through the life-cycle activities. In addition, metrics for requirement volatility, such as the percentage of requirements that are changed, can be prepared by maintaining a detailed history of the requirements changes and the rationale for each one. Finally, one reality of project work is the inevitability of defects in the deliverable and the concomitant need for rework to correct them.

Thus, project progress documents must track activities conducted to make changes in the deliverable in order to resolve any physical or performance defects. (Instruments 2–C and 2–D) Further, there is a potential risk, especially in new product development or in systems development projects, that the resulting product will not perform fully in line with its intended purpose. Thus, the relevance and applicability of the deliverable must be continually verified.

During the early stages of the project, the project manager should prepare a statement of detailed project requirements for client approval and signoff. The frequency and nature of the requests for change must be tracked to assess the completeness of the process for analyzing the requirements and defining the scope. If both the requirements analysis process and the scope definition process are comprehensive, there probably will be fewer change requests during the life of the project.

In turn, a comprehensive scope definition will reduce the number of unplanned quality audits and project reviews. Thus, the audit should be considered an effective quality assurance tool for the project manager, rather than a "gotcha game" (Levin 1998). Using these proactive processes, defects detected during acceptance tests should decrease, as should the time and cost required to fix them.

Documents that record the evolution of project requirements and project scope allow direct or indirect tracking of the number of requirements changes made throughout the project. This tracking enables verification of whether changes were prompted by a need to define client requirements that were not detailed initially, or whether they can be attributed to significant changes in client requirements during the life of the project. Proper metrics also allow assessment of the number of meetings held with stakeholders to identify requirements and the extent of stakeholder participation, as indicated by the number of stakeholders who signed off on the project requirements.

Monitoring project requirements activities involves quantifying the progression of requirements from concept to formulation, to design, to testing, and finally to acceptance. This process ensures that there is always an approved and current set of requirements at any given point in the project life cycle, even when the client's needs or the project environment changes. Also, defining and redefining project requirements in a methodical fashion increases the likelihood that the resulting product will meet the required functionality.

Metrics associated with scope definition address the nature and size of the project and possibly the level of complexity of the change control plans. The number of changes to project scope, the desired deliverable quality, assumptions, and constraints can form the basis for a suite of metrics. Further, the completeness of the scope statement should be monitored during the initiation stage of the project, perhaps even through the execution stage. As an indirect measure of overall project success, it is possible to devise a suite of metrics for timeliness in resolving ambiguities of the project scope and for the number of times that scope issues had to be escalated to the project's executive management.

Finally, a project is not considered complete until the client officially accepts it. Therefore, client signoff on project deliverables must be obtained, signifying that most, if not all, client requirements were met with the deliverable. More important, this document should explicitly highlight the extent to which the deliverable meets the client's current or stated needs.

Planning is an iterative process throughout the life of each project, and plans are expected to change as new information is acquired. Accordingly, it is important to assess whether templates used for planning are sufficient or if changes are needed.

Metrics can be formulated to assess plan revisions necessitated by changes to subsidiary plans, such as the Procurement Management Plan, the Staffing Management Plan, or the Quality Management Plan. Further, for purposes of future projects, it often is helpful to track the extent to which stakeholders were involved in the planning process. An additional metric, tracking the specific contributions of stakeholders in developing these plans, can be extremely useful in characterizing the project environment.

DETAILED PROJECT PLANS

The project scope document is the formal project description developed in response to the client's needs. (Instrument 2–E) The Work Breakdown Structure (WBS) is a useful tool for graphically depicting project elements and providing a framework for the project (see Figure 2–3). If it is prepared to the appropriate level of detail, and particularly if it is oriented toward

Figure 2-3
Work Breakdown Structure

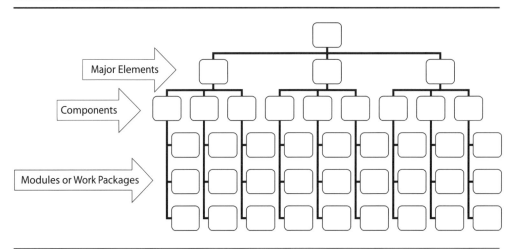

deliverables, the WBS can accurately describe the scope of work. In turn, a clear scope statement can serve as the basis for detailed project planning, methodical project execution, accurate responsibility assignment, and informed progress tracking.

Information for preparing the WBS comes from the project's scope statement, historical files of past projects, and other files containing the original and final project objectives of previous similar projects. Given that project information is normally developed on a gradual basis, the WBS should be treated as an evolving document that is updated throughout the project life cycle.

The WBS provides a common framework for conducting specific tasks related to project elements. When logically constructed, it enhances monitoring, controlling, and reporting processes. (Instrument 2–F) For example, a WBS facilitates the process of integrating project plans for time, resources, and quality. An effective WBS encourages a systematic planning process, reduces the possibility of omitting key project elements, and simplifies the project by dividing it into manageable units.

When the WBS is used as the common basis for scheduling and estimating, it facilitates communication among the professionals implementing the project. In fact, methodical use of the WBS ultimately leads to more effective schedules and estimates. Although the WBS is not a metric per se, it can be used effectively to enhance estimates and schedules. (Instrument 2–G)

To develop a WBS, the project must first be divided into three to nine components, with seven considered typical. In turn, each of these elements is divided into smaller, identifiable modules. This process is repeated until the project deliverable has been divided into many manageable, identifiable units. A metric can be established to assess the effectiveness of the WBS in facilitating project activities. In addition, a set of metrics can measure the effectiveness of developing a WBS template for use on future projects.

Similarly, in-house resources should be cataloged in a methodical manner by creating a Resource Breakdown Structure (RBS). The RBS tabulates the resources available to, or needed in, projects of a certain type. Developing the RBS involves dividing the pool of resources into entities specific enough that the RBS can serve as a shopping catalog for the resources needed to craft each WBS element.

The RBS is developed by first dividing all the project resources into major categories such as labor, material, equipment, and tools. Then, each category is broken down into its logical components until the lowest-level element is a specific identifiable specialty (see Figure 2–4). The RBS is not a metric per se, but it provides the foundation for and means by which methodical cost analysis can be conducted using logical categorizations and summaries.

Developing a detailed project estimate begins at the lowest level of the WBS. Here, the cost of each element is calculated by multiplying the quantity of each required resource by its unit cost, which is obtained from the RBS (see Figure 2–5).

This type of cost estimate is called a "bottom-up estimate," and it is derived from detailed information contained in the WBS and RBS at the time

Figure 2-4
Project Resource Breakdown Structure

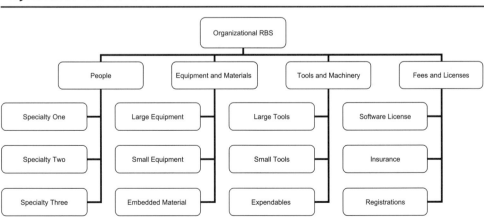

Figure 2-5
Bottom-Up Estimating

- Determine how much of any resource is required for each Work Breakdown Structure element.
- Summarize resource requirements and their associated costs to the intermediate elements and ultimately to the project.

    Thus, at any level of the project, a list of resources, their amount, and their cost is available.

    Likewise, the total demand for each resource over the entire project can be determined by summing the resource requirements along the Resource Breakdown Structure lines.

of the estimate. This calculation clearly indicates the category of the re-source, its intensity, and its duration. For example, if a project needs three chemists for a period of four days to create a chemical compound, then the category is chemist, the intensity is three workers, the duration is four days, and the effort is 12 worker-days. At a unit cost of $300 per worker per day, the cost is $3,600.

While total project cost could be computed by adding all these costs together, doing so is somewhat unwieldy and is not reflective of higher-level information that is easily obtained. Therefore, the next step involves moving up a level to determine—by simple addition—the total quantity of resources necessary for all elements on the next WBS level. The process repeats, proceeding from bottom to top, until each element of the WBS is tagged with the total resources required, grouped by resource category.

Once the calculations are extended to Level Zero, the project's total cost has been determined, as has the cost of all intermediate elements of the WBS. In addition to cost, the resource utilization values of all intermediate components defined in the WBS are available.

As in any estimating method, it is important to check the estimate against experiential data and the subjective knowledge of project professionals. The first key question to ask is, "Is the estimate of total project cost reasonable?" Since inaccurate estimates often result from inadvertent omissions of key elements in the WBS and the RBS, correction of the estimate primarily comprises filling logical gaps in the WBS. In addition, refining the WBS, by way of enhancing the estimates of the current elements, adds precision to the project estimate. (Instrument 2–H)

The WBS also serves as the foundation for the network diagram and the project schedule. Before developing the project schedule, the project manager and project team must define the logical sequence of WBS elements in a precedence table. This allows the network to be populated with anticipated dates for starting and completing project components.

Schedule metrics can be based on the most detailed activities of the project or its aggregate components. Using WBS terminology, schedules can be developed for the lowest level of the WBS or any one of its intermediate levels.

A detailed schedule network is not a metric in and of itself. However, it provides the foundation for metrics that assess the pace and productivity of the project. Scheduling-related instruments deal with formalized procedures in developing a logical sequence for project elements, identifying the critical path of project execution, and developing a prediction for the project delivery date.

Combining the predictions for resource expenditure with resource cost and sequencing of activities provides a wealth of project information. The combination of these indicators provides a resource demand forecast and a cash flow forecast. Then, based on these results, and in light of organizational constraints for cash flow and resource availability, it is possible to adjust project plans by reducing resource demand or, in rare cases, making organizational adjustments in favor of project progress.

CONCEPTUAL PLANS

As discussed, the most accurate, reliable project estimate can be developed when all WBS elements have been identified with a reasonable degree of reliability and when the RBS has been defined with an adequate degree of specificity. However, the amount of information required for a detailed estimate will not be available until a major portion of the project has been designed and implemented. Nevertheless, project stakeholders must have indications of project cost and duration in order to approve initial project implementation.

Project authorization decisions necessitate a preliminary estimate, even though this estimate is compiled prior to many essential actions, including clarification of project objectives, definition of project scope, full articulation of requirements, clear definition of functions, and formulation of system architecture. Thus, a tentative, abbreviated project plan must be developed during the project's inception in order to formulate a rough estimate of cost and duration for purposes of preliminary decisions. Then, as information regarding the project deliverable is enhanced, a more reliable project estimate can be developed. Depending on the organization, the first estimate is sometimes called preliminary, conceptual, or order of magnitude.

In the absence of detailed project information, project managers use a variety of tools and techniques to formulate estimates. These tools and techniques are usually based on models with proven success in previous estimating efforts on this or other projects. These models use mathematical expressions, ranging from simple to complex, to estimate cost, duration, and resource demands of one single activity, an assembly, or an entire project as a function of one or more input variables.

Estimating models compute the values of a set of dependent outputs as a function of the values of a set of independent inputs, which might initially be sparse in amount and low in accuracy. The selection of the technique depends on organizational policies, the project manager's experience, and the amount of information available to the project manager at the time of the estimate. The techniques often used for preliminary project estimates are ratio, analogous, range, modular, and parametric (Rad 2002) estimating techniques (see Figure 2–6).

The timing of the estimate affects how much information is available and the degree to which the information is reliable. As a result, the accuracy of available information will determine the level of sophistication of the estimate.

When little project information is available, the only feasible tool is the analogous estimate, or the ratio estimate, which focuses on the entire project. When more information becomes available, then a parametric tool can be used to estimate the WBS elements down to Level Two or Level Three. Finally, when enough information is available, a detailed bottom-up estimate can be prepared (see Figure 2–7).

Figure 2-6
Techniques for Rough Estimates

Ratio Estimating
- Estimate the cost and duration of the new project on the basis of one of its quantified attributes, which is multiplied or divided by an empirical factor

Analogous Estimating
- Estimate the cost of the new project from the cost of previous similar projects, using an empirical formula
- Estimate the duration of the new project from the duration of previous similar projects, using an empirical formula

Range Estimating
- Provide the possible range of the detailed estimate of the project
- Use a variation of this method for a most likely estimate, sometimes called three-point estimating

Parametric Estimating
- Estimate the cost and duration of the new project from a combination of quantified attributes of the project, through formulas that use these attributes to calculate cost, duration, and resource demand

Figure 2-7
Choice of the Model

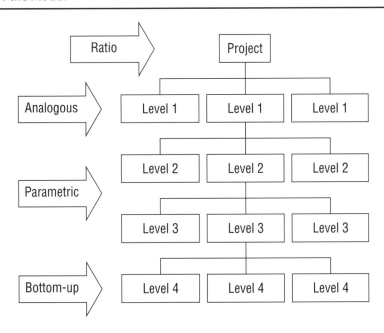

The ratio estimating technique is premised on the existence of a linear relationship between project cost and duration and one or more basic features of the proposed deliverable. The basic features can be related to either physical attributes or performance characteristics. Although ratio estimating is deceptively simple, given an appropriate base of historical data, it can be a powerful tool in developing quick estimates for prospective projects. For example, experience has shown that the cost of major turbines and generators in a power generation plant is nearly 30% of the total cost of the plant. Likewise, in a construction project, the total cost of the project is twice that of the materials and embedded equipment.

Further examples include: high-level design of a systems development project is nearly 30% of the total cost of the project; only 20% of the cost and effort of a systems project is spent in coding; 75% of the cost of a systems development project is labor; and engineering design of a facility is nearly 8% of the project's total budget. In addition, extensive effort has been devoted to developing a relationship between the estimated lines of code, or the number of function points, and the total cost of a systems development project. However, this ratio is highly specific to the operating system and the system architecture.

The terms "parametric estimating" and "modular estimating" refer to two estimating models that are essentially quite similar in application, principle, and underlying structures. They possess different names because they come from different industries. For purposes of this book, "parametric estimating" is used to refer to both these techniques collectively (see Figure 2–8).

Models used for software and systems development projects use some or all of the following data in arriving at a tentative estimate for the project: system complexity, system size, personnel skill, resource availability, specificity of project objectives, clarity of requirements, operating system features, environmental characteristics, and the extent of new technologies involved in the project (see Figure 2–9). Models used for construction and industrial projects use the following data to predict project cost and duration: industry and project type, capacity and quantity, external and usable size, overall weight, project location, and the extent to which novel materials, tools, and techniques are required for the project (Rad 2002) (see Figure 2–10).

Among the most useful models for making conceptual estimates of the cost and duration of a project based on previous similar projects are the three-quarter rule, the square-root rule, and their modified counterparts (Rad 2002; Gates 1976) (see Figure 2–11). These techniques are premised

---

Figure 2-8
Modular and Parametric Models: Input Indices

Physical Characteristics
- Flow capacity
- Storage capacity
- Load capacity
- Amount of equipment
- Size of equipment
- Height
- Weight

Performance Attributes
- Speed
- Accuracy
- Error tolerance
- Reliability
- Friendliness
- User satisfaction

Figure 2-9
Estimate Parameters: Systems Development Projects

Input
- Reliability
- Database size
- Project complexity
- Error rate
- Number of queries
- Function points
- Labor skills

Output
- Analysis cost
- Implementation cost
- Transition cost
- Testing cost
- Labor cost
- Phase duration
- Project duration

Figure 2-10
Estimate Parameters: Construction and Industrial Projects

Input	Output
• Project type	• Design cost
• Roof type	• Structure cost
• Equipment type	• Equipment cost
• Frame material	• Labor cost
• Exterior material	• Needed crafts
• Ground conditions	• Crew size
• Desired floor space	• Phase duration
• Geographic location	• Project duration

on the existence of a mathematical power relationship between the ratios of cost, size, and duration.

Even when the historical files contain only one similar project, the equations presented in Figure 2–11 allow development of a tentative estimate of cost and duration, respectively. In addition, these techniques presume that data for several similar projects will follow a straight line on a log-log scale.

Therefore, in cases where some historical data are available for cost and capacity, a graph similar to that shown in Figure 2–12 can be constructed in order to plot the existing data on a log-log scale. In turn, once a pattern line is drawn through the existing data, the cost of future projects can be estimated by using the pattern line. Likewise, Figure 2–13 can be constructed from existing data for cost and duration, and its pattern line can be used to predict the duration of future projects if their total cost is known.

PROJECT QUALITY

Quality refers to physical attributes when thinking of quality control of deliverables. However, quality also can refer to those non-physical attri-

Figure 2-11
Analogous Estimating

Metrics
- Three-Quarter Rule
  $$C_p = C_e (S_p/S_e)^{.75}$$
- Square-Root Rule
  $$T_p = T_e (C_p/C_e)^{.5}$$

Variables
- $T_p\, T_e$ = Project Duration
- $C_p\, C_e$ = Cost
- $S_p\, S_e$ = Size or Capacity Index

p = proposed
e = existing

Figure 2-12
Modified Three-Quarter Rule: Estimating Cost from Capacity or Size

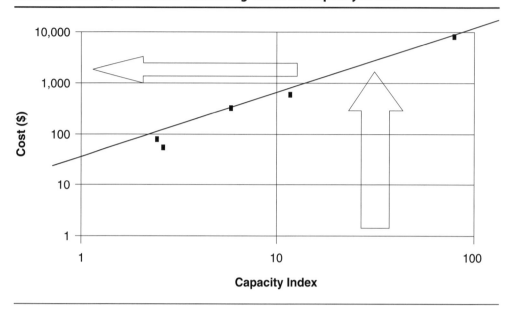

Capacity Index

Figure 2-13
Modified Square-Root Rule

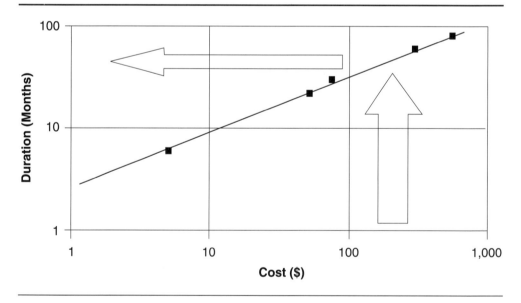

Cost ($)

butes that directly or indirectly result in client satisfaction. The continuum between these two somewhat different concepts has been variously called quality control, quality assurance, quality management, and total quality management (TQM). In other words, although quality control refers to the process of monitoring the physical quality of products, TQM refers to good business practices that result in client satisfaction because superior products and services were delivered. (Instrument 2–I)

The acronym TQM is sometimes used in service environments where no physical product is involved. For purposes of this book, quality refers to the physical attributes of the project components. However, planning for project quality should be more than a plan for spot-checking, or even full-scale measuring, of the physical quality of the end product. A formalized quality plan should include clearly stated criteria for each work package. In turn, the client should use these criteria during the evaluation and acceptance of the product or service. (Instrument 2–J)

For purposes of progress monitoring, review gates can be established at identifiable milestones to verify that the project deliverable meets its intended specifications before continuing further in the process. Quality metrics can be established to determine progress in meeting the objectives of these review gates, even before getting to the specific review gate. (Instrument 2–K) Metrics that fit this category could be used to track trends in defects in deliverable components, grouped by severity or status. The availability of these data will help the project team identify, research, and resolve quality issues in a timely manner.

The emphasis here should be on ways to ensure that the quality of the project deliverable is in line with client expectations. This is usually achieved by establishing an infrastructure that is conducive to producing consistently high-quality results through formalized procedures, relevant guidelines, and specialized training.

The literature identifies volatility of project scope and quality as the leading cause of implementation errors, and eventually, as the leading cause of variance from the project plan (Rad 2002). Thus, the success, or lack thereof, of scope and quality issues tends to overshadow project performance in other areas. Naturally, the client's satisfaction with scope and quality will be enhanced by the team's diligence in developing a detailed scope definition during the early stages of the project.

To that end, client satisfaction could be directly linked to the team's success in implementing a methodical procedure by which the scope is verified, modified, enhanced, and finalized. With respect to performance in cost or schedule, the client's perception of success is normally based on the original values, the final values, and the relative magnitude of the variance between the two. Given that some variance in cost and schedule is justified, it is only the unjustified portion that becomes the basis for judgments as to whether or not the project was a success relative to that specific attribute and by how much.

To achieve an in-depth understanding of client involvement and satisfaction, each client could be asked to complete a survey at the end of the project. This survey would address project performance in terms of all its requirements, the overall success in meeting those requirements, and the client's general satisfaction with the project deliverables.

To minimize the cost of quality in projects, the components of the cost of quality must first be identified. (Instrument 2–L) The two major categories of cost are those related to (1) prevention of defects and (2) remedy of failures if prevention efforts are insufficient. The cost of prevention includes costs related to training, process improvement, modeling, qualifying, certification, and inspections. The cost of defects includes the costs of error analysis, rework, modifications, recalls, and retesting. The annual enterprise cost of quality, in any of the preceding areas, gives a clear indication of whether new efforts in quality are necessary. (Instrument 2–M)

CONTRACTS

For many organizations, specific contracts may be awarded for selected project work packages. For others, outsourcing is the primary way in which business is conducted. Organizations that outsource an extensive amount of their development and expansion work tend to regard projects as a subset of the contracts with which these products are commissioned. As such, project performance is often viewed in terms of the legalities of the contract rather than the deliverables and business objectives that first motivated the project.

A more appropriate approach is to consider a contract as a way of commissioning project deliverables. Then, a contract becomes the legal instrument by which an organization acquires products and services from an outside source.

For project purposes, a contract is an administrative mechanism by which the project is conducted by personnel who reside outside the corporate boundaries of the performing organization. Under this mindset, the contract becomes subordinate to the project, and performance is viewed in project terms rather than contract terms.

The project team, working in conjunction with the organization's procurement department, can establish metrics to track each contractor's progress in meeting schedule, cost, and technical performance goals. Project contract documents comprise two major types: administrative and technical. The administrative part deals with the legal responsibilities of both parties and the processes and procedures for enforcing various contract clauses. The technical part deals with the technical content of the project. The technical content of the contract, and issues that directly affect the implementation pace of the deliverable, should be the focus of the project management metrics dealing with contracts.

There are two basic types of project contracts (see Figure 2–14). The first is the fixed-price or lump-sum contract, which requires detailed specifications. Usually, the contractor offering the lowest price is chosen. In this mode of contracting, the prospective contractor offers to deliver the specific project deliverable for a fixed price. The contractor guarantees the fixed price and thereby assumes all financial risk in implementing that project. That is, of course, if the initial set of client objectives and project specifications is spelled out with sufficient detail and if the project environment remains reasonably stable during the life of the project. Under ideal circumstances, this type of contract gives the contractor incentives to avoid waste, reduce costs, increase productivity, and improve profits.

The second type of contract is a cost-plus contract, under which the contractor is reimbursed for costs incurred in performing project activities.

Figure 2-14
Types of Contracts: Expanded

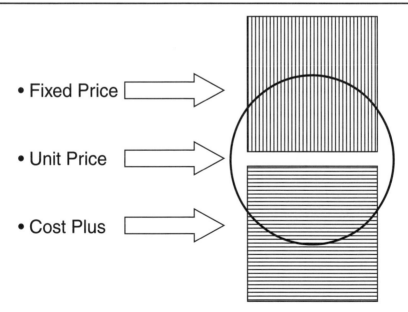

The contractor is also paid a fixed or variable fee. There are variations of this type of contract in which the fee is tied to performance-based incentives arising from early delivery or cost-cutting measures. Regardless, the client assumes a large portion of the project performance risk—and the financial risk—of the project in this type of contract.

Because of the obvious shortcomings of these two basic forms of contracts, a third category has emerged that incorporates some of the best features of the two while minimizing their shortcomings. Under this mode of contracting, the contactor quotes a price for each unit of each activity or deliverable. For example, under a unit pricing scheme, the client and the contractor might agree that the contractor will be paid $100 for each specialist hour, $2,000 for each personal computer, $35 for each foot of pulled network wire, etc. Aptly, this type of contract is called a unit-price contract.

In many ways, a unit-price contract is a compilation of hundreds of fixed-price contracts, thus allowing the client to change the overall scope with some ease. Sometimes this type of a contract is called a time and material contract.

Contractor performance is measured with two somewhat separate sets of indices. The first deals with project performance in terms of cost, schedule, and quality. These performance indices can compare the actual values of these attributes with their planned values. These indices also can evaluate the sophistication of a contractor's plans for successfully completing project activities and the contractor's expertise in interpreting the technical requirements of the project.

The second set of indices deals with the contractor's behavior in terms of responsiveness to a client's request for minor scope changes, more timeliness in communications, and greater efficiency in resolving conflicts and ambiguities (see Figure 2–15). The availability of such indices, with or without a model, enables clients to provide feedback to contractors as to whether or not their expectations were met. In many ways, the people issues of the external project, such as a subjective perception of project success, are very similar to those of an internal project. Thus, many people metrics of internal projects are applicable to outsourced projects.

MONITORING PROJECT PROGRESS

Most project indices relate to the monitoring phase of the project, although the foundations for these indices must be formed during the planning phase. Metrics can be used to assess tradeoff decisions among the three

Figure 2-15
Contractor Evaluation Indices: Example

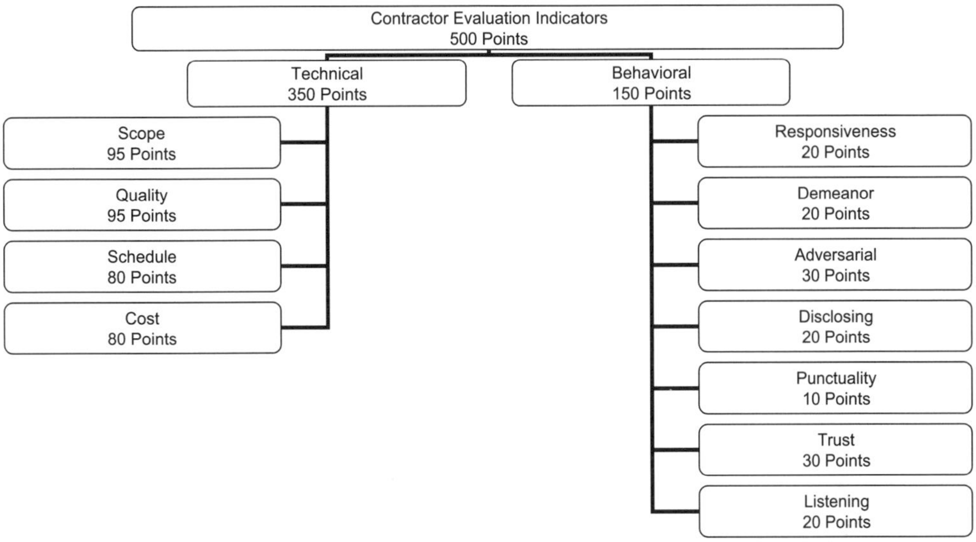

areas of scope, cost, and time throughout the life of the project. (Instrument 2–N)

One common example of such a tradeoff occurs when the team must determine whether a project's schedule should be compressed in response to a desired early delivery date. If schedule compression is needed, the impact of compression on resource requirements and budget is of interest. Using the cost estimating data, a metric can be established to record the initial project cost estimate and the updated estimates as the project moves through its paces. The values provided by this metric can help improve the quality of future estimates on similar or related projects. (Instrument 2–O)

While it is important to track and monitor project progress, the tracking process can easily become an end in itself. Thus, a metric should be devised to determine the effectiveness of the processes used to track and control schedule and cost. (Instrument 2–P)

It is often useful to track the number of key milestones completed and missed. This can be done by baselining the project schedule and tracking milestones against the specific WBS element and control account identification number. Differences in the scheduled delivery date and actual delivery date can thus be tracked. This information can be used to determine why delivery dates were missed. Thus, preventive action can be taken on future similar projects, and sometimes on the current project if it is a large, complex one. (Instrument 2–Q) At the organizational level, the number of people who use the schedule for tracking and controlling can be assessed.

As the project progresses through its life cycle, it is imperative to assess the project's rate of progress regularly. The earned value technique provides this crucial piece of information. The technique's premise is that the client will be fully informed of the pace of project progress with a combined accounting of how much time and money have been spent so far and how many deliverables have been delivered to date.

Although the earned value technique was initially developed for monitoring the status of outsourced projects toward achieving the goals of the project, it can serve as an equally powerful tool in determining the rate of progress on internal projects. Therefore, computation of earned value must be integrated into the progress monitoring system of every project, internal or external.

In fixed-price contracts, the contractor is focused on a very specific deliverable for a specific payoff. Therefore, in cases involving fixed-price contracts, the concept of earned value is generally used to calculate the amount of incremental payment that is due the contractor.

By contrast, on projects that are conducted through cost-plus contracts, the objective of the contractor is compliance with the directions and instructions of the client, even if they are incremental, incomplete, and possibly inconsistent over the life of the project. In cost-plus contracts, the contractor is paid for expenses regardless of the amount of progress toward the stated or intended project goal. Thus, the earned value will compute the real progress of the project and the real cost of that progress, but it might not impact the contractor's payment.

Nevertheless, the project's final cost and duration can be predicted based on project progress as of any point in the project. Availability of such predictions at the early stages of the project can facilitate informed project decision making regarding increased resource allocation or termination.

The first step in the earned value process is to formulate a list of values during the project's planning stages. These values are usually expressed in terms of the monetary value of each element. Then, at reporting milestones, progress credited to each constituent element is determined, using measurement of the quantified progress. If progress is not directly quantifiable, any of the crediting methods shown in Figure 2–16 can be used.

The total earned value will be the sum of the products of the value amounts and credited progress. The value that is earned for each WBS element can

Figure 2-16
Progress Reporting for Non-Measurable Activities

The 0%–100% Rule
• The team will not be credited for progress unless the deliverable is fully delivered.
The 20%–80% Rule
• The team will get 20% for starting the task. Full credit will be applied upon delivery.
The 50%–50% Rule
• The team will be credited for half of the deliverable for starting and half upon delivery.
The 30%–30%–40% Rule
• Not Started   Team will be credited for 0%.
• Just Started   Team will be credited for 30%.
• In Progress   Team will be credited for 60%.
• Completed   Team will be credited for 100%.

---

be determined by summing the progress made in each of the tasks for a particular WBS element. Thus, at any point during the life of the project, the amount of progress can be determined, as indicated by the earned value of the project, by summarizing the earned value of lower-level components along the WBS structure.

During the early stages of the project, and for small projects, this process involves only a few elements at the first or second WBS levels. For fully developed projects, the process involves a large set of all the lower-level components of the project, extending to Level Four, Level Five, and even lower on the WBS.

Figure 2–17 symbolically depicts the procedure for establishing an earned value system for a deliverable element. It shows that, independent of what was supposed to have been completed by the time of the review, the elements under review have completed between 14% and 90% of their assigned target delivery value. Thus, if the weight of all these elements is the same, the total value for this project would be 37%; if this were a fixed-price contract, the contractor would be due 37% of the contract value.

PROJECT RISK

Risk management remains one of the more elusive aspects of project management. Although several schemas are available for the process, the nature of implementation varies substantially from organization to organization in response to unique environmental features.

Essentially, the risk management process involves activities dealing with identifying the risks, quantifying the impact of those risks on the project, and mitigating the influence of those risks on the project's progress. (In-

Figure 2-17
Value Earned in Deliverable Modules

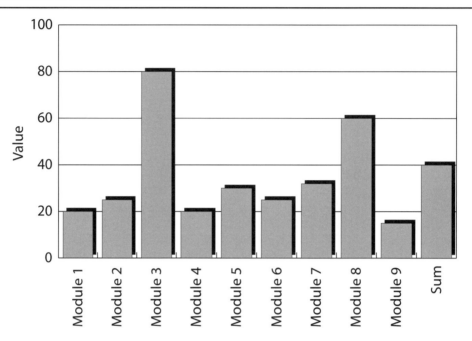

struments 2–R and 2–S) Risk metrics can be divided into metrics that categorize the nature of risk events, metrics that categorize the probability of occurrence of those events, and metrics that predict the impact of the risk events on the project's outcome.

Each project will have certain risks associated with it. A risk tracking form can help determine the number of risks identified, the risks that actually occurred, the effectiveness of the risk responses employed, and the actual impact of the identified risks on the project. These kinds of data can be incorporated into a risk project repository database, which in turn can help identify the types of risks that may be expected on certain types of future projects at certain phases in their life cycle. (Instrument 2–T)

For each identified risk, a response plan should be established to detail the specific response that should be employed if and when the identified risk occurs. Accordingly, a suite of metrics can be established for evaluating the effectiveness of risk response plans. The indices of this suite would quantify the number of workarounds required, the type of mitigation actions that were implemented, and the team's ability to mitigate the risks with appropriate contingency plans. (Instruments 2–U, 2–V, 2–W, and 2–X)

An interesting advantage of a well-constructed risk metrics system is that it enables project team members to identify important events and trends as preludes to separating problems from opportunities. The availability of such information allows team members to exploit emerging opportunities and construct plans to mitigate problematic events.

Within the context of a project, it might first appear that the client and the project team define success differently. The client is usually focused on the physical attributes of the project deliverables, whereas the project team is concerned with the means and modes by which those deliverables are designed and crafted. Further, sometimes the definition of success can vary during different phases of the project. A responsive, timely deliverable can be a primary indicator of both client and team success.

From the vantage point of the client, project success is measured by how closely targets of scope, quality, cost, and duration are met. A WBS-like structure can be used to highlight the client-focused elements of project success (see Figure 2–18). Although their relative importance will undoubtedly vary from one organization to the next, it is possible to develop a general weighting scheme for these elements (see Figure 2–19).

Client-centric project performance metric systems include those that describe the various attributes of scope, cost, and schedule. Metrics useful for this purpose include those that monitor progress in terms of the quality and extent of deliverables, including variances in cost and schedule.

Figure 2-18
Project Success Indicators: Client View

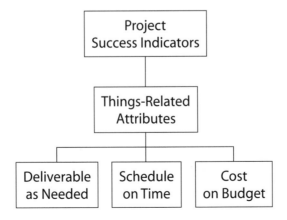

Figure 2-19
Illustrative Project Success Indicators: Client View

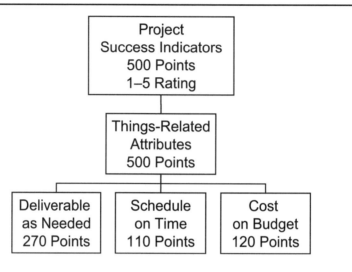

PROJECT SUCCESS FACTORS

Project success factors, as viewed by the extended project team, can be divided into two major categories: those that deal with things and those that deal with people (see Figure 2–20). The major feature of things issues is that they are somewhat easy to quantify; therefore, they lend themselves to tabulation, plotting, and evaluation by a variety of metrics.

In addition, the mission of the project manager is to develop processes and procedures for effecting acceptable levels of client satisfaction, vendor satisfaction, and team morale. A detailed knowledge of such people attributes provides the foundation for the team to measure its success in managing cost, schedule, quality, and scope.

The things metrics most useful to the project manager, and possibly to the project team, tend to include operational issues, such as sophistication of processes, effectiveness of processes, and, ultimately, the impact of those processes on the project deliverable. Such indices allow all team members to maintain more effective control over costs and schedules by reducing risks, recognizing opportunities, and improving quality.

Overall, the team then has a better likelihood of achieving significant project objectives to the satisfaction of the client. Summing team performance

Figure 2-20
Project Success Factors: Team View

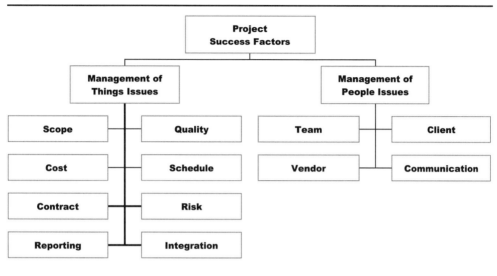

in these areas provides a barometer of how well tasks were conducted. Figure 2–21 shows a suggested weighting scheme for success indices of a project. (Instruments 2–Y and 2–Z)

Figure 2-21
Illustrative Project Success Factors: Team View

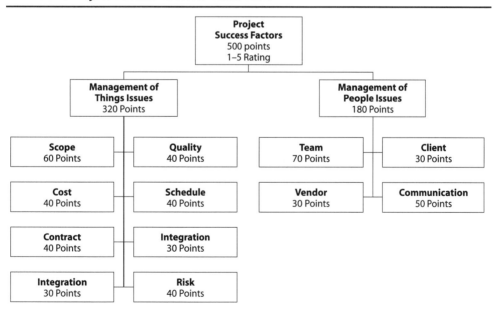

Things metrics are the most familiar metrics available for characterizing projects. By and large, these metrics describe the project deliverable and the efficiency with which it is crafted. The deliverable, as characterized by the WBS, can be quantified and tracked with reasonable accuracy. The metrics for means and modes of delivery include those dealing with managing elemental cost, project cost, and project schedule. Finally, metrics dealing with project delivery issues include the sophistication of the project team in managing project risk, quality, and contracts.

Project Charter

Strategic Objectives of the Project

Business Case

Project Scope and Deliverables

Requirements

Assumptions

Constraints

Assigned Project Manager and Level of Authority

Participation by Functional Departments

Major Risks

Major Milestones

Conceptual Budget

Responsibilities:
- Project Sponsor
- Project Manager
- Project Team
- Key Stakeholders

Approvals:

Project Manager	Signature	Date

Director, Project Management Office	Signature	Date

Vice President	Signature	Date

Project Sponsor	Signature	Date

Stakeholder	Signature	Date

Stakeholder	Signature	Date

Requirements Documentation Form

Client Information

Business Objectives of Project Deliverables

Requirements

Project Description

Deliverables

Project Boundaries

Acceptance Criteria

Acceptance Tests

Constraints

Assumptions

Major Risks

Order-of-Magnitude Cost Estimate

Major Milestones

Approval Requirements

Defect Identification Log

Defect	Date	ID Number	Reason Defect Occurred	Defect Priority	Value to the Project

Example:
  Customer
  Complaint
 	
Test Defect
 	
Internal Failure
 	
External Failure
 	
Inspection
 	
List Other:
			Example:
			  Requirement
			  Error
			
			Design Error
			
			Architecture
			Problem
			
			Tooling
			Problem
			
			List Other:
				Identify by
				Severity
				Multiplied by
				the Likelihood
				of Occurrence
					Assess by a
					1–5 scale,
					with 1 being
					the lowest

INSTRUMENT 2–D

Defect Tracking Log

Use this instrument to record project team progress in identifying defects and in successfully resolving identified defects.

Defect Number	Defect ID Owner	Status (Open, Pending, Resolved, Deferred, Complete)	Person Assigned to Verify Correctness	Stakeholders Notified	Date Required to Correct	Estimated Time to Correct	Actual Time to Correct	Actual Date Corrected	Estimated Cost to Correct	Actual Cost to Correct

INSTRUMENT 2–E

Abbreviated Project Planning Checklist

Use this instrument as a quick, high-level reminder to perform all the tasks required during the planning phase of the project.

✓ Documented business goals and objectives

✓ Project scope statement

✓ Major deliverables

✓ Work Breakdown Structure (WBS)

✓ Top-down cost estimates

✓ Major milestones and target dates

✓ Budget

✓ Description of project management approach or strategy

✓ Responsibility assignments for each WBS element

✓ Performance measurement baseline for technical scope, schedule, and cost

✓ Key or required staff and their expected cost and/or effort

✓ Subsidiary management plans

- Change management
- Communications management
- Contract management
- Cost management
- Documentation
- Performance, evaluation, and test
- Process improvement plan
- Procurement management
- Quality management
- Resources
- Risk management
- Schedule management
- Scope management
- Staffing management
- Training

Work Breakdown Structure Dictionary

Client:

Project Manager:

Team Member in Charge:

WBS Number:	Code or Account Idenfier:
WBS Element:	Revision Number/Date:

Statement of Work:

Responsible Organization:

Names of Tasks Associated with This WBS Element:

Contract Information (if applicable):

Quality Requirements:

Duration:

Deliverables:

Other Team Members Assigned to This Element:

Estimated Hours:	Estimated Cost:

Required Materials:

Estimated Amount:	Estimated Cost:

Required Equipment:

Estimated Amount:	Estimated Cost:

Technical References:

Approvals

Project Manager	Date
Responsible Team Member	Date
Stakeholder 1 (if applicable)	Date
Stakeholder 2 (if applicable)	Date
Stakeholder *N* (if applicable)	Date

Work Breakdown Structure Development Checklist

Use this checklist during WBS development to ensure that items are not inadvertently omitted.

✓ Divide the work into three to nine categories.

✓ Divide each category into three to nine packages.

✓ Divide each package into three to nine modules.

✓ Continue to divide as long as logically possible.

✓ Ensure that the numbering schemas for WBS elements represent the hierarchical structure.

✓ Recognize that not all branches need go to the same level, but the significance of all the lowest-level items in the overall project should be similar.

✓ Ensure that deliverable elements are logical, unique, and distinct.

✓ Ensure that each WBS element at the lowest level represents a single, tangible deliverable.

✓ Ensure that each intermediate WBS element represents an aggregation of all subordinate WBS elements listed below it.

✓ Recognize that the level of significance of all lowest-level elements should be the same.

✓ Refine the WBS on a regular basis as the project team develops more information about the deliverables.

✓ Develop the WBS Dictionary.

✓ Update the WBS when any work scope change occurs.

✓ Update the scope statement, if required, based on development of the WBS.

INSTRUMENT 2–H

Effectiveness of the Work Breakdown Structure

The overall level of utility of using a Work Breakdown Structure (WBS) and the WBS Dictionary is the average of the scores reported for the items below. Using feedback on performance on current or past projects can help improve the chances of success on future projects.

1—Not at all
2—Marginally
3—Partially
4—Mostly
5—Fully

Item	1	2	3	4	5
1. The WBS defined the total scope of the project.					
2. The WBS, WBS Dictionary, and scope statement served as the scope baseline for the project.					
3. Deliverables in the WBS were defined so effort was not duplicated.					
4. Each WBS component was assigned to a specific unit or individual to complete.					
5. The WBS included all the project deliverables.					
6. Each item in the WBS had a unique identifier.					
7. Deliverables in the WBS were defined to the level describing how they would be produced.					
8. Project management items were included in the WBS.					
9. The WBS coding structure was linked to the project schedule.					
10. The WBS coding structure was linked to the finance and accounting system.					
11. Each WBS component was cross-referenced to other components in the WBS Dictionary, as appropriate.					

Item	1	2	3	4	5
12. A WBS template was used to develop the project WBS.					
13. Technical experts and other project stakeholders contributed to WBS development.					
14. The WBS Dictionary contained information on the WBS components.					
15. Scope changes were assessed based on the approved WBS.					
16. If there was a major scope change on the project, the WBS, WBS Dictionary, and scope statement were updated accordingly.					
17. The WBS served as the foundation for the schedule activity list.					
18. Refinements to the WBS were made based on developing the activity list, as appropriate.					
19. The WBS, with the activity list, was the basis for schedule development.					
20. The WBS was the main input in activity resource estimating.					
21. The WBS and the WBS Dictionary were used to organize cost estimates and ensure all work was estimated.					
22. The WBS and the WBS Dictionary were key inputs to cost budgeting.					
23. The WBS was used as a way to communicate with project stakeholders.					
24. The WBS was the foundation for performance reporting.					
25. The WBS and the WBS Dictionary were used for risk management planning.					
26. The WBS and the WBS Dictionary were used for risk identification.					
27. The WBS and the WBS Dictionary were used to plan purchases and acquisitions.					
28. The scope statement was reviewed after the WBS was developed to see if any changes were required.					
29. The Scope Management Plan was reviewed after the WBS was developed to see if any changes were required.					
30. The WBS Dictionary was used to verify that the deliverables being produced and accepted were included in the approved project scope.					

Item	1	2	3	4	5
31. The WBS was used in closing the project.					
32. The final, enhanced WBS was placed in the organization's archives for use by future projects.					
33. The WBS was more client-centric than team-centric.					
34. The elements of the WBS were mostly deliverables, not activities or milestones.					
35. The WBS was used to assign responsibility for project segments to individuals and organizations.					

Importance of Quality Initiatives to the Enterprise

Use this form to evaluate the degree to which the organization places emphasis on quality initiatives. Regular evaluation should provide occasions for celebration, as ratings should increase with the benefit of feedback.

Rate the following in terms of its importance in the organization:

1—Not at all
2—Marginally
3—Partially
4—Mostly
5—Fully

Item	1	2	3	4	5
1. Is quality an important component of each project?					
2. Are customer requirements assessed for quality requirements?					
3. Are documentation requirements for quality specified by the customer?					
4. Are acceptance criteria specified for the project deliverables, including performance requirements and essential conditions?					
5. Does the project follow the organization's quality policy?					
6. Are data collected on the cost of quality?					
7. Is quality assurance a separate function outside the project team?					
8. Do the Quality Assurance Manager and the Project Manager meet regularly?					
9. Are the Quality Assurance Manager and the Project Manager able to reach agreement on outstanding issues?					

Item	1	2	3	4	5
10. Is the quality assurance function at a high level in the organization?					
11. Is a representative from the quality assurance staff aligned with the project team?					
12. Does the quality assurance staff have the needed training in project management concepts?					
13. Does the project team have the needed training in quality management concepts?					
14. Is quality improvement a critical success factor for each team member?					
15. Is quality assurance viewed as a value-added activity?					
16. Is quality control viewed as a value-added activity?					
17. Are data collected from quality control tools analyzed and evaluated?					
18. Is a defect log maintained as part of a problem-tracking system?					
19. Are reviews undertaken periodically to see whether results conform to requirements?					
20. Are any causes of nonconformance identified, researched, and resolved?					
21. Are quality metrics collected on every project?					
22. Does executive management provide proactive quality oversight project management activities?					
23. Does each project prepare a Quality Management Plan that is reviewed by appropriate stakeholders?					
24. Is the scope statement reviewed for quality requirements?					
25. Is a process improvement plan prepared as a subset of the Project Management Plan?					
26. Are standard quality checklists available?					
27. Are completed checklists part of the project's final records?					
28. Is continuous process improvement an objective for each project team member?					
29. Does process analysis focus on root-cause analysis?					
30. Are project work results monitored and verified according to quality standards so corrective action can be taken as required?					

Item	1	2	3	4	5
31. Does the project focus on both prevention and inspection?					
32. Are quality metrics used to improve quality, cost, and delivery time continuously and simultaneously?					
33. Has a quality baseline been established?					
34. Do project team members view quality as a key responsibility?					
35. Are quality management procedures prepared for each project?					
36. Is a quality audit conducted on each project to identify areas of quality improvement and lessons learned?					
37. Are quality indicators developed to help determine potential areas of improvement?					
38. Are quality measurement results displayed openly for all appropriate stakeholders to view?					
39. Does the organization participate in internal and/or external benchmarking forums?					
40. Are quality improvements implemented according to integrated change control procedures?					
41. As a result of implementing quality improvements, are other documents updated as required?					
42. Are existing quality standards reviewed on a regular basis to assess effectiveness and efficiency?					
43. Is quality regarded as simply a statistical exercise rather than general enterprise culture?					
44. Are project managers and project team members consistently rewarded for offering improvements to the enterprise quality plan?					
45. Is there an agreement by everyone that high quality and high profits are tied together?					

INSTRUMENT 2–J

Quality Assurance Survey

Assess the following factors and determine their level of importance with regard to the project:

1—Never
2—Rarely
3—Sometimes
4—Most of the time
5—Always
NA—Not Applicable

Factors	Definitions	1	2	3	4	5	NA
Correctness	Does the project satisfy its specifications and meet the customer's requirements and objectives?						
Reliability	Does the project fulfill its intended purpose?						
Flexibility	Can the project's product be used for other items in addition to its intended purpose?						
Efficiency	Is the project one that can be used productively?						
Usability	Is the project one that does not require significant effort on the part of its end users?						
Maintainability	Will the customer need extensive effort to maintain the product?						
Reusability	Can the organization reuse aspects of the project in future projects?						
Operability	Is it easy to operate the project's product?						
Life Cycle	Does the product have a long life cycle?						
Continuity	Can the product be used in other than optimal conditions?						

Factors	Definitions	1	2	3	4	5	NA
Innovation	Does the product include new or enhanced features?						
Cost	Is the product's unit cost substantially less than products with similar features?						
Timeliness	Does the timetable for project delivery meet market demands?						
Technological Obsolescence	Does project technology require continual updates?						
Social-Economic-Environmental Sustainability	Does the project's product have any unintended negative impacts?						

Quality Management Planning Checklist

Use this instrument to guide the project's quality management aspects. While users need not follow the instrument sequentially, unaddressed items might indicate an opportunity for improvement in future projects.

Overall Quality Management Aspects

✓ Project Scope
  • Describe the project; include the scope statement or provide a summary description of the overall project, its objectives, the customer, a summary of the requirements, and the acceptance criteria.
✓ Project Quality Policy
  • Define the project's quality policy.
✓ Quality Assurance Manager
  • Identify the Quality Assurance Manager for the project and state whether this person is assigned to the project full or part time.
  • Provide a summary of this Quality Assurance Manager's responsibilities.
  • Discuss the relationship of the Quality Assurance Manager to the Project Manager.
  • Discuss the relationship of this manager to the Quality Control Manager.
✓ Quality Control Manager
  • Identify the Quality Control Manager for the project and state whether this person is assigned to the project full or part time.
  • Provide a summary of the Quality Control Manager's responsibilities.
  • Discuss the relationship of the Quality Control Manager to the Project Manager.
  • Discuss the relationship of the Quality Control Manager to the Quality Assurance Manager.
✓ Project Quality Team Responsibilities
  • Identify the responsibilities of the project quality team as a whole.
  • List any specific task-related quality responsibilities, such as responsibility for acceptance tests or audits and use of checklists, benchmarking, cost-benefit analysis, and experiments.
✓ Cost of Quality
  • Specify the estimated quality costs in terms of prevention costs, appraisal costs, and failure costs.

✓ Quality Management Plan Review and Update
  • Describe how quality assurance and quality control will be handled on the project.
  • Specify how often the Quality Management Plan will be reviewed and when it will be updated during the project.
  • Specify who will receive copies of the Quality Management Plan and how it will be disseminated.
✓ Quality Metrics
  • Define the specific quality metrics that will be used in quality assurance and quality control.
✓ Quality Baseline
  • Establish the project's quality baseline.
  • Describe how updates to the quality baseline will be handled.
✓ Process Improvement Plan
  • Describe the process improvement plan to be followed to ensure that non-value-added activities are not performed.
  • Discuss how quality improvement will be identified.
  • Describe how lessons learned will be collected and documented.

Quality Assurance of Project Deliverables

✓ Deliverable Description
  • Describe the project deliverables.
✓ Test and Acceptance Process
  • Discuss any planned test and acceptance processes and how they will verify the quality of the deliverable items.
✓ Acceptance Criteria
  • Describe the acceptance criteria for project deliverables and how these criteria will be used to assess project quality.
✓ Project Audits and Quality Reviews
  • Discuss the planned schedule of project audits and quality reviews.
  • Discuss how audit results and review outcomes will feed back into project planning activities.
  • Discuss how lessons learned will be identified.
✓ Tools and Techniques
  • Discuss how process analysis will be used to examine any problems, constraints, and non-value-added activities.
  • Discuss any other quality assurance tools and techniques that will be used.
✓ Change Management
  • Describe how changes will be handled based on identified quality improvements.
  • Describe how quality standards will be updated based on identified quality improvements.

Project Processes and Quality Control

✓ Project Monitoring and Quality Control
  • Discuss the in-process monitoring and control processes planned for the project and how they will affect project quality.

- Discuss how project-related data concerning quality will be gathered and used to control project quality.
- Discuss how quality improvements will be identified.

✓ In-Process Quality Monitoring and Inspections
- Discuss how project quality will be measured as part of each work process in the project.
- Discuss the use of inspections as a quality control tool and technique.
- Discuss how deliverables will be validated.
- Discuss other quality tools to be used.

✓ Change Management
- Describe how changes will be handled based on the results of quality control measurements.
- Describe how the quality baseline will be updated.
- Describe how other aspects of the project will be updated, such as standard checklists.
- Describe how lessons learned will be documented.

INSTRUMENT 2-L

Quality Cost Analysis Form

Use this instrument to document the cost of maintaining quality deliverables for the project.

WBS Work Package	Work Package Purpose	Customer Requirements	Measurements	Level of Effort	Estimated Cost	Work Package Cost of Quality							
						Prevention		Appraisal		Internal Failure		External Failure	
						Planned	Actual	Planned	Actual	Planned	Actual	Planned	Actual

Project Quality Checklist

Use this instrument to record a summary of the activities involved in managing the quality issues of a project. Since this instrument yields primarily numeric results, the comparison of two projects will show which one is more sophisticated and will likely be indicative of future performance.

✓ Number and type of revisions to the Quality Management Plan

✓ Number of stakeholders involved in preparation of the Quality Management Plan

✓ Number of problems discovered through quality inspections

✓ Amount of rework required

✓ Number of inspections conducted

✓ Number of lessons learned and areas of potential improvements discovered through quality audits

✓ Completeness of quality management activities compared to the plan

✓ Efforts and funds in quality activities as compared to the plan

✓ Extent of processes established to verify that quality improvements identified on each project are in fact implemented in the enterprise

Change Order Request Form

Date:

Project Name:

Project Manager:

Person Requesting the Change:

E-Mail: Phone:

Identify the Category of the Reason for the Change:

  Business Strategy

  Customer Request

  Design Philosophy

  Project Environment

  Technology Used for the Project

  Project Implementation Efficiency

  Other (please identify)

Describe the Change:

Describe the Recommended Change's Impact on:

Scope

Quality

Project Duration

Project Cost

State the Actions Necessary to Implement the Change:

State the Date by Which Implementation of the Change Is Required:

Revise Budgeted Hours:	from	to	
Revise Budgeted Equipment and Materials:	from	to	
Revise Completion Date:	from	to	
Revise Scope and Quality:	from	to	

Project Change Management Checklist

Use this checklist as a guide for managing changes in project attributes and circumstances.

Overall Project Status
✓ What are the current values for project schedule, cost, and performance?
✓ What are the current values for schedule, cost, and performance objectives of the individual work packages?
✓ Is the client pleased with the results of the project?
✓ If there are significant variances in the project performance, can these variances be remedied with
  • Additional personnel?
  • Reallocated personnel?
  • Additional funds?
  • Changes in deliverable attributes?
  • Changes in schedule?
✓ If there are positive variances, celebrate them and acknowledge the team's efforts.

Project Duration
✓ Is an overrun of the current duration baseline projected?
✓ What is the cause of the variance?
✓ Is a delay acceptable to the client?
✓ If a delay is not acceptable, can additional resources be acquired?
✓ What are the cost implications of additional resources?
✓ Is additional funding the only way to maintain the original delivery date?
✓ If a delay is acceptable to the client, will the delay result in an improved deliverable?

Project Cost
✓ Is an overrun of the current cost baseline projected?
✓ What is the cause of the variance?
✓ Is a cost increase acceptable to the client?
✓ If a cost increase is not acceptable, can the project scope and/or schedule be modified?
✓ If a cost increase is acceptable to the client, will the increased cost result in an improved deliverable?

Project Deliverable
✓ Is a shortfall of the current scope and quality baseline projected?
✓ What is the cause of the variance?
✓ Is a deliverable shortfall acceptable to the client?
✓ If a variance is not acceptable, can additional funds be acquired, or can the project be delayed?
✓ If a scope shortfall is acceptable to the client, will the shortfall result in improved cost and schedule performance?

Project Status Report

Use this instrument periodically to record the status of project activities supporting accomplishment of stated goals.

Project Name:

Project Description:

Project Manager:

Project Sponsor:

Strategic Importance:

Expected Outcomes:

Project Stage:

- Concept

- Feasibility

- Development

- Design

- Implementation

- Closing

Work Accomplished During Current Period:

| WBS Number | Description | Status | Date Started | Date Completed |

Work Expected to Start During Period but Delayed:

| WBS Number | Description | Reason for Delay | New Start Date |

Work Expected to Be Completed During Period but Not Finished:

| WBS Number | Description | Reason for Delay | New End Date |

Work Expected to Start in Next Period:

| WBS Number | Description | Concerns/Issues (if any) |

Overall Project Risk:

- High

- Medium

- Low

Current Problems and Concerns:

| Date | Problem | Comments |

Emerging Problems, Alternative Solutions, Impacts:

Earned Value:

PV	EV	AC	SV	CV	SPI	CPI	ETC	EAC

Recommendations/Actions Needed by Whom and When:

Cost, Scope, and Schedule Impact of Approved Change Orders:

Explanation of Unapproved Variances in Cost and Schedule:

Updated Cost Estimate of Major Project Modules:

Updated Delivery Dates of Major Project Modules:

WBS	PV	EV	AC	SV	CV	SPI	CPI	ETC	EAC

INSTRUMENT 2–Q

Project Management Checklist

Use this instrument as a guide for performing all the necessary tasks for each phase of the project. The extent to which items are deliberately skipped might signal an opportunity for future enhancement.

Initiating Phase	Yes	No
• Prepare a project charter to		
– Describe the business need for the project	_____	_____
– Describe the purpose of the project	_____	_____
– Identify the project team's obligations to the client	_____	_____
– Identify and assign a Project Manager	_____	_____
– Provide a summary milestone schedule	_____	_____
– Identify key stakeholders	_____	_____
– Identify assumptions and constraints	_____	_____
– Identify key functional organizations that need to participate	_____	_____
– Present a summary budget	_____	_____
– Describe the Project Manager's authority and responsibility	_____	_____
• Prepare a preliminary scope statement to		
– Describe the project and deliverable requirements	_____	_____
– State project boundaries	_____	_____
– Present a high-level scope	_____	_____
– List project constraints and assumptions	_____	_____
– Present an initial Work Breakdown Structure (WBS)	_____	_____
– Present project milestones	_____	_____
– Present an order-of-magnitude cost estimate	_____	_____
– Describe configuration management requirements	_____	_____
– State acceptance criteria	_____	_____
– State approval requirements	_____	_____

Planning Phase		
• Prepare a project plan that includes		
– Project management approach or strategy	_____	_____
– Scope statement	_____	_____
– Baselines (scope, schedule, cost, quality)	_____	_____
– Major milestones and target dates	_____	_____
– Key or required staff, expected cost and/or effort, and calendars	_____	_____
– Change management approach	_____	_____
– Maintenance of the integrity of baselines	_____	_____

	Yes	No
– Key management reviews	_____	_____
– Other subsidiary plans (scope, schedule, cost, quality, process improvement, staffing, communication, risk, and procurement)	_____	_____
– Open issues and pending decisions	_____	_____
• Establish a performance measurement baseline for technical scope, quality, schedule, and cost	_____	_____
• Perform a stakeholder analysis and identify those stakeholders who have an interest in or an influence over the final outcome of the project to gain their participation in developing the plan	_____	_____
• Document project constraints, such as a predefined budget, availability of funds, imposed dates, resource availability, resource skills required, or contractual provisions	_____	_____
• Document any assumptions made by the project team	_____	_____
• Document relevant policies, such as those involving quality management, personnel management, procurement management, safety and health, environmental, and financial management	_____	_____
• Establish a project management information system	_____	_____
• Establish a configuration management system to describe		
– How to submit proposed changes	_____	_____
– Tracking methods to use for review and approval of proposed changes	_____	_____
– Approval levels for change authorization	_____	_____
– Method to validate approved changes	_____	_____
• Establish a change control system to define how deliverables and documentation are controlled, changed, and approved	_____	_____
• Prepare a Scope Management Plan that describes how to		
– Prepare a scope statement	_____	_____
– Create the WBS from the scope statement	_____	_____
– Obtain formal verification and acceptance of the completed project deliverables	_____	_____
– Control change requests	_____	_____
• Prepare a scope statement that includes the		
– Project justification	_____	_____
– Product description	_____	_____
– Project requirements	_____	_____
– Project objectives	_____	_____
– Project deliverables	_____	_____
– Acceptance criteria	_____	_____
– Assumptions	_____	_____
– Constraints	_____	_____
– Initial identified risks	_____	_____
– Initial project organization	_____	_____
– Preliminary cost estimate	_____	_____
– Configuration management requirements	_____	_____
– Approval requirements	_____	_____

	Yes	No
• Prepare a WBS to organize and define the total scope of the project and assign a unique identifier to each item in the WBS	_____	_____
• Prepare a WBS Dictionary that describes each work package with		
– Contact information	_____	_____
– Quality requirements	_____	_____
– Technical references	_____	_____
– Schedule dates	_____	_____
– Cost estimates	_____	_____
– Staff assignments	_____	_____
• Establish a scope baseline with the approved scope statement, WBS, and WBS Dictionary	_____	_____
• Prepare a Resource Breakdown Structure (RBS) to assign work packages to individuals and to show the resources to be used on the project	_____	_____
• Prepare a Risk Breakdown Structure to show identified project risks by risk category	_____	_____
• Prepare an Organizational Breakdown Structure (OBS) to show the work packages assigned to specific organizational units	_____	_____
• Prepare and review acceptance criteria with the client	_____	_____
• List each activity to be performed on the project	_____	_____
• Identify activity attributes, including		
– Activity identifier	_____	_____
– Code of accounts	_____	_____
– Description	_____	_____
– Predecessor activities	_____	_____
– Successor activities	_____	_____
– Relationships	_____	_____
– Leads and lags	_____	_____
– Resource requirements	_____	_____
– Imposed dates	_____	_____
– Constraints	_____	_____
– Assumptions	_____	_____
– Person responsible	_____	_____
– Activity type	_____	_____
• Ensure that all dependencies are documented	_____	_____
• Ensure that dependencies include those specified by the client as well as any that involve a relationship with non-project activities or those of another project	_____	_____
• Define dependencies in terms of		
– External dependencies	_____	_____
– Discretionary dependencies	_____	_____
– Mandatory dependencies	_____	_____
• Use the identified risks in the preparation of the activity duration estimates and modify them as required to ensure that the effect of risks is included in the baseline duration estimate for each activity	_____	_____

	Yes	No
• Consider the use of contingencies and buffers in the preparation of the schedule	_____	_____
• Document the basis of the assumptions made in developing the elemental estimate	_____	_____
• State the probability that an activity may finish earlier or later than planned	_____	_____
• Prepare a project schedule and identify critical path activities	_____	_____
• Document the		
– Schedule milestones	_____	_____
– Schedule activities	_____	_____
– Activity attributes	_____	_____
– Identified assumptions and constraints	_____	_____
– Resource requirements by time period	_____	_____
– Contingency reserves	_____	_____
• Prepare a calendar for the project	_____	_____
• Prepare resource calendars for a specific resource or a category of resources	_____	_____
• Identify key events as requested by the client and major milestones to note any interfaces with work outside of the project	_____	_____
• Prepare a Schedule Management Plan that identifies how changes to the schedule will be managed	_____	_____
• Establish a schedule baseline	_____	_____
• Describe the types and quantities of resources required for each activity in a work package	_____	_____
• Prepare a cost estimate for all resources (not solely labor) that will be charged to the project	_____	_____
• In the cost estimate for each activity, consider		
– Effect of risk	_____	_____
– Activity duration estimates	_____	_____
– Cost-estimating policies	_____	_____
– Activity resource estimates	_____	_____
– Resource rates	_____	_____
– Available historical information	_____	_____
• Ensure that the cost estimate is supported by		
– A reference to the WBS	_____	_____
– The basis for the estimate	_____	_____
– A description of how the estimate was developed	_____	_____
– A description of the scope of work	_____	_____
– A description of any assumptions	_____	_____
– A description of any constraints	_____	_____
– Other items, such as an allowance for inflation and range of possible results	_____	_____
• Assign the estimate to the chart of accounts	_____	_____
• Prepare a Cost Management Plan to describe how cost variances will be managed on the project	_____	_____
• Establish a cost baseline as a time-phased budget to be used to measure and monitor project cost performance	_____	_____

	Yes	No
• Establish contingency reserves	_____	_____
• Establish project funding requirements as derived from the cost baseline	_____	_____
• Reconcile the expenditure of funds with any funding limits	_____	_____
• Use the prevailing corporate quality policy or have the project team prepare one for the project based on client expectations	_____	_____
• Set up a process to collect data on efforts required to achieve product/service quality in terms of		
– Prevention costs	_____	_____
– Appraisal costs	_____	_____
– External and internal failure costs	_____	_____
• Prepare a Quality Management Plan to define the		
– Organizational structure for quality initiatives	_____	_____
– Responsibilities	_____	_____
– Processes	_____	_____
– Resources needed to implement quality management	_____	_____
• Establish quality metrics to be used in quality assurance and quality control	_____	_____
• Set up checklists and use them to facilitate client acceptance of project deliverables	_____	_____
• Prepare a quality checklist to verify that the required steps in a process/procedure have been followed	_____	_____
• Prepare a process improvement plan to detail the steps to analyze processes to describe value and non-value-added activities that includes		
– Process boundaries	_____	_____
– A flowchart	_____	_____
– Metrics	_____	_____
– Targets for improved performance to guide the process improvement activities	_____	_____
• Establish a quality baseline to record the quality objectives of the project and to measure and report quality performance	_____	_____
• Assess organizational, technical, logistical, political, and interpersonal interfaces as the Staffing Management Plan is prepared	_____	_____
• Prepare a resource assignment matrix (RAM) to assign roles and responsibilities for specific activities to individuals	_____	_____
• Use the activity resource estimates and prepare a Staffing Management Plan to describe when and how human resources will be brought on and taken off the project team that includes		
– Training requirements	_____	_____
– Recognition and rewards	_____	_____
– Strategies for complying with policies and regulations	_____	_____
– Safety policies and procedures	_____	_____
• Prepare a project organization chart	_____	_____
• Prepare position descriptions	_____	_____
• Prepare a project team directory that lists all team members and other project stakeholders	_____	_____

	Yes	No
• Track actual staff assignments versus planned assignments; assess whether there are qualified staff for all aspects of the project	_____	_____
• Set up a process to track the direct billing and the actual utilization rate	_____	_____
• Set up a process for time tracking	_____	_____
• Determine those stakeholders who are both involved in, or have influence over, the project, or whose interests may be positively or negatively affected by the project; determine the information needs of each stakeholder	_____	_____
• Use the results of the stakeholder analysis, as well as an assessment of communication requirements and technology, to prepare the Communications Management Plan, including		
– Methods used to gather and store information	_____	_____
– The information distribution description and structure	_____	_____
– Schedule for distributing information	_____	_____
– A glossary of terms	_____	_____
– Issue escalation processes	_____	_____
– Methods to access the information needs between scheduled communication	_____	_____
• Analyze, through interviews, policies, and procedures, stakeholders' tolerance for risk as the project Risk Management Plan is prepared		
• Hold a meeting with the project team and other key stakeholders to develop the project Risk Management Plan and to foster a commitment to risk management throughout the project	_____	_____
• Prepare a Risk Management Plan to cover risk activities throughout the project that includes items such as		
– The methodology	_____	_____
– Risk categories	_____	_____
– Roles and responsibilities	_____	_____
– Risk budget	_____	_____
– Stakeholder risk tolerances	_____	_____
– Analysis scoring and interpretation, reporting formats, and tracking methods	_____	_____
• Set up a classification system for use in risk identification, such as		
– Technical	_____	_____
– Quality or performance	_____	_____
– Project management risks	_____	_____
– Organizational risks	_____	_____
– External risks	_____	_____
• Identify risks through methods such as		
– Documentation reviews	_____	_____
– Interviews	_____	_____
– Checklists	_____	_____
– Assumption analysis	_____	_____
– Diagramming techniques	_____	_____

	Yes	No
• Prepare a list of all identified risks and maintain it throughout the project	_____	_____
• Prepare a risk register or risk tracking log that lists		
– Identified risks	_____	_____
– Root causes	_____	_____
– Risk categories	_____	_____
– Risk owners and assigned responsibilities	_____	_____
– Agreed-upon response strategies	_____	_____
– Actions to take to implement the selected response	_____	_____
– Triggers	_____	_____
– Budget and schedule to implement the response	_____	_____
– Contingency reserves	_____	_____
– Fallback plans	_____	_____
– Residual risks	_____	_____
– Secondary risks	_____	_____
• Establish triggers to indicate whether a risk has occurred or is about to occur	_____	_____
• Prepare a probability/impact risk rating matrix	_____	_____
• Establish criteria for use in prioritizing risks	_____	_____
• Based on the risk analysis, determine an overall risk ranking for the project and repeat the analysis periodically during the project to assess trends	_____	_____
• Prepare a forecast listing possible completion dates or project duration and costs, with associated confidence levels	_____	_____
• Prepare a prioritized list of quantified risks and repeat the analysis during the project to focus on trends in the results	_____	_____
• Prepare a risk response plan appropriate to the severity of the risk and identify an owner for the risk responses	_____	_____
• Ascertain whether several risks may be driven by a common cause to see if it may be possible for one response to mitigate several risks	_____	_____
• Develop a contingency plan in advance to help reduce the cost of an action should the risk occur	_____	_____
• Define and track risk triggers; prepare a fallback plan if the risk has a high impact or if the strategy may not be fully effective	_____	_____
• Based on the analysis and the risk thresholds, use the data to determine the buffer or contingency that is required to reduce the risk of overruns to an acceptable level	_____	_____
• Prepare a make-or-buy analysis to determine whether to outsource purchases and acquisitions; consider both direct and indirect costs	_____	_____
• Based on the results of the make-or-buy analysis, if outside vendors are to be used, prepare a Procurement Management Plan; include items such as		
– The types of contracts to be used	_____	_____
– The need for independent estimates	_____	_____
– Roles and responsibilities	_____	_____
– Management of multiple providers	_____	_____
– Assumptions	_____	_____

	Yes	No
– Constraints	_____	_____
– Needed lead times	_____	_____
– The direction to develop a contract WBS	_____	_____
– Format for the contract statement of work	_____	_____
– Pre-qualified sellers	_____	_____
– Metrics	_____	_____
– How the procurement will be coordinated with other aspects of the project	_____	_____
• Document make-or-buy decisions	_____	_____
• Work with the Procurement Department to ensure that input from the project team is included to plan contracting	_____	_____
• Establish evaluation criteria to rate or score proposals	_____	_____

Executing Phase

	Yes	No
• Establish a work authorization system to use to initiate work on a work package or a specific activity	_____	_____
• Establish a system to collect information on deliverables and integrate it with the performance reporting system	_____	_____
• Set up a system that includes those stakeholders who should be notified when the Project Management Plan is updated during the project	_____	_____
• Establish a method to implement		
• Approved corrective actions	_____	_____
• Approved preventive actions	_____	_____
• Approved change requests	_____	_____
• Approved defect repairs	_____	_____
• Validation of defect repairs	_____	_____
• Perform a structured review of quality management activities, as well as other project management activities, through the use of quality and project audits; use the audits to focus on quality and project improvements	_____	_____
• Identify needed improvements from an organizational and technical standpoint through process analysis, as noted in the process improvement plan	_____	_____
• Use client satisfaction surveys to identify needed process improvements during the project and after its completion	_____	_____
• Determine actions that can promote team building and implement them throughout the project to improve team performance	_____	_____
• Establish a team-based performance evaluation system for the project	_____	_____
• Establish a process that ensures that the Project Manager and other team members provide input into the performance appraisals of project staff	_____	_____
• Set up a process to request team member feedback on progress in terms of individual performance, team performance, and overall project performance	_____	_____

	Yes	No
• Have each team member prepare an individual development plan that is reviewed and followed, with a focus on improving skills and competencies	_____	_____
• Review the Project Manager's authority and responsibility as stated in the project charter	_____	_____
• Review the team charter or team ground rules prepared for use in performing team work	_____	_____
• Establish an issue log	_____	_____
• Ensure that each stakeholder receives required information in a timely manner and that there are minimal unexpected requests for project information	_____	_____
• Establish a method to document and use lessons learned	_____	_____
• See if qualified lists are available for approved vendors for project purchases	_____	_____
• Set up weighting and screening systems, as appropriate, for use in selecting sellers	_____	_____
• Award contracts	_____	_____
• Prepare a Contract Management Plan for significant purchases and acquisitions and to cover contract administration activities	_____	_____
• Determine whether the Procurement Management Plan is being followed or whether it requires an update	_____	_____

Controlling Phase

	Yes	No
• Establish a process to compare actual progress against the Project Management Plan	_____	_____
• Assess progress to determine whether corrective or preventive actions are needed	_____	_____
• Manage implementation of changes as they occur	_____	_____
• Set up an integrated change control system for use on the project	_____	_____
• Establish an earned value management system to integrate the project's scope, schedule, and resources; use it to assess whether variances to the plan require corrective action	_____	_____
• Document lessons learned	_____	_____
• Prepare documentation for use by the client to formally sign off on and accept each deliverable	_____	_____
• Follow the integrated change control process and document lessons learned and the types of corrective action selected	_____	_____
• Revise and reissue the scope baseline documents (scope statement, WBS, and WBS Dictionary) as an adjusted baseline in response to any major scope changes	_____	_____
• Set up a schedule change control system that includes the procedures to use to change the project schedule, including those who must approve all schedule changes	_____	_____
• Regularly track the schedule variance (SV) and schedule performance index (SPI) through earned value analysis	_____	_____
• Perform variance analysis to compare target schedule dates with the actual/forecast start and finish dates	_____	_____

	Yes	No
• Use project management software to track planned dates versus actual dates and to forecast the effects of schedule changes	_____	_____
• Re-baseline and reissue the schedule if the schedule delays are severe	_____	_____
• Use root-cause analysis to identify causes of variations and to assist in any needed project recovery actions	_____	_____
• Set up a cost change control system with the paperwork, tracking systems, and approval levels needed to authorize changes to the cost baseline	_____	_____
• Regularly track the cost variance (CV) and cost performance index (CPI) using earned value for all control account plans	_____	_____
• Use earned value analysis and regularly track the estimated cost at completion (EAC) to forecast the most likely total project costs based on project performance and quantitative risk analysis	_____	_____
• Use earned value analysis to regularly track the estimate to complete (ETC) to determine the estimate to complete the remaining work for a schedule activity, work package, or control account	_____	_____
• Conduct project performance reviews	_____	_____
• Compare actual project cost performance to planned or expected performance	_____	_____
• Update the cost estimates and cost baseline as appropriate	_____	_____
• Examine project performance over time to determine if performance is improving or deteriorating	_____	_____
• Determine what is required to bring expected performance in line with the project plan	_____	_____
• Re-baseline the approved cost baseline if cost variances are severe to provide a realistic measure of performance	_____	_____
• Notify appropriate stakeholders when cost estimates are revised	_____	_____
• Update the Project Management Plan as needed as the result of cost estimate changes	_____	_____
• Set up a process to document the causes of variances and the reasons corrective actions were selected	_____	_____
• Request feedback regularly on the project to avoid the need for rework and to lead to client acceptance decisions	_____	_____
• Prepare cause-and-effect diagrams to see how various factors might be linked to potential problems or effects	_____	_____
• Determine whether or not processes are stable for predictable performance	_____	_____
• Use flowcharts to analyze how problems occur	_____	_____
• Determine the number of defects generated by type or category of identified cause	_____	_____
• Determine trends in processes over time and variations	_____	_____
• Identify the possible relationships between changes observed in two variables	_____	_____
• Conduct inspections to determine whether deliverables conform to standards	_____	_____

	Yes	No
• Prepare status reports to describe where the project now stands as requested by the client and project sponsor and as detailed in the project Communications Management Plan	_____	_____
• Conduct analyses of project performance and issue change requests as needed	_____	_____
• Establish reports for use in risk monitoring and control	_____	_____
• Use a project risk audit to examine and document the effectiveness of the risk response	_____	_____
• Ensure that project risk is an agenda item at each project meeting to determine if additional risk responses are required	_____	_____
• Assess the number of workarounds that have occurred; document and incorporate them into the project plan and risk response plan	_____	_____
• Analyze reserves to determine if the remaining reserve is adequate	_____	_____

Closeout Phase

	Yes	No
• Prepare a complete set of indexed project records for archiving, as appropriate	_____	_____
• Set up a process for the client's formal acceptance of all deliverables	_____	_____
• Provide contractors with written notice that the contract has been completed	_____	_____
• Follow an administrative closure procedure	_____	_____
• Follow a contract closure procedure	_____	_____
• Conduct a final project review to analyze project success, effectiveness, and lessons learned	_____	_____
• Update the knowledge management system based on the lessons learned from the project	_____	_____
• Assign responsibility for contract administration to include		
• Authorizing work	_____	_____
• Monitoring work	_____	_____
• Ensuring changes are properly approved	_____	_____
• Ensuring proper signature authority	_____	_____
• Verifying the adequacy of the vendor's work	_____	_____
• Set up a contract change control system that includes		
• Required paperwork	_____	_____
• Tracking systems	_____	_____
• Dispute resolution procedures	_____	_____
• Proposed contract changes	_____	_____
• Approval levels for authorizing changes	_____	_____
• Conduct performance reviews of the seller's progress in terms of		
• Scope	_____	_____
• Quality	_____	_____
• Schedule	_____	_____
• Cost	_____	_____
• Conduct inspections and audits to identify any weaknesses in the contractor's work	_____	_____
• Set up a performance reporting system for use by contractors	_____	_____
• Establish a payment system with the needed reviews and approvals	_____	_____

	Yes	No
• Establish a records management system for use with each contract	_____	_____
• Ensure that contract documentation is complete for inclusion with the final project records	_____	_____
• Ensure that the person responsible for contract administration provides the vendor with formal notification that the contract has been completed	_____	_____

INSTRUMENT 2–R
Risk Identification Checklist

Use this instrument as the basis for categorizing project risks. Use these categories as a first approximation, then enhance and modify them to be in line with the needs and policies of the organization.

Categorize the risks into categories such as:

- **Business Impact**—risks associated with constraints imposed by management or the marketplace
- **Client Needs**—risks associated with changes in attributes of the deliverable as suggested by the client or in client-imposed dates that affect the deliverable
- **Client Characteristics**—risks associated with the sophistication of the client and the Project Manager's ability to communicate with the client effectively
- **Deliverable Size or Capacity**—risks associated with the overall size or capacity of the product to be built or modified and the expected quality level
- **Development Environment**—risks associated with the availability and quality of the tools to be used to build the product
- **Legal and Regulatory**—risks associated with possible legal or regulatory changes that may affect the project
- **Organization**—risks associated with the performing organization, such as those involving dependencies with other projects, resources that are supporting multiple projects and are needed at specific time frames, availability of funding, and project prioritization within the organization
- **Project Management**—risks associated with project management activities such as estimating, planning, scheduling, controlling, and communicating, with an emphasis on constraints and assumptions
- **Staff Size and Experience**—risks associated with the overall technical and project experience of the people who will do the work, particularly as external forces affect the size and nature of the project team
- **Technology**—risks associated with the complexity of the system to be built or product to be delivered, the inevitable rapid changes in the technology, and the extent to which the latest technology must be incorporated into the deliverable

Characterizing Project Risk

Use this instrument as a first-order guideline for categorizing project risks. Note: There are several ways to categorize risk. Pick a strategy that is compatible with the organization.

1. Source of Risk
   a. Within the project
   b. Outside the project
   c. Outside the enterprise

2. Probability of Occurrence
   a. Qualitatively
   b. Quantitatively

3. Impact of Occurrence
   a. On schedule
   b. On cost
   c. On scope
   d. On quality
   e. On the project team

4. Response Plan
   a. Avoid
   b. Accept
   c. Transfer
   d. Mitigate
   e. Exploit
   f. Share
   g. Enhance
   h. Contingent responses

INSTRUMENT 2–T

Risk Tracking Form

Use this form to record and monitor the distribution of risk among the Work Breakdown Structure (WBS) elements. Cumulative entries will show the progression of this ongoing activity over the life of the project.

WBS Component and Number	Risk Item	Risk ID Number	Risk Owner	Rank This Period	Rank Last Period	Triggers	Risk Response Plan	Consequences: Actual or Potential

INSTRUMENT 2–U

Risk Ranking Form

Use this instrument to identify and prioritize project risks. Review for correctness on a regular basis.

Work Breakdown Structure Component and Number	Risk Item	Root Causes	Risk Category (Technical, External, Organizational, Project Management, or Other—please explain)	Impact on Project Objectives (Scope, Quality, Time, Cost)	Risk Impact (Very Low, Low, Moderate, High, Very High)	Probability of Occurrence (10%, 30%, 50%, 70%, 90%)	Impact Value	Overall Risk Score	Priority Ranking

INSTRUMENT 2–V

Risk Monitoring and Control Checklist

Use this instrument to record the intensity and sophistication of the risk activities of the project. Since there is no weighted scoring, and this is a first approximation, a general summary of positive/affirmative responses is sufficient as the rating. An absolute ranking is not as significant as an increase or decrease in ranking during two successive assessments.

	Yes	No
• Were risk responses implemented as planned?	_____	_____
• Was the risk response action effective as expected?	_____	_____
• Was a new response required?	_____	_____
• Were the project assumptions valid?	_____	_____
• Were risk triggers used?	_____	_____
• Were risk policies and procedures followed?	_____	_____
• Were change requests analyzed to determine whether approved changes generated new risks or changes in previously identified risks?	_____	_____
• Were reports on possible risks prepared throughout the project?	_____	_____
• Was risk an agenda item at team meetings?	_____	_____
• When the project scope changed, was the change evaluated for possible risk impacts?	_____	_____
• Were project risk reviews or audits conducted?	_____	_____
• Were results from earned value analyses used to determine whether there was a need for updated risk analysis?	_____	_____
• Were project status reports analyzed to determine whether there were impacts on the risk management process?	_____	_____
• Was it necessary to use workarounds for unidentified or accepted risks?	_____	_____
• Was it necessary to use a contingency plan?	_____	_____
• Were change requests issued to handle workarounds or contingency plans?	_____	_____
• Throughout the project, were comparisons of the amount of contingency reserves remaining to the amount of risk remaining made to see if the remaining reserve was adequate?	_____	_____
• Was a risk database or repository established?	_____	_____
• Were risk identification checklists updated?	_____	_____

	Yes	No
• Were lessons learned collected on the actual outcomes of the risk analysis and responses? Were they included in the project closure documents?	_____	_____
• Were templates, such as the organization's Risk Management Plan or Risk Response Plan, analyzed to determine whether changes to them would be beneficial for future projects?	_____	_____

INSTRUMENT 2–W

Risk Response Plan Tracking

Use this instrument for each risk in the risk response plan to track the effectiveness of the plan.

Risk Event	WBS Element and Number	Risk Owner	Effect on Project Objectives (major, intermediate, minor)	Response Selected (avoid, accept, transfer, mitigate, exploit, share, enhance)	Contractual Agreements	Time for the Response	Risk Trigger	Risk Budget	Contingency Reserves (time and cost)	Contingency Plans	Fallback Plans	Expected Residual Risks	Secondary Risks

Risk Map

Use this instrument to develop a tabular and visual map of project risks. Often, visual display of data enhances the decision-making process.

Classify each risk:

1—Negligible	If the risk does occur, the project management team will passively accept it and not take any action.
2—Marginal	If the risk does occur, the project management team will actively accept the risk and use a contingency plan that it has developed.
3—Probable	The risk is likely to occur, but the project management team plans to avoid it to protect the project objectives from its impact.
4—Critical	The risk is expected to occur and, when it occurs, it is expected to affect the project objectives. Financial exposure is expected, and the project team has a transfer response prepared, which it will execute.
5—Catastrophic	The risk is expected to occur and, when it occurs, it will adversely affect the overall project objectives. A risk owner has been identified and risk triggers have been established. A mitigation response has been prepared. Contingency funds are available.

Event Occurrence	Event Impact/Probability
Unlikely	Not expected to occur unless there are unusual situations
Possible	Expected to occur once or twice during the project
Probable	Expected to occur several times during the project
Likely	Expected to occur often during the project
Highly Likely	Expected to occur regularly throughout the project

Then, over time, prepare a risk index for each project. The Project Management Office can use the index at the enterprise level to assess the types of risks that have occurred and are expected to occur and to reevaluate the classification scheme.

Risk Index

Count the number of occurrences in each risk class.

Risk Event Occurrence	Risk Class				
	1 Negligible	2 Marginal	3 Probable	4 Critical	5 Catastrophic
Unlikely					
Possible					
Probable					
Likely					
Highly Likely					

INSTRUMENT 2–Y

Brief Post-Delivery Project Audit

Use this instrument to assess the sophistication of the project management activities, as a pre-lude to enhancing project procedures for future projects. The score for each area is simply the sum of positive/affirmative responses. With continuous improvements in project procedures, the audit scores should continue to increase.

Project Planning and Execution	Yes	No
• Was the project objective clear?	_____	_____
• Was a detailed Project Management Plan prepared?	_____	_____
• Did the Project Management Plan cover the full life cycle from initiating to closing?	_____	_____
• Was work to be done authorized as planned?	_____	_____
• Was a project management information system established and used?	_____	_____
• Was the project management methodology followed?	_____	_____
• Were resources available when required?	_____	_____
• Were changes implemented based on a defined approach?	_____	_____
• Were corrective and preventive actions assessed for effectiveness?	_____	_____
• Were risk responses adequate?	_____	_____
• Did the project receive top management support throughout its life cycle?	_____	_____
• Was the client fully informed throughout the project of:		
– Project progress?	_____	_____
– Project scope changes?	_____	_____
– Project cost changes?	_____	_____
– Project duration changes?	_____	_____
– Project quality changes?	_____	_____
• Were project communication channels established?	_____	_____
• Was project communication effective and timely?	_____	_____
• Was information about the project provided in a timely manner?	_____	_____
• Was a schedule baseline established?	_____	_____
• Was a quality baseline established?	_____	_____
• Was a scope baseline established?	_____	_____
• Did the project have a detailed budget?	_____	_____

Project Deliverable	**Yes**	**No**
• Was the client satisfied with the final:		
– Deliverable?	_____	_____
– Cost?	_____	_____
– Duration?	_____	_____
• How well did the final project attributes match the original Project Management Plan?	_____	_____
• What were the major variances from the original Project Management Plan?	_____	_____
• Of the variances listed, which ones were caused by:		
– Shortfalls in planning requirements?	_____	_____
– Shortfalls in skills of team members in planning?	_____	_____
– Quality issues?	_____	_____
– Unforeseen risks?	_____	_____
– Changes in client requirements?	_____	_____
– Unforeseen and unpredicted events?	_____	_____

Learning from the Experiences of this Project

	Yes	**No**
• Which project procedures need to be changed for future projects?	_____	_____
– To minimize variances from the original Project Management Plan:		
• For deliverables	_____	_____
• For costs	_____	_____
• For schedules	_____	_____
– To make general improvements in organizational project management	_____	_____
– To analyze and understand project scope	_____	_____
– To document project requirements	_____	_____
– To meet quality standards	_____	_____
– To meet requirements of regulations and standards	_____	_____
– To determine whether the project activities complied with the organizational policies, procedures, and processes	_____	_____
– To minimize non-value-added activities	_____	_____
– To create preventive actions for similar problems	_____	_____
– To promote continuous process improvement	_____	_____
– To ensure that the project is linked to the organization's strategic plan	_____	_____
– To improve the quality, reliability, availability, and timeliness of the data in the project management information system	_____	_____
– To collect and distribute performance information	_____	_____
– To enhance contract administration and partnering with subcontractors	_____	_____
– To enhance stakeholder analysis and management	_____	_____
– To improve communication on project issues	_____	_____
– To maintain the integrity of baselines	_____	_____

	Yes	No
– To document the impact of requested changes	_____	_____
– To validate defect repair	_____	_____
– To ensure that changes are integrated across all aspects of the project	_____	_____
– To ensure that formal client acceptance is received	_____	_____
– To enhance the knowledge, skills, and competencies of the project team members	_____	_____
– To ensure that the project manager has the needed authority to execute the project	_____	_____
– To identify the effectiveness of the team's ground rules as expressed in its charter	_____	_____
– To identify the effectiveness of specific risk responses	_____	_____
– To enhance the information in the lessons learned/knowledge management repository	_____	_____

INSTRUMENT 2–Z

Abbreviated Project Closeout Checklist

Use this instrument as a quick guide for the actions that need to be performed as part of the project closeout.

	Yes	No
✓ Prepare performance evaluations for each team member.	_____	_____
✓ Reassign team members.	_____	_____
✓ Update the personnel skills database.	_____	_____
✓ Archive key project documentation.	_____	_____
✓ Disseminate the lessons learned.	_____	_____
✓ Close out financial documents and records.	_____	_____
✓ Conduct financial audit.	_____	_____
✓ Prepare final financial report.	_____	_____
✓ Conduct a procurement audit.	_____	_____
✓ Provide vendors with formal acceptance of deliverables.	_____	_____
✓ Review the project's Work Breakdown Structure.	_____	_____
✓ Conduct a quality audit.	_____	_____
✓ Complete the issue and defect management database.	_____	_____
✓ Complete the process measurement database.	_____	_____
✓ Document the final approved project scope.	_____	_____
✓ Complete the configuration management database.	_____	_____
✓ Complete all outstanding action items.	_____	_____
✓ Prepare and document required customer acceptance.	_____	_____
✓ Transmit records to storage.	_____	_____
✓ Release all equipment and materials.	_____	_____
✓ Prepare a final project report.	_____	_____
✓ Submit the final report to the customer.	_____	_____
✓ Receive formal acceptance from the customer.	_____	_____
✓ Submit a final report to the sponsor.	_____	_____
✓ Update the lessons learned/knowledge management database.	_____	_____

CHAPTER 3

Project People Metrics

Project team members are the backbone and skeletal structure upon which projects are successfully implemented. The premise is that people make a project happen. Therefore, project management is (or should be) primarily about people and how they work together in support of a project's objectives and ultimately in support of the organization's goals. Team support of the organization occurs directly in the area of managing project things and indirectly in handling enterprise issues such as infrastructure support and upper management endorsement.

A motivated team can successfully discharge continuous improvement duties in areas including client satisfaction, flexibility, and productivity (Lynch and Cross 1995). Thus, it is somewhat surprising that many organizations do not include people factors in defining project metrics. The purpose of performance metrics within the context of people issues is to identify opportunities for motivating desired behaviors in team members. By definition, organizations with higher levels of maturity will have metrics that are dedicated to people-related issues at both the project and organization levels.

PEOPLE AS INTELLECTUAL RESOURCES

Organizations must use the sum total of all their resources to sustain success. Traditionally, physical resources, such as buildings and machinery, have been considered part of the resource pool. Ideally, people resources of the organization should be regarded as intellectual resources.

Intellectual resources relate to the knowledge, experience, and behavior of employees. Therefore, many of the organization's most important resources are somewhat intangible, such as organizational learning, market knowledge, and staff morale. These seemingly intangible resources provide the organization opportunities for continuous growth and development toward the more global objective of maintaining—or enhancing—its competitive edge.

Intellectual resources are critical success factors and, because they have far-reaching and subtle strategic importance, their value should be measured (Drucker 2000). Naturally, the overall organizational resource structure also should include the organization's infrastructure that supports employees' efforts.

Skandia was one of the first companies to explicitly recognize organizational intellectual capital and use it as a foundation for measuring key performance indicators (Edvinsson and Malone 1997). Such measurement, coupled with the use of a balanced reporting approach, represented a significant milestone in how people were viewed within organizations. It also signaled a shift from the industrial era to a knowledge economy by using a more systematic description of the company's potential ability to transform intellectual capital into financial capital.

Skandia's intellectual capital model, called the Skandia Intellectual Navigator, focuses on five areas: financial, client, process, renewal, and human. The latter four areas collectively constitute the company's intellectual capital. The literature suggests that attention to people issues, such as coaching, mentoring, and training, has positive effects on the bottom line. People-oriented work practices have contributed to reported market value increases of as much as $18,000, sales increases of up to $27,000, and profit increases of as much as $3,000 per employee (Geaney and Engel 1996).

The People Capital for Project Management instrument adapts the concepts advanced by Skandia. (Instrument 3–A) It can assist an organization in recognizing the intellectual capital that people bring to projects and ultimately to organizations. Notably, this instrument also addresses enterprise issues, as it examines the interaction between people capital and organizational success.

WHAT ARE PEOPLE METRICS?

People metrics, which characterize and quantify the behavioral attributes of people, do not lend themselves to easy quantification. Consequently, there are fewer project people metrics than project things metrics.

Project people metrics can include indicators of procedures for conflict management, communication, collaboration, teamwork, and technical competency. People metrics also can deal with the features of the enterprise environment that promote leadership, integrity, and professional responsibility. Regardless, project people metrics are intended primarily to assess, directly or indirectly, whether team members are executing their tasks well. Generally, project people metrics can be viewed as metrics that measure the friendliness of the organization toward the project team and the friendliness of team members toward one another.

By assessing the management style of the organization, it is possible to evaluate environmental friendliness toward the team. Douglas McGregor (1960) stated that people can be categorized as either disliking work (Theory X) or enjoying work and seeking opportunities to do their best (Theory Y). The Organizational Management Style Inventory adapts this behavioral theory to the project management environment. (Instrument 3–B)

A team charter also can be an effective means of setting the stage for a team environment that is conducive to team members being mutually supportive and accountable for the missions of the project. (Instrument 3–C) By definition, organizations with higher levels of maturity have metrics that are dedicated to people-related issues at both the project and organization levels. According to Edvinsson and Malone (1997), these must be well-reasoned, well-designed metrics; moreover, they must be teleological, or with a special purpose in showing where the company is and where it should be. The mere fact that some organizations will select certain metrics over others points to their biases in the area of human resources.

Not surprisingly, there are other barriers to selecting and using people metrics. Miller and Wurzburg (1995) suggest that barriers include the lack of transparency in the cost of labor and the difficulty of measuring the productive capacity of the knowledge, skills, and abilities that people acquire through expertise and education. Further, organizations cannot easily capitalize training costs or the benefits of increased knowledge and learning. Therefore, the added benefits of having competent people support the organization's projects do not clearly move into the balance sheet of financial reports. Thus, without a sophisticated method to measure and value people resources, there is a risk of misallocating resources within an organization.

People are simultaneously participants in the metrics program and sources of its data. People metrics cannot have the desired benefits unless their development recognizes this basic fact. Project people must be involved in planning and executing the metrics system if tools are to be successful. Thus, each project participant must clearly understand the objectives of the project metrics and the ways in which these metrics, directly or indirectly, affect the organization's objectives.

Finally, project teams must be empowered to define metrics that they believe are of value. Likewise, they should be permitted to recommend starting or stopping the use of certain metrics as they deem appropriate. Naturally, such empowerment would be counterproductive in organizations that have not achieved higher levels of project management maturity.

MOTIVATION

Literature on human behavior contains several models and theories that can be adapted and applied within the project management environment. Although generally called "motivation theories," they are best described as "primary personality attributes" when used in the project management environment.

One especially relevant motivation theory addresses the need for achievement, affiliation, and power as part of performing project management activities (McClelland 1961; Boyatzis 1982). The need for achievement is characterized by a desire to seek attainable but challenging goals and a strong desire for positive feedback on performance. The need for affiliation is characterized by a desire to be part of a group with friendly relationships and to have roles that involve human interaction.

Finally, the need for power is characterized by a desire to have an impact and be viewed as influential and effective. For example, if assignments with measurable objectives are given to two team members with achievement and power motivations, the achievement-oriented member is likely to produce successful results, whereas the power-motivated person is likely not to, at least not until he or she negotiates to craft the assignment to his or her standards. (Instrument 3–D)

Figure 3–1 is a stylized depiction of the personal preference style attributes of a team of four. With this information, the project manager should be able to match the duties of team members to their strong points and inclinations. Alternatively, such knowledge should allow the project manager to predict the behavior of a certain team member in a future situation. The following anecdotal illustration highlights the major differences in the three motivation styles in the development and management of a team charter.

The achievement-oriented individual, who is interested in team goal setting, will be the one who initially develops the team charter. However, once the project is under way, the power-oriented individual, who is interested in being a leader, will call frequent meetings to modify the objectives and content of the charter to ensure that they continue to relate to the organization's strategic vision and mission. The affiliation-oriented person, who is interested in providing an amicable working environment, will try to moderate the efforts of these two individuals, facilitate meetings, and mentor individuals as they join the team so they understand the team's operating protocols as delineated in the team charter (Rad and Levin 2003).

Figure 3-1
Predominant Personality Attributes

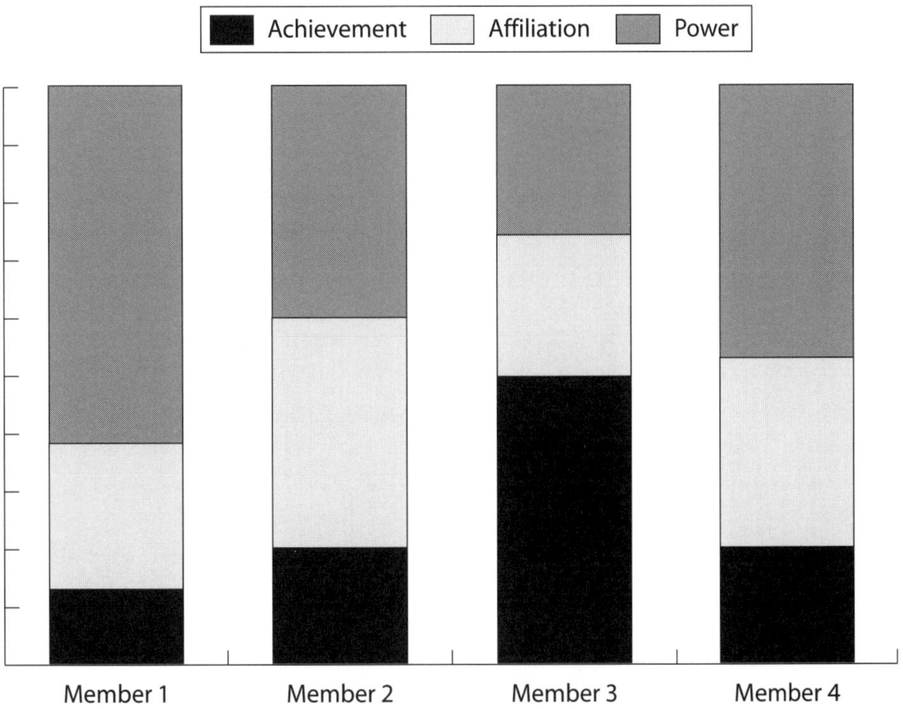

PERFORMANCE

The primary focus of the project team is, or should be, the project's final deliverable. However, the team focuses on the deliverable in light of the processes that ensure delivery of the desired product in the most cost-effective and efficient manner, while maintaining harmony and teamwork within the team.

The mission of the project team is to plan the delivery of the desired product through adoption of best practices and consistent procedures. The team is expected to implement those plans in a dynamic environment and to manage all the emerging issues that influence team performance in delivering the desired product.

Most appraisal systems have been developed with individual performers in mind. In projects where the team is the unit of performance, it is often difficult to determine the line of demarcation between team performance and individual activities. Team performance indicators should include indices that measure performance features that are under the team's control and at the same time lead to the organization's success. Further, performance metrics must be compatible with the maturity ranking of the team and/or the organization.

Many personnel appraisal systems have features that could potentially impact the performance of project personnel negatively. Such negative impact could be significant if these appraisal standards interfere with improvements in employee performance, fail to address organizational improvements, are poorly designed, and are not friendly toward team spirit. The ideal performance measurement system reflects the organization's culture, fosters continuous improvement, and promotes career development.

Project success depends on effective team performance. In turn, the collective performance of the team depends on the individual performance and behavioral traits of each team member. Accordingly, each team member must understand the overall team objectives, as well as his or her own individual objectives.

Each team member's roles and responsibilities must be defined in terms of the nature of the individual results needed to support the team's work processes. To that end, a formalized people metrics system provides a logical basis for responses to questions such as:

- What attributes of work are considered quantitative, and what attributes are considered qualitative?

- If a qualitative approach is followed for metrics, how can performance be monitored to ensure it meets or exceeds expectations?

- Are different types of metrics systems required for co-located teams and virtual teams?

- How can appraisal systems become team friendly?

- What combination of metrics is required for organizational success?

- How can an appraisal system become team oriented, rather than individual oriented?

Using instruments that address these issues, a team member can obtain a more detailed appreciation of his or her technical performance and general behavior. In addition, such information can help team members understand how other team members react to everyday project situations.

The intent is not to acquire a tool to change people's behavior, although sometimes that can happen as part of the self-assessment process. Rather, the goal is to obtain a clearer picture of the behavioral attributes of team members, knowing that personal challenges and characteristics of a team environment can become sources of frustration and stress that can impact team performance. A set of metrics, and its accompanying guidelines, can teach team members how to cope with these different behaviors and use the inevitable team conflicts innovatively and progressively.

A multiple feedback approach facilitates the process of aligning individual team member behavior with the collective behavior of the project team. This approach is variously known as a 360° evaluation, multi-rater, full-circle, or multi-level feedback system. It refers to a general process of gathering observations concerning performance from many different individuals. In a 360° evaluation, the project manager, functional manager, team members, client, and others, as appropriate, conduct separate appraisals of the same person. (Rad and Levin 2003)

As team members and stakeholders have unique perspectives on one another's performance, a 360° evaluation typically provides a much more realistic, comprehensive evaluation (see Figure 3–2). Two approaches to such an evaluation are provided. (Instruments 3–E and 3–F)

To support project teamwork, each team member should have the opportunity to evaluate other team members using either of the two instruments. The two primary focuses of a 360° evaluation are (1) to improve the work performance of the project team, and (2) to mitigate the negative effects of personal challenges and issues. The results of a 360° evaluation exercise enable team members to improve working relationships within the team. Further, they elucidate the developmental needs of team members and indicate what new tools and techniques would support team effectiveness.

Ideally, the performance-related items to be evaluated should be collectively determined by the team members during the project kickoff meet-

Figure 3-2
360° Evaluation

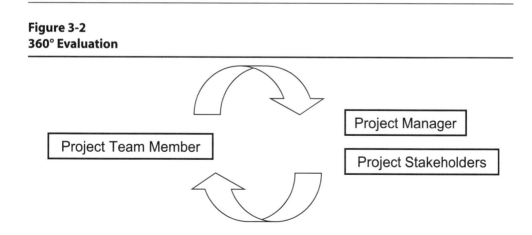

ing. Team members could either design an entirely new system or tailor an existing organizational rating system.

If team members have a direct involvement in the design or customization of the evaluation instrument, they are far more likely to value the resulting data and subsequent recommendations. If the entire team is involved in determining the specific rating items at the beginning of the project, then the biases of individual team members will be averaged out. In addition, the team, as a unit, should develop a procedure governing use of the rating process.

Team input, as compiled through this type of instrument, can be particularly useful for recognition and awards. Further, periodic ratings allow the team to determine whether changes are necessary in project processes or in the behavior of individual team members. Naturally, the frequency of the ratings depends on the length of the project and the preferences of the project team.

Sometimes it is desirable to conduct the rating process anonymously. For example, on a newly formed team, it is often useful to keep the identities of each team member confidential so that feedback is honest. However, on mature teams, particularly ones with a culture of open communication, there should be enough trust and emotional comfort among team members to identify the raters. Open evaluations provide the foundation for direct feedback, mentoring opportunities, and continuous improvement.

Each team member can use the 360° instrument for a self-assessment with minor tailoring. The results obtained allow an individual to see how others perceive him or her. Then, the team member can compare those views with his or her own self-assessment and ultimately identify his or her strengths and weaknesses.

Alternatively, the assessment focus can be solely on ways to improve overall team performance, without identifying specific individuals. Using this approach, each team member rates other team members anonymously. Then, a neutral third party analyzes the anonymous ratings and presents the summarized results to the entire team.

TEAMWORK

Teamwork is that elusive concept that allows all team members to focus collectively on project success. Through the movement toward management-by-projects and greater use of virtual teams, project work is becoming more people-centric rather than location-centric. Therefore, team-related issues, such as team building, teamwork, team organization, team turnover, and team experience, are now far more critical to successful project performance (Sanvido, Grobler, Parfitt, and Guvenis 1992). Efficiency and quality can be maximized through optimal allocation of people resources that have the right attitude, mindset, and motivation for that specific environment.

To promote teamwork, it is necessary to understand the behavioral traits that contribute to teamwork, team spirit, and team harmony (Rad and Levin 2003). A Collaborative Leadership instrument facilitates this understanding by highlighting the behavioral attributes of team members, particularly as these attributes relate to teamwork and proper team interaction. (Instrument 3–G) The Teamwork Attributes instrument, which characterizes a team member's behavior across ten different personality attributes, complements it. (Instrument 3–F)

Different team members will have unique strengths and weaknesses across each attribute. However, by being aware of the differences, team members should relate to each other better, and hopefully, collaborate more efficiently.

COMMUNICATIONS MANAGEMENT

Successful conduct of a project requires the transfer of voluminous amounts of information among multiple stakeholders. Consequently, communications play a major role in project success, and proper communications planning significantly influences all performance attributes of a project (Alarcon and Ashley 1992).

Metrics comprise a significant component of the project communications management processes, and communication-related tasks are estimated to comprise over 90% of a project manager's job. Therefore, it is essential to assess the effectiveness of project communications management activities.

A project Communications Management Plan should be developed that lists the reports that will be routinely prepared and disseminated. By extension, data should be collected to determine whether clients or executive managers have requested additional information beyond the standard reports, or whether the existing reports are useful and timely. In addition, the timeliness and frequency of project review meetings, the ease of access to reports, the ability to tailor reports in response to stakeholder requirements, and the number of requests for ad hoc reports should be assessed. (Instrument 3–H)

Each organization has a unique collection of communications tools and techniques, ranging from text files, to spreadsheets, to advanced project management scheduling software programs, to complex organizational databases and portals. Project personnel might need training in advanced features of software tools in order to exploit these communications tools to their fullest. Then, the project team should regularly analyze the magnitude of schedule and cost variances and the number of schedule and budget revisions.

On a regular basis, the team should evaluate the effectiveness of the cost/schedule management plans using the information provided by the metrics suite. Moreover, the usefulness of the reporting tools should be evaluated by determining if additional reports are necessary for a clear and complete look at the project.

COMPETENCY

In any project, there are major variations in the ability of project participants to do their jobs. When deemed *competent,* it means the project manager or team member is operating at an acceptable level of performance.

Competence does not mean that the project professional possesses perfect knowledge of all areas. Competence also involves knowing what you do not know, having the courage to express concerns about these potential deficiencies, and obtaining assistance when needed. Thus, competence involves the ability to assess personal strengths and then to sharpen skills in areas needing improvement. (Instrument 3–I) Organizations should foster a positive attitude toward improvement such that employees believe that competent people are capable people possessing a goal of superior performance in all areas, although they might not have yet attained that goal yet.

Competency can be regarded as both a people issue and a project issue. It is a people issue because it relates to how well a team member is prepared to perform assigned tasks. On the other hand, competency can be regarded as a project issue because, when the competencies of all project personnel are summed, an average competency can be achieved, which represents the competency of the team for the project. Then, summing the competency of all teams provides an indicator of the organization's ability to deliver useful and innovative products in an effective manner.

Clearly, measuring individual competency, as well as organizational competency, provides the road map toward improvement. As organizations become more knowledge-intensive, and as continuous improvement becomes a prerequisite for success, the importance of knowledge and skills takes on greater significance.

Organizational project management success depends on the active involvement of personnel at various levels of the organization, at the right time, with the appropriate competency, and with high vigor (see Figures 3–3 and 3–4). From the goal-oriented vantage point of the project, competency can be categorized in four separate areas: sophistication in handling the technical content of the project, the project things issues, the project people issues, and the enterprise issues

Figure 3-3
Project Management Competency

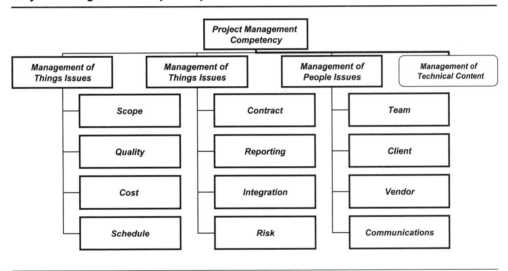

Figure 3-4
Areas of Project Management Competency

	Initiate	Plan	Execute	Control	Close
Scope	Skilled	Skilled	Skilled	Skilled	Skilled
Quality	Skilled	Skilled	Skilled	Skilled	Skilled
Cost	Skilled	Skilled	Skilled	Skilled	Skilled
Time	Skilled	Skilled	Skilled	Skilled	Skilled
Risk	Skilled	Skilled	Skilled	Skilled	Skilled
Integration	Skilled	Skilled	Skilled	Skilled	Skilled
Human Resources	Skilled	Skilled	Skilled	Skilled	Skilled
Communications	Skilled	Skilled	Skilled	Skilled	Skilled
Procurement	Skilled	Skilled	Skilled	Skilled	Skilled

Examples of technical skills are those necessary to understand the intricacies of dealing with areas such as Web technology, construction equipment, or fiber optics design. Competency in things skills involves state-of-the-art knowledge of management of project facets such as quality, schedule, risk, and scope. Competency in people skills can be demonstrated in graceful handling of communications, conflict management, and team-building issues. Team members must additionally possess, or develop, leadership attributes such as trustworthiness, charisma, loyalty, and openness.

The attributes dealing with the management of enterprise issues involve political savvy, knowledge of organizational culture, and skill in building networks with project stakeholders (see Figure 3–5). Generally speaking, a successful team member must have competencies in dealing effectively with the parent organization. Finally, the people associated with a project must be able to interact with, be committed to, and support the enterprise's strategic visions, goals, and objectives.

The appropriateness and sophistication of the project team's practice are at the heart of any successful project. Accordingly, repeated success occurs when project teams start with good processes and continue to learn and improve their personal practices. As an example, the Siemens Corporation estimated that its project success rate increased by 30% after project management training (Ward 2002).

To work toward a competency improvement program in project management, the first step is to establish a baseline of knowledge, skills, and competencies for each project management function. This baseline then serves as

Figure 3-5
Team Member Performance

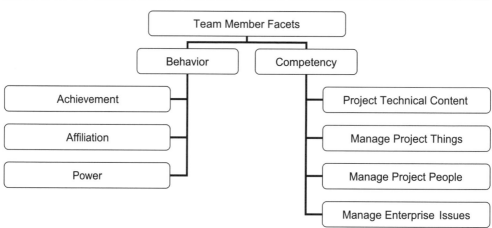

the framework for a personal improvement program, allowing individuals to measure specific improvements in their professional profile (Levin 1999).

A common technique is to identify successful project managers in the organization and assess their skills as a first approximation for the competency model. To the extent possible and practicable, attempts should be made to determine which critical skills facilitated the success of these particular managers, and how these exceptional project managers acquired these skills (see Figure 3–6).

Care should be taken not to identify those project managers who simply appear to be successful because they are charismatic leaders, but rather to identify those who have managed projects that have been deemed successful based on specific project indices. Therefore, clear and specific criteria to measure the success of project managers, and the success of the project team, are required.

One important additional feature of this exercise involves determining what further skills would have been necessary to produce an even higher level of success for a project. This information highlights the project management skills that future successful project mangers need to possess. It is highly useful to prioritize these skills in relation to the organization's objectives and goals. Then, using subsets of these skills, organizational standards for junior, intermediate, and senior levels of project managers can be established. (Instrument 3–J)

Figure 3-6
Organizational Competency in Project Management

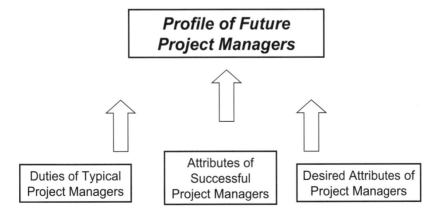

Another way to determine desired project management competencies is to develop a prioritized list of between seven and ten activities that occupy a project manager's time. Then, this list is reconciled with another list of between seven and ten tasks that are, or should be, the responsibility of a project manager. This exercise can be performed by a focus group of experienced project managers, just as the 3M Company did (Storeygard 1995). Figure 3–7 presents the ten critical success factors this focus group developed for project managers.

MATURITY OF TEAMS AND ORGANIZATIONS

Since the performance of the team is the sum total of the performance of its individual members, the sophistication and maturity of a team can be inferred, or calculated, from indices used at the individual level. Figure 3–8 depicts the relationship between a project's success and the maturity of the hosting environment.

Given that project management maturity can be regarded as both an organizational attribute and a people attribute, it is important to consider the context when developing or using maturity metrics. If these metrics are used for people purposes, the spirit of measurement is how much they improve the progress of a given person or a given project. By comparison, the organizational vantage point requires measurement of the effectiveness of these functions toward collective organizational goals. (Instruments 3–K and 3–L) The project management maturity of an organization is directly and predictably related to the success of the collective projects of that organization, which in turn is related to the success of individuals.

At the lower end of the maturity scale is an organization that has no procedures for its teams, no historical data, and no history of meeting cost,

---

Figure 3-7
Critical Success Factors for Project Managers

- Client/team/management communications
- Assignment of the right people to the right task
- Project planning to meet identified constraints
- Project estimating to meet identified constraints
- Client commitment/involvement/ownership
- Documentation
- Technology currency and awareness
- Stress management
- Monitoring and controlling deliverables
- Organizational astuteness

Figure 3-8
Team Maturity

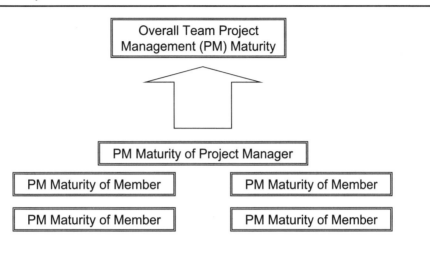

schedule, and quality targets on projects. This organization ranks somewhere between 0 and 1 (see Figure 3–9). Most maturity models overlook this stage, hoping that such an organization does not exist. At the upper end of the maturity spectrum is the mature organization that consistently completes its projects ahead of time and under budget. Such an organization can boast about its cadre of motivated, competent people who are the primary reason for its project success.

An anecdotal example of an organization making its way from immature to mature is the one in which, despite a lack of proper procedures and competent people, projects miraculously do meet their targets. While these events should be celebrated, it would be unwise to expect them to be repeated with any regularity. The only predictable way for an organization to have successful projects is for that organization to possess procedures that all team members follow (see Figure 3–10).

VIRTUAL TEAMS

As the number of companies with offices and plants around the world grows, multi-location virtual teams are becoming more popular. Such project teams might be cross-disciplinary, or they might comprise two separate departments such as production and research. Regardless, the key fact is that organizations can and must redefine themselves to optimize strategies and resources in response to competitive business pressures across borders.

Figure 3-9
Success and Maturity for Projects Teams

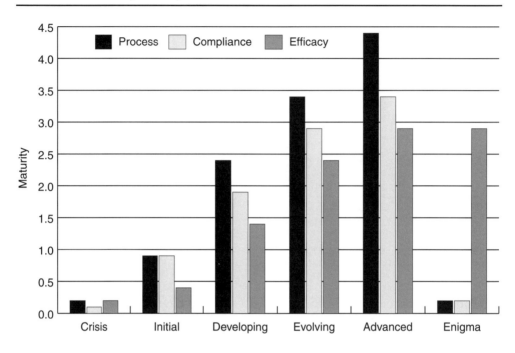

Figure 3-10
Success and Maturity for the Organization and Projects

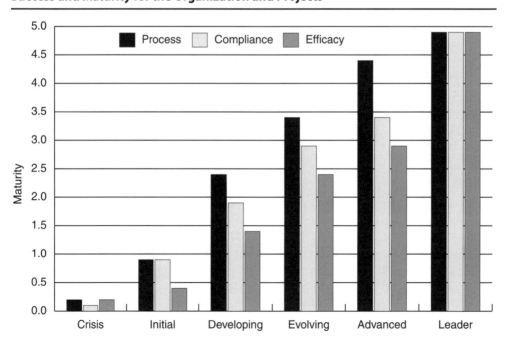

Virtual teams are different from traditional teams. Thus, it stands to reason that importing traditional procedures to a virtual team will minimize that team's effectiveness in handling project issues. Sometimes the mismatch is not immediately evident because efficiencies in the conduct of individual work remain the same regardless of project team texture (see Figures 3–11 and 3–12). However, a unique set of metrics is necessary to handle the special issues that virtual teams face (Rad and Levin 2003). This set can contain traditional procedures modified for the virtual environment; procedures so modified will yield efficiencies equal to those obtained by streamlined traditional teams.

People metrics quantify the performance and behavioral attributes of project people. The premise behind their use is that success in the delivery of things is an indirect manifestation of success in handling the people issues of the project. The more team members know about each other's attributes, the smoother the team will function. This mutual knowledge will fuel continuous improvement in relationships and ultimately in performance.

Figure 3-11
Stylized Comparison of Virtual and Traditional Teams: Undernourished Virtual Team

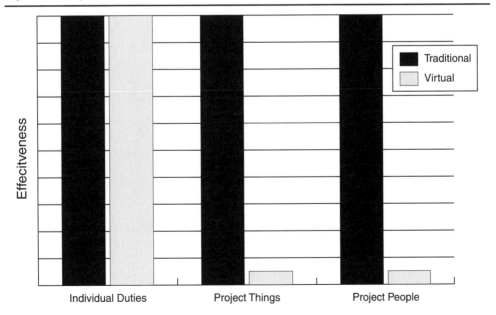

Figure 3-12
Stylized Comparison of Virtual and Traditional Teams: Reasonably Nourished Virtual Team

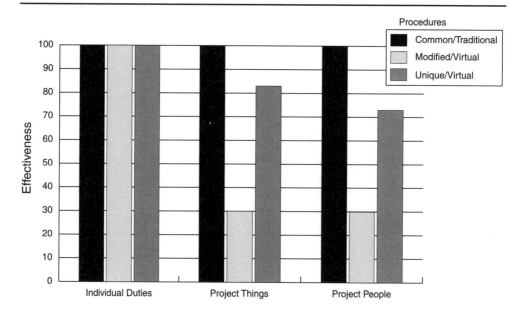

INSTRUMENT 3–A

People Capital for Project Management

Use this instrument to determine the extent to which an organization regards its people as valuable assets and necessary capital for maintaining competitiveness.

Determine the score for each area and then sum all scores to get a total score.

1—Not at all
2—Once in a while
3—On occasion
4—Often
5—Always

	Not at all	Once in a while	On occasion	Often	Always
1. INNOVATION					
1. Does the project's product or service differentiate it from its competitors?					
2. In developing the product or provisioning the service, do the Project Manager and team look for improvements in the overall project management process used?					
3. Are subproducts or additional services generated throughout the project?					
4. Is the project viewed as a way to move the organization into new markets and opportunities?					
5. Do the Project Manager and team use existing processes but look for ways to improve them and enhance existing standards of project management practice in the organization?					
2. VISION					
1. Does the Project Manager ensure that the project's vision supports the organization's vision?					
2. Does the Project Manager ensure that team members and major stakeholders hold comparable concepts of the project vision?					

	Not at all	Once in a while	On occasion	Often	Always
3. Does the Project Manager ensure that team members understand the corporate vision and the role of the project in support of this vision?					
4. Does the Project Manager ensure that the project's goals and objectives are supportive of the organization's strategic goals?					
5. Does the Project Manager review the organization's strategic goals periodically to ensure that the project's goals and objectives remain supportive?					
3. CULTURE					
1. Do most people on the project team demonstrate similar attitudes?					
2. Do project team members tend to behave in a similar fashion while working on the project?					
3. Do project team members deal with problems in a similar way?					
4. Do team members hold similar perceptions of the purpose of the project and its importance to the organization?					
5. Do project team members regularly share knowledge relative to project work?					
4. COMPANY VALUES					
1. Are organizational goals known, communicated to, and shared by the project team?					
2. Does the Project Manager follow an organizational standard that emphasizes open communication without retribution on all issues?					
3. Is there agreement between the Project Manager and the team regarding project goals in support of organizational goals?					
4. Does the project have a statement of values or code of conduct that reflects that of the organization?					
5. If there are discrepancies between actual behavior and the project's values, does the Project Manager and team use this information to determine whether changes are needed in the statement of values or code of conduct?					

	Not at all	Once in a while	On occasion	Often	Always
5. COLLABORATION ACROSS THE ORGANIZATION					
1. Does the Project Manager identify stakeholders across the organization so that the team can work with them throughout the project?					
2. Is the organization's atmosphere a synergistic one that supports project work?					
3. Are disruptions attributable to a lack of collaboration with other units in the organization minimal, if any?					
4. Do methods of communication facilitate communications with others on project work, even when working in a virtual environment?					
5. Do project team members feel that working relationships with internal stakeholders are positive?					
6. RELATIONSHIPS WITH CUSTOMERS					
1. Is the project customer driven rather than Project Manager/ team driven?					
2. In working on the project, does each team member recognize the potential for additional customer work in terms of other products or services?					
3. Do the Project Manager and team regularly contact their counterparts in the customer's organization in order to anticipate their demands?					
4. Do customer representatives regularly meet with their counterparts on the project team whenever needed, rather than just at scheduled times?					
5. Are customer requests for project information fulfilled in a timely manner?					
7. OTHER CUSTOMER METRICS					
1. What is the annual purchase rate for project management work?					
2. What is the rate of repeat customers for project management work?					
3. What is the investment in customer service versus the increased rate of customer satisfaction?					

	Not at all	Once in a while	On occasion	Often	Always
4. What is the ratio of customers with complaints versus those without complaints regarding project work?					
5. What is the ratio of customers lost versus new customers in terms of sales for project management work?					
6. What is the value of business development expenses for new and existing customers?					
7. What is the value of the company's market share for project management work versus that of its competitors?					
8. What is the investment in terms of technologies to ensure high levels of customer satisfaction (e.g., access by the customers to the project management information system, use of common platforms)?					
9. What is the percentage of dollars invested to promote strategic partnerships with customers in project work?					
10. What is the cost of sales to revenue in terms of business development initiatives that lead to project work?					
8. TEAM EMPOWERMENT					
1. Is project team member responsibility commensurate with authority?					
2. Does the project team operate as a self-directed team following a team charter or other ground rules it develops?					
3. Can the project team make decisions without having to consult other managers regarding project direction?					
4. Is the project team responsible for its actions as a team?					
5. Do project team members have the authority to perform their assigned tasks on the project?					
9. MOTIVATION					
1. Does the Project Manager need to proactively take initiative to motivate project team members?					
2. Are specific incentives required for project team member motivation?					

	Not at all	Once in a while	On occasion	Often	Always
3. Does the project team perceive that the project environment is challenging such that it is the team member's primary source of motivation?					
4. Do project goals and objectives suffice as motivators for project team members?					
5. Is working on a project viewed as a positive motivating force because of the organization's friendliness toward projects?					
10. TEAM MEMBER SATISFACTION					
1. Are team members anxious for the project to end so they can return to their functional unit?					
2. Is project work considered desirable relative to one's long-term career path?					
3. Are team members sorry to enter the closing phase of the project because they have enjoyed their work on the project?					
4. Do project team members seem pleased with their assignments to project work?					
5. Do project team members feel that their work on projects is valued throughout the organization?					
11. QUALITY FOCUS					
1. Do project team members consider excellence in their work a measure of their success?					
2. Do project team members consistently strive to meet customer expectations in light of constraints?					
3. Do customers typically find that the team's work is acceptable and does not need extensive rework?					
4. Does the project team establish a quality policy for its work?					
5. Does the project team focus on continuous improvement of processes as well as products of the project?					
12. CONTINUOUS IMPROVEMENT					
1. Do project team members suggest ideas for continuous improvement to the organization's project management practice?					

	Not at all	Once in a while	On occasion	Often	Always
2 Are project team members active in related professional organizations as a way to obtain and share knowledge in professional communities?					
3. Are project team members expected to apply skills and knowledge from training to their project work?					
4. Do project team members mentor and coach others in their areas of expertise?					
5. Does the organization encourage internal forums for exchange of ideas within its project management community?					

13. OTHER TEAM METRICS

1. What is the market value of a project team member?	$0–$25K	$25K–$50K	$50K–$75K	$75K–$100K	>$100K
2. What is the value added per team member salary?	0%–5%	5%–10%	10%–15%	15%–20%	>20%
3. What are the profits per team member from the project?	0%–5%	5%–10%	10%–15%	15%–20%	>20%
4. What is the age distribution of project team members?	All below 25, or all above 55	75% above 50, or 75% below 30	75% above above 45, or 75% below 35	50% above 40, 50% below 40	Equally distributed
5. How many project team members leave the organization each year?	>20%	15%–20%	10%–15%	5%–10%	0%–5%
6. How many project team members receive at least 40 hours of related training?	0%–5%	5%–10%	10%–15%	15%–20%	>20%
7. What is the annual direct cost (course materials, fees, logistics) of training per team member?	$0–$500	$500–$1K	$1K–$2K	$2K–$4K	>$4K
8. What is the indirect cost of training?	$0–$1K	$1K–$2K	$2K–$3K	$3K–$4K	$4K–$5K

9. How many project team members are from different nationalities/cultures?	<5%	5%–15%	15%–25%	25%–50%	>50%
10. To what extent does the organization support (per year, per employee) involvement in professional activities such as those of the Project Management Institute (PMI®), the Association for the Advancement of Cost Engineering (AACE), the Software Engineering Institute (SEI), and the Institute of Electrical and Electronics Engineers (IEEE)?	$0–$500	$500–$1K	$1K–$2K	$2K–$4K	>$4K

Organizational Management Style Inventory

Use to assess the friendliness of the organization's management style toward project management. Projects thrive and succeed in friendly environments but fail in hostile ones.

Use the numbers to indicate the proximity of your organizational attitude to either of the two extremes that are indicated by each statement. The total summary of the scores is not nearly as significant as the amount of change and direction of change between two successive assessments.

View	1	2	3	4	5	View
1. Management feels that most people do not like project work.						1. Management feels that people view their project work positively and enjoy working on it.
2. There is little empowerment; most team members work for managers who micromanage each assigned work package.						2. On each project, there is a sense of team spirit; team members are empowered to do their assigned work on specific work packages with limited, if any, supervision.
3. Most team members avoid responsibility; rather than sign up for a specific work package, they prefer review modes with limited accountability.						3. Most team members willingly accept responsibility for assigned work packages and volunteer to help others to ensure project success.
4. Most team members do not value personal achievement in assigned work.						4. Most team members strive to accomplish assigned work in an exemplary fashion, meeting scope, quality, time, and cost objectives.
5. Most team members lack imagination and creativity and do not put forth new ideas.						5. Most team members search for breakthroughs and enjoy brainstorming-type sessions that promote creativity and innovation.
6. Most team members are motivated primarily by monetary rewards.						6. Most team members view monetary rewards as a benefit, but they also value project work and its challenges.

View	1	2	3	4	5	View
7. Most team members lack the desire to meet quality objectives.						7. Most team members recognize the importance of quality and actively participate in developing project quality policy and a quality plan.
8. Most team members do not set personal goals or objectives for project work.						8. Most team members develop and follow an individual development plan, viewing objectives and goals as aids to continuous improvement.
9. Most people prefer ongoing operational activities to project work.						9. Most people find project work stimulating and request it instead of ongoing operational activities.
10. Project Managers generally use reward and penalty powers.						10. Project Managers generally use legitimate, expert, or referent power.
11. Most team members will not willingly work overtime when it is required to complete a key project deliverable.						11. There is a sense of dedication to the project; team members will willingly work additional hours to complete deliverables.
12. If project team members are not fully engaged, they do not seek additional tasks to perform.						12. Team members value productivity; when awaiting completion of other tasks, they willingly request additional work or help others finish their assigned tasks.
13. Most Project Managers make decisions without consulting the team.						13. Most Project Managers value the insights of the team and seek their suggestions and ideas before making a final decision.
14. Project Managers want a cohesive team that conforms to organizational values.						14. Project Managers value a diverse team (i.e., one that does not foster "group think") and look for new ideas.
15. Most project team members are passive and do not suggest alternative, innovative approaches.						15. Most project team members are active contributors in many aspects of the project.
16. Project Managers are viewed as getting things done through others.						16. Project Managers are viewed as helping team members achieve their personal goals so they can direct their efforts toward the project and the organization's strategic goals.

View	1	2	3	4	5	View
17. Functional managers prepare performance appraisals without input from Project Managers or team members.						17. Project Managers prepare performance appraisals in conjunction with functional managers and team members, using a 360° approach.
18. Project Managers and team members resist change.						18. Project Managers are change agents, seeing projects as a way to transform the organization.
19. Self-respect is not valued.						19. Self-respect is valued, as is deserved respect from one's peers.
20. Project Managers are viewed as leaders in all aspects of the project.						20. There is an emphasis on collaborative leadership throughout the project.
21. Only the Project Manager performs planning.						21. The project team actively participates in the planning process.
22. The Project Manager is assigned after the project is officially chartered in the organization.						22. The Project Manager is assigned early in the project's initiating process to enable participation in project charter and scope statement development.
23. The Project Manager develops the vision and strategy for the project but does not communicate them to the project team.						23. The Project Manager ensures that everyone knows the importance of the project to the organization's strategic goals and motivates team members to achieve that vision and strategy.
24. Most team members are unaware of how the project affects people and the environment.						24. Most team members understand the ramifications of the project in terms of its social, economic, and environmental context.
25. Project management is not valued as an asset to the organization.						25. Projects are viewed as assets to the organization, as project management has a leadership role in the organization.
26. Most people learn project management tools and techniques on the job.						26. The organization values project management and is committed to an ongoing project management education and training program.
27. Most team members believe they must adhere to strict policies and procedures.						27. Most team members view policies and procedures as guidelines that can be tailored to the specific needs of the project.

View	1	2	3	4	5	View
28. Few management systems are in place to assist in overall project management.						28. Management systems are in place to facilitate project management (e.g., financial systems designed for accounting, tracking, and reporting on projects; human resource management systems).
29. The organization is known for being risk-averse.						29. There is a high tolerance for risk, which is viewed as an opportunity.
30. The organization has a hierarchical structure that focuses on authoritarian management.						30. The organization is structured in a way that is project-focused, with an emphasis on participatory management.
31. On projects, one project constraint dominates activities.						31. On projects, there is a balance of the competing demands of scope, quality, cost, and time.
32. It is rare to involve customers and other stakeholders in projects.						32. Shared ownership is the goal, with active participation by all project stakeholders, including customers.
33. The project plan is rarely updated once completed and reviewed.						33. The project plan is an iterative document that is updated regularly in response to new information and project changes.
34. A specialized group or the Project Manager does cost estimating.						34. Project Managers solicit team member participation in the cost-estimating process through a bottom-up approach and use experts as appropriate.
35. A project calendar is developed for each project that does not consider individual needs.						35. Both project and resource calendars are prepared and used as part of the schedule development process.
36. The project adheres completely to the organization's quality policy.						36. The project team reviews the organization's quality policy for applicability to the project and determines whether any changes are required for it to be useful.
37. Audits conducted throughout the project are viewed as "gotcha" games; emphasis is solely on compliance.						37. Project audits are viewed as useful tools and techniques, with an emphasis on using results for continuous improvement.

View	1	2	3	4	5	View
38. Little or no emphasis is given to risk management.						38. The project team actively participates in risk management through brainstorming sessions, interviews, and document reviews and participates in the development of the Risk Management Plan.
39. Project communication channels are vertical and follow established processes.						39. The organization emphasizes open communication; thus, there is a horizontal flow of communication without rigid adherence to organizational reporting structures.
40. Project stakeholders are not identified or managed in a pro-active way.						40. The project team emphasizes close coordination with its stakeholders and identifies methods of communication for each stakeholder.
41. The Project Manager only meets with team members on a regularly scheduled basis.						41. The Project Manager stays in touch with the work of each team member and practices a style of management by walking around, even if it is a virtual team.
42. Conflicts are viewed in a negative fashion as something to be avoided; when they do occur, the Project Manager tends to use a forcing or competing resolution style.						42. Conflicts are viewed as leading to increased creativity and more informed decisions; the Project Manager fosters a collaborative conflict resolution style.
43. There is little, if any, recognition of the importance of the project team and its contributions.						43. The organization values project teams and considers them key assets; as a result, team recognition and reward are fostered.
44. Team ground rules, such as use of a team charter, are not established on projects.						44. Team members prepare a team charter that establishes the procedures for its operation; team members share responsibility for following procedures.
45. The Project Manager rarely conducts team-building activities.						45. Team-building activities with a variety of approaches are used frequently; they are viewed as essential to building greater trust and better working relationships.

View	1	2	3	4	5	View
46. There are limited opportunities for the team to meet and share experiences.						46. "War" rooms are set up for co-located teams, and web-based team rooms are established for virtual teams so team members can easily exchange project information.
47. Most team members are unaware of the contributions by other team members or their areas of expertise.						47. The knowledge, skills, and competencies of project team members are known and recognized, as team members regularly seek the input of others on their project work.
48. Staff turnover is high.						48. Staff turnover is low, as there is an emphasis on the importance of continual development of people in accomplishing the organization's strategic objectives.
49. Most people do not know why they were specifically assigned to be on a project team.						49. Most people are pleased to be assigned to a project team and view their assignment as one based on their interests and areas of expertise.
50. The Project Manager assigns specific roles and responsibilities to team members.						50. Project team members are involved in determining their roles and responsibilities.
Summary Score						

Team Charter

Project Manager
_____

Phone   Fax   E-Mail   .
_____

Project Scope Statement

_____

Project Commitment Statement

_____

Description of Project Manager's Roles and Responsibilites

_____

Description of Project Sponsor's Roles and Responsibilities

_____

Description of Client Roles and Responsibilities

_____

Description of Stakeholder 1 Roles and Responsibilities

_____

Description of Stakeholder 2 Roles and Responsibilities

_____

Description of Stakeholder _N_ Roles and Responsibilities

_____

Team Member Responsibility Assignment Matrix

WBS Work Package #	Team Member A	Team Member B	Team Member C	Team Member D
Activity				
Activity				
Activity				
Activity				

Team Performance Objectives

_____

Team Measures of Success

_____

Scope and Boundaries of Team's Work

_____

Project Time Frame

_____

Deliverables

_____

Conflict Resolution Process

_____

Decision-Making Process

_____

Communication Process

_____

Administrative Activities Process

_____

Issue Escalation Process

_____

Approvals:

Project Sponsor
Signature   Date

Project Manager
Signature   Date

Team Member #1
Signature   Date

Team Member #2
Signature   Date

Team Member *N*
Signature   Date

INSTRUMENT 3–D

Personal Orientation and Preferences Style

Three choices follow each scenario. Select the one that most closely approximates your approach.

1. Assume you are working on a project. You must meet with the Project Manager to obtain feedback on your work thus far. Ideally, you would prefer that this feedback reflect how
   a. Cooperative or helpful you are
   b. Your work contributed to project success
   c. Your performance on assigned tasks was received in terms of its quality

2. On a project, you have a
   a. Tendency to take risks, believing that risks typically are opportunities
   b. Moderate tolerance for risk, taking only calculated risks
   c. Low tolerance for risk, avoiding risks if possible

3. Assume you are working on a project and have a conflict with another team member over a technical issue. In this situation, you typically would resolve the conflict through a
   a. Competing or win-lose type of approach
   b. Collaborating or win-win type of approach
   c. Compromising or giving in for the short-term type of approach

4. You prefer to work on a project performing roles that involve
   a. Interdependent tasks in which you work often with other team members
   b. Tasks in which you are primarily responsible for their outcome, from beginning to end
   c. Interactions with stakeholders both internal and external to the project

5. Assume you are in a meeting with the project team and a decision must be made. In this situation, you tend to
   a. Take the lead and strive to bring the issue to closure
   b. Provide technical input to the decision but do not feel you should be responsible for making the final decision
   c. Work to ensure that everyone has an opportunity to contribute their ideas and concerns

6. Generally, there are many ways to receive approval for work done on projects. On your work, you prefer to receive approval from
   a. Subject-matter experts
   b. Project sponsors and external stakeholders
   c. Team members

7. Assume you are working on a project, and several tasks have been assigned as your primary responsibility. In response, you would
   a. Try to show people, regardless if they are peers or superiors, a better way to complete the work
   b. Help team members complete their work, if requested to do so, even if this might delay completion of your own assigned tasks
   c. Tend to think about how to accomplish something significant and difficult even if it is outside your own assigned tasks and responsibilities

8. During the kick-off meeting for your project, the team prepares a team charter and sets team norms as to how work is to be done and how conflicts are to be resolved. You would tend to
   a. Follow the group norms explicitly
   b. Experiment with new approaches and then inform the team of a better way to get things done
   c. Follow your own approach to complete your assigned tasks, even if it differs from the group's norms

9. In setting goals, you tend to
   a. Favor goals that are attainable (i.e., neither too high nor too low)
   b. Set challenging, but attainable, personal goals
   c. Clarify the team's goals in such a manner that they represent your own goals and then persuade others to work toward these goals

10. Assume you are meeting fellow team members for the first time. At this point, you typically
    a. Trust that because they have been assigned to the project they will complete their assigned tasks on schedule and according to plan
    b. Expect others to devote as much time to each task as you do
    c. Talk about past projects or tasks in which you were successful and suggest that people follow these approaches

11. Working on a project, you are interested in
    a. Participating in as many decisions as possible that affect the project, even if the decisions involve issues that are outside the scope of your assigned tasks
    b. Working primarily on the tasks that are your assigned responsibility, as they are the ones over which you have the greatest control
    c. Working primarily to encourage teamwork and cooperation among team members

12. Assume that you have had a disagreement with another team member on a technical issue relating to one of your assigned tasks. In this situation, you would
    a. Try to resist reacting defensively to your team member's concerns and keep an open mind
    b. Tend to view this team member in a competitive way
    c. Typically react positively to the information about your work, even if it is somewhat negative

13. On a project, in terms of rewards and recognition, you
    a. Feel rewards are as essential as the accomplishment of the work itself
    b. Focus primarily on your own personal achievement rather than the overall rewards of project success
    c. Want to be recognized as the person who makes the greatest overall contribution to the project's success

14. When assigned to a project team, you feel frustrated more by the
    a. Tasks that remain to be completed
    b. Inability to make friendly, long-lasting relationships with team members
    c. Lack of opportunities to meet and interact with internal and external stakeholders

15. In a team meeting, you view your role primarily to be one of
    a. Soliciting the thoughts, opinions, feedback, and ideas of other team members
    b. Stating complex information, thoughts, and ideas simply, clearly, and concisely
    c. Taking the initiative to identify and resolve any work-related problems that need to be solved

16. In order to complete your assigned tasks as efficiently as possible, you
    a. Follow the overall project schedule as closely as possible
    b. Prepare your own detailed schedule for your assigned tasks, striving to complete your tasks ahead of schedule
    c. Focus first on completing work due today or over the near term and then focus on work to be done in the future

17. If you could select a project to work on, you would prefer to work on one that was authorized because of a
    a. Technological advance
    b. Social need
    c. Customer request

18. If you do not believe that you are contributing to the work done by the project team, or if you do not believe that your work is valued, then
    a. You find that your productivity tends to decrease overall
    b. You spend a lot of time thinking about how you should be doing your assigned tasks in order to improve your results
    c. You approach team members and clearly express and request information that will enable you to fulfill your assigned responsibilities

19. If you are making a presentation to a customer, you tend to
    a. Express your ideas in a way that persuades others to accept your points of view
    b. Explain your work as clearly and succinctly as possible
    c. Restate and clarify important points and questions

20. If a team member approaches you and asks for assistance such as mentoring or training, you tend to
    a. Drop your own assigned tasks to come to the aid of your team member
    b. Be the person the team member contacts immediately since you have already volunteered to help should such a situation arise
    c. Explain that you are pleased to help once your own tasks are completed

21. When you are working on a project, your own personal goals are
    a. Carefully measured so that they can be accomplished
    b. In line with those of the project team
    c. In line with the organization's strategic goals

22. On your current assignment, you cannot seem to master the technical intricacies of the work involved. In such as situation, you
    a. Ask team members for assistance
    b. Simply try harder
    c. Ask to be reassigned to a task in which you are sure you can make a contribution and achieve recognition

23. In receiving feedback, you are most interested in knowing how
    a. Well you are doing on your assigned tasks
    b. Much your team members like and value your contributions
    c. Your work is viewed by the project sponsor and other internal and external stakeholders

24. Assume two team members can only "agree to disagree." They ask you to help resolve a current conflict. In this situation, you tend to
    a. View the conflict in terms of its technical issues and point out why each person's opinions may not be correct
    b. Work with the team members collaboratively and help them resolve the conflict, even if it means that the overall working relationships established by the team may need to be changed
    c. Work with the team following a confrontational-type approach to conflict resolution that fosters a forthright discussion of the issues at hand

25. Assume you work for a company that has a Project Management Center of Excellence with a mandatory project management methodology for all company projects. In this situation, you typically are
    a. Not very concerned about the methodology, focusing instead on your own assigned tasks
    b. Interested in following the methodology, as you feel it is essential to achieve the project's goals and objectives
    c. Interested in the project management methodology only if you believe you can significantly enhance it and be recognized for your contributions in this regard

26. Working on a project team, you experience a sense of frustration if you
    a. Cannot take charge
    b. Feel that your efforts to help other team members are rebuffed
    c. Cannot complete your assigned tasks to your expected level of quality

27. You feel that, in general, team decisions should be based on
    a. Consensus among the team members
    b. The goals and objectives of the project and the organization
    c. The available technical information supporting the decision

28. You are most pleased as a project team member when you perceive that
    a. Your ideas and approaches to the task at hand are the correct ones
    b. Your leadership in an important situation with project stakeholders has proven to be effective
    c. Your efforts to assist others in completing their assigned tasks are viewed as instrumental to their success

29. Typically, in working on a project, you tend to
    a. Want to help others, even to the degree that you may get in their way
    b. Want to be independent and often rebuff the attempts of others to assist you
    c. Direct others and exert your authority over them

30. If you are having a conflict on a technical issue with people on your team whom you respect for their technical expertise, you
    a. Work to maintain harmony rather than assert your own point of view
    b. Strive to dominate regardless of their opinions and feelings
    c. Strive to keep your options open and acknowledge their feedback in a constructive way

31. If something goes wrong on a project, you believe it is primarily due to
    a. Lack of dedication and hard work
    b. Lack of teamwork
    c. The failure of others to acknowledge your approach or point of view

32. Ideally, you feel best about your work on a project team when you
    a. Believe your work has resulted in a technical breakthrough or innovation that otherwise would not have occurred
    b. Have been able to provide leadership to others on the project and guide them through some difficult moments during the project
    c. Have been able to mentor other team members and enable them to complete their work successfully

33. Assume you are working on a project team. At the kickoff meeting, you are more interested in
    a. Determining what you need to do to accomplish your assigned tasks
    b. Getting to meet and know the other team members
    c. Seeing how this project fits in with the organization's overall strategic goals

34. When your project team might not meet its planned schedule or budget, you tend to work
    a. With the team to redefine the project's goals and objectives
    b. With the team to suggest that it meet and mutually agree on better ways to work together
    c. Harder to see if you can get the project back on track

35. During a team meeting to discuss project status and upcoming milestones, you tend to primarily
    a. Work to ensure that everyone has an opportunity to participate in the meeting, often drawing out those people who may not speak up
    b. Provide information about the technical issues affecting the project
    c. Focus the team on the goals and objectives of the project and on what must be done to ensure overall project success

36. Working on a project team, you prefer that your team members perceive that you are the person who
    a. Can best provide leadership, especially if it is a self-directed team
    b. Will want to support the other team members and provide assistance whenever requested
    c. Is respected for technical ability and desire to meet the project's performance requirements

37. Recognizing that team decisions tend to be more complete than individual team member decisions, you strive during team problem solving and decision making to
    a. Provide technical data to assist in the decision-making process
    b. Make sure the atmosphere is a cooperative one that values everyone's participation and contribution
    c. Focus the team on the objectives at hand and on the specific issues to be resolved

38. The ideal role for you to assume on a team is one in which you are
    a. Perceived as being assertive in helping the team meet project goals and objectives
    b. Considered the technical expert who consistently completes all work as assigned
    c. The thoughtful person whom other team members contact whenever they are having a personal problem

39. If you have a disagreement with another team member on a technical issue, you tend to
    a. Be open-minded throughout the disagreement, working to find an answer that represents a middle ground between the two positions
    b. Look objectively at the data the other person presents in order to understand his or her point of view
    c. Consider the opposite view but push for your solution to the problem

40. Your project team has established ground rules regarding working relationships among team members. Three team members now feel the approach for ensuring participation at team meetings is not working, as one person tends to dominate the discussions and their ideas and concerns are not being addressed. You do not feel this is a major issue. When asked for your view, you
    a. Suggest a quick-fix that ensures that everyone participates
    b. State that you do not see it as a problem and try to refocus them on the technical tasks that need to be completed
    c. Make a strong case that the group process is working well and is not in need of change at this time

41. If you are in a meeting with a group of project stakeholders and there is a heated discussion regarding a possible scope change to the project, you tend to
    a. Organize your thoughts logically and make a strong case for your position
    b. Be sensitive to the issues of other project stakeholders and not take a firm stand
    c. Try to gain the trust of stakeholders and lead the group toward merging their perspectives

42. Your project has the opportunity to be the first in your company to use a new technology in its work. The alternative is to remain with the current approach, which has been used successfully on many projects in the past. If the new technology is selected, it might be possible to complete the project in half the time. If it does not work, the schedule will slip by at least three months. In this situation, you would
    a. Favor using the new technology
    b. Use the new technology in parallel with the current approach to ensure it can be used without serious problems
    c. Favor using the current approach

43. Working on a project team, you would prefer to
    a. Have little external structure, except knowing the general goals and objectives and when tasks need to be completed to keep on schedule
    b. Have the opportunity to establish a defined structure for the team's work and encourage team members to adopt it
    c. Work within a defined structure for your work, with someone available for consultation whenever desired

44. You are specifically interested in tasks
   a. That reflect high levels of responsibility, with challenging, varied, and integrative work
   b. With clearly defined objectives, where you can determine how best to accomplish them
   c. That you can succeed in and that provide the opportunity to work with others

45. You prefer to be recognized for your achievements that stress your
   a. Specific contributions to the project team and your steady performance
   b. Ability to get results
   c. Technical contributions in your field of expertise

46. If you are asked to do administrative tasks on a team, you generally feel that
   a. They are necessary to perform but not enjoyable or desirable to do
   b. You should complete them in a manner that shows you can handle them effectively and efficiently
   c. They are necessary tasks, so you approach them positively as a way of showing you are contributing to the overall success of the team

47. If you can select the type of project on which you will work, you tend to pick a project that provides an opportunity to
   a. Work closely and interdependently with others
   b. Personally contribute to the success of the organization
   c. Perform work that you feel is personally challenging

48. You are more concerned with the
   a. Intrinsic context of the work
   b. Technical content of the work
   c. External environment in which the work is done

49. You primarily value approval from
   a. Someone who understands and relates to the type of work that you do
   b. Your Project Manager or project sponsor
   c. Other project team members

50. You tend to identify primarily with
   a. The organization and its overall success or failure
   b. The other members of the project team
   c. Your professional peers

INTERPRETING THE QUESTIONNAIRE

Use the chart below to see where you rank in terms of your preferred motivational approach. To determine a total score, put a checkmark in the appropriate column for each answer and then count the checkmarks that appear in each of the three columns. The overall totals will indicate your motivation profile.

Question/Answer	Affiliation	Power	Achievement
1	A	B	C
2	C	A	B
3	C	B	A
4	A	C	B
5	C	A	B
6	C	B	A
7	B	A	C
8	A	B	C
9	A	C	B
10	A	C	B
11	C	A	B
12	A	B	C
13	A	C	B
14	B	C	A
15	A	C	B
16	A	C	B
17	B	C	A
18	A	C	B
19	C	A	B
20	A	B	C
21	B	C	A
22	A	C	B
23	B	C	A
24	B	C	A
25	B	C	A
26	B	A	C

Question/Answer	Affiliation	Power	Achievement
27	A	B	C
28	C	B	A
29	A	C	B
30	A	B	C
31	B	C	A
32	C	B	A
33	B	C	A
34	B	A	C
35	A	C	B
36	B	A	C
37	B	C	A
38	C	A	B
39	A	C	B
40	A	C	B
41	B	C	A
42	C	A	B
43	C	B	A
44	C	A	B
45	A	B	C
46	C	B	A
47	A	B	C
48	A	C	B
49	C	B	A
50	B	A	C
TOTAL			

360° Assessment Tool

Use this instrument to assess your collaborative and teamwork behavior. Ask others to rate you using this form. Compare the ratings of different people. Most important, reconcile other people's view of you with your own view of yourself.

Repeat this process at least annually.

	1 Never	2 Seldom	3 Sometimes	4 Often	5 Always
1. Possesses a strong *commitment* to the goals and objectives of the project					
a. Completes assigned tasks according to the project schedule when faced with competing priorities between project work and other assigned work					
b. Recognizes how assigned tasks support the project's goals and objectives and the organization's strategic goals and objectives					
c. Establishes objectives for the project that are aligned with the organization's strategic goals and objectives					
d. Keeps track of details and follows up on action items and tasks					
e. Affirms priorities frequently so less important tasks do not dominate more important ones					

	1 **Never**	2 **Seldom**	3 **Sometimes**	4 **Often**	5 **Always**
f. Considers risk as an opportunity to enhance overall project value					
g. Plans ahead and follows through to complete work on schedule					
h. Considers organizational and project constraints and project assumptions in planning and executing assigned tasks					
i. Completes requests from other project team members in a timely manner					
j. Puts forth more effort and takes more initiative than expected in order to complete assigned project work					
k. Takes corrective actions as required to ensure that all work is done on schedule and meets performance specifications					
l. Works to develop a reputation as someone who is reliable and dependable in all aspects of project work					
m. Works to prepare the project team's charter and other team policies and procedures					
n. Takes initiative in identifying and resolving project-related problems					
o. Improves one's own results on assigned tasks in order to contribute fully to project team work					
Commitment Summary					
2. Establishes and supports a _collaborative_ environment for project work					
a. Encourages cooperation and teamwork on the project					
b. Seeks the opinions of others on work in progress or completed					

	1 Never	2 Seldom	3 Sometimes	4 Often	5 Always
c. Seeks the advice of subject-matter experts in areas where personal expertise is lacking					
d. Makes it easy for others to disclose information, share ideas, and talk openly about problems and concerns					
e. Takes initiative in offering both informal and formal assistance to other team members					
f. Develops cooperative, rather than competitive, working relationships with other team members					
g. Involves others in decision-making and problem-solving tasks, when appropriate					
h. Maintains friendly relationships with other team members					
i. Determines innovative ways to optimize cooperation among project team members					
j. Strives to unite the team in common actions and rewards					
k. Ensures that all team members participate in discussions concerning the team's mission, scope, and deliverables and how best to work toward success					
l. Encourages team members to work toward consensus before decisions are made					
m. Expresses confidence in the team's ability to meet or exceed project goals and objectives					
n. Examines different perspectives and alternatives on issues being discussed					
o. Appreciates the views and ideas of other team members					

	1 Never	2 Seldom	3 Sometimes	4 Often	5 Always
Collaborative Environment Summary					
3. Demonstrates _credibility_ in all aspects of project work					
a. Is thoughtful in personal interactions in team situations					
b. Shows respect for other team members					
c. Helps team members establish trust					
d. Handles project issues according to team-defined procedures					
e. Provides information affecting others' work promptly					
f. Expresses confidence in the skills and abilities of others					
g. Displays a nonjudgmental attitude toward the ideas and work of other team members					
h. Prepares for project team meetings					
i. Is able to cope in situations that are ambiguous or uncertain					
j. Takes time to gather and analyze information before making decisions affecting the project					
k. Demonstrates high performance standards, acting as a role model for others on the team					
l. Organizes and manages time productively					
m. Takes responsibility for one's own statements and points of view					
n. Has a well-developed sense of personal standards and principles to guide behavior					

	1 Never	2 Seldom	3 Sometimes	4 Often	5 Always
o. Works to ensure that technical and performance goals are met, even if this means compromises in cost and schedule					
Credibility Summary					
4. Promotes effective *communications* among project team members and stakeholders					
a. Recognizes the most important information and communicates it to others concisely and clearly					
b. Summarizes what others have said to clarify understanding					
c. Prepares written communication that all members of the project team can understand					
d. Seeks additional information when clarification is needed					
e. Provides clear, concise, and logical answers to questions from other team members					
f. Encourages other team members to express diverse points of view					
g. Does not dominate project team meetings					
h. Listens to what others say in an understanding way					
i. States opinions in a persuasive, clear, and logical manner					
j. Establishes processes for interpersonal communication among project team members					
k. Appreciates and recognizes individual differences in communications with project team members					
l. Asks open-ended questions to encourage information exchange					

	1 **Never**	2 **Seldom**	3 **Sometimes**	4 **Often**	5 **Always**
m. Establishes and manages formal and informal communications networks with project stakeholders					
n. Considers the nature of the alliance with the people involved in the communication					
o. Views other team members as persons of equal worth, so communication is based on reciprocal and mutual respect					
Effective Communications Summary					
5. Establishes a sense of *community* within the project team with a focus on professional responsibility in all activities					
a. Shows an awareness of the social and cultural contexts of problems					
b. Shares information appropriately within the professional community					
c. Shows sensitivity to project confidentiality requirements					
d. Elicits and respects the values of others					
e. Exhibits sensitivity to persons from different cultures					
f. Shows awareness of the impact of different values, obligations, moral rights, and personal principles in decisions that are made					
g. Identifies the most appropriate corrective action for unethical behavior					
h. Exercises tolerance and compromise in interactions with team members and stake-holders					

	1 **Never**	2 **Seldom**	3 **Sometimes**	4 **Often**	5 **Always**
i. Adheres to legal requirements and ethical standards in project work					
j. Models the desired skills, behavior, and attitude to follow on project work					
k. Exercises appropriate judgment in order to protect the community and project stakeholders					
l. Gathers, analyzes, and integrates information in order to determine methods of fair resolution if there are competing requirements and objectives					
m. Exhibits empathy toward other team members, especially in the face of competing pressures among project objectives					
n. Recognizes that team decisions are generally more complete than decisions made by one person and works to involve others, as appropriate					
o. Shares lessons learned and best practices with other team members in an unobtrusive manner					
Sense of Community Summary					
6. Emphasizes *continuous improvement* in personal and team skills and knowledge					
a. Leverages the contributions of others and available resources to the greatest extent possible in order to increase personal knowledge and skills					
b. Redefines problems so they are viewed as possible opportunities					
c. Looks for opportunities to continually upgrade knowledge and skills					

	1 Never	2 Seldom	3 Sometimes	4 Often	5 Always
d. Performs a self-assessment of strengths and weaknesses					
e. Seeks feedback from project team members on project performance					
f. Values feedback on working relationships					
g. Provides feedback to other team members regarding working relationships and project performance in a nonthreatening manner					
h. Uses constructive comments provided by others to their maximum extent					
i. Applies new information and practices to improve project performance					
j. Determines changes to the team's procedures, as defined in its charter, to increase their effectiveness					
k. Determines changes to the organization's project management methodology to increase its effectiveness					
l. Identifies lessons learned throughout the project and communicates them to other team members, as appropriate					
m. Compiles internal and external best practices in project management and makes them available to project team members					
n. Provides mentoring and coaching to other team members, as appropriate, in order to transfer knowledge and best practices					
o. Strives to keep options open, and looks for new alternatives or breakthroughs to obtain desired performance results on technical project issues					

	1 Never	2 Seldom	3 Sometimes	4 Often	5 Always
Continuous Improvement Summary					
7. Strives for effective *conflict resolution* among team members					
a. Seeks agreement on specific actions when conflicts arise among team members					
b. Discusses possible win-win solutions to help resolve conflicts on the project team					
c. Helps involved team members generate possible alternatives if asked to help resolve a conflict					
d. Remains neutral when asked to resolve a conflict between other team members					
e. Focuses on issues, not personalities					
f. Tries to avoid the need to escalate the resolution of conflicts to those outside the project team					
g. Displays openness to conflicting opinions and flexibility when presenting points of view					
h. Resists reacting defensively, and keeps an open mind when others disagree					
i. Uses creativity to resolve differences among team members					
j. Identifies conflicts to maximize achievement of project objectives					
k. Exercises judgment in determining the fair resolution of project conflicts among team members					

	1 Never	2 Seldom	3 Sometimes	4 Often	5 Always
l. Productively challenges existing paradigms when conflicts arise, so that they are viewed as opportunities rather than solely as problems to be solved					
m. Fosters an attitude that conflict can be useful in reducing the risk of intellectual compliance or a tendency toward "group think"					
n. Ensures that conflicts are addressed in a way that people do not withdraw from one another and that overall team motivation is strengthened					
Conflict Resolution Summary					
8. Demonstrates *curiosity* and *creativity* in project activities					
a. Strives to generate new ideas and creative solutions to problems					
b. Suggests changes to existing processes and procedures in order to minimize bureaucracy and maximize effectiveness					
c. Identifies any team-related barriers to effectiveness so they can be removed					
d. Determines innovative ways to optimize cooperation among project team members					
e. Seeks opportunities for adding value to the project's product or service					
f. Considers alternatives and generates contingency plans when solving problems					
g. Pilots the use of new tools and technologies to facilitate project work					
h. Challenges existing approaches in order to determine optimum ways to meet project objectives					

	1 Never	2 Seldom	3 Sometimes	4 Often	5 Always
i. Acquires new knowledge to refine/expand potential alternatives to problems					
j. Seeks innovative solutions to meet project goals and objectives					
k. Shows genuine interest in the work under way by other team members in order to contribute new ideas, whenever appropriate					
l. Experiments with new approaches in order to later inform team members of possible changes in team processes to promote effectiveness					
m. Helps the team establish guidelines, rather than strict rules and procedures, to promote flexibility and innovation in project work					
n. Asks probing questions during team meetings or one-on-one communications so that discussions go beyond a general level					
o. Listens to as many stakeholders as possible, even to those who may not have a direct interest in the project's outcomes, in order to broaden perspectives					
Curiosity and Creativity Summary					
9. Recognizes the *contributions* of other team members to the project's goals and objectives					
a. Writes or calls team members when they accomplish something significant on the project					
b. Acknowledges the contributions of others to assigned work					

	1 Never	2 Seldom	3 Sometimes	4 Often	5 Always
c. Recognizes team members who champion ideas as well as those who support the ideas of others					
d. Recognizes and appreciates individual differences					
e. Analyzes internal and external influences on team performance to remove any negative barriers					
f. Takes actions to reduce any negative impacts on project performance					
g. Compares project outcomes against the defined scope and uses this information to recognize the work of other team members					
h. Works with the team to establish agreed-upon performance measurement criteria both for team members and for individuals					
i. Provides feedback that is constructive and recognizes success					
j. Works to help unite the team in common actions and rewards					
k. Develops "win-win" strategies for both individual and team goals					
l. Works to ensure that everyone has an opportunity to contribute ideas and concerns					
m. Requests information from others in order to fulfill assigned responsibilities in a timely manner					
n. Works to ensure that all project tasks, even administrative ones, are considered essential to overall project success					

	1 Never	2 Seldom	3 Sometimes	4 Often	5 Always
o. Recognizes that one's personal success is dependent on overall team success in achieving project goals and objectives					
Contributions of Others Summary					
10. Shows *consideration* toward other team members during the project					
a. Treats other team members in a fair and consistent manner					
b. Shows a willingness to take time to listen to and understand the points of view expressed by other team members					
c. Shows genuine concern and interest, even when there is a disagreement with another team member					
d. Avoids making personal accusations toward other team members					
e. Realizes the importance of taking the time to provide advice and direction to others					
f. Provides feedback focused on problems or solutions, not on personalities					
g. Remains attentive and interested in team meetings and conference calls even if one's own work progress is not being discussed					
h. Demonstrates empathy toward others					
i. Communicates in a manner that is not condescending					
j. Shares beliefs and feelings with others on the team (i.e., is self-disclosing)					
k. Is in control of any personal differences in interpersonal relationships					

	1 Never	2 Seldom	3 Sometimes	4 Often	5 Always
l. Provides opportunities to promote long-lasting relationships among team members					
m. Volunteers services and support to others from the earliest stages of the project					
n. Works to ensure that other team members recognize that assistance is instrumental to team success					
o. Refrains from attributing self-serving motives to other team members					
Consideration Toward Others Summary					
TOTAL SCORE					

INSTRUMENT 3–F

Teamwork Attributes

Use this instrument to assess collaborative and teamwork behavior. Ask others to rate you using this form. Compare the ratings of different people. Most important, reconcile other people's view of you with your view of yourself.

Rate attributes using the scale below. Repeat this process at least annually.

1—Never
2—Seldom
3—Sometimes
4—Often
5—Always

I. EXEMPLARY OVERALL PROJECT PERFORMANCE

Item	1	2	3	4	5
1. Project performance exceeded the customer's overall quality requirements.					
2. The project did not experience any unplanned scope creep.					
3. All schedule milestones were met, and no deliverables were late.					
4. The project was completed within or under budget.					
5. The project's objectives were aligned with the organization's strategic goals.					
6. Tasks were completed as planned, even when faced with competing priorities from other projects or initiatives.					
7. Details were tracked, and action items were followed until completed.					
8. Meetings held on the project were considered useful, as preparation was done beforehand.					
9. High performance standards were demonstrated, acting as a role model for others on the team.					
10. Lessons learned were collected, analyzed, and then shared with others in a way that was not obtrusive and contributed to overall team success.					
11. Feedback was sought from others on project performance for continuous improvement.					

Item	1	2	3	4	5
12. Conflicts were viewed proactively to maximize achievement of project objectives.					
13. To broaden perspectives, there was an emphasis on listening to as many stakeholders as possible, even to those who did not have a direct interest in the project's outcomes.					
14. Action was taken, as appropriate, to reduce any negative impact on project performance.					
15. Team and individual performance assessments were conducted.					
16. A collaborative environment was fostered with the customer through-out the project life cycle.					
17. A goal-setting process served to provide measurable goals with clear expectations.					
18. Risks were viewed as opportunities, and the response strategies selected were appropriate.					
19. A partnering relationship was established with subcontractors and vendors.					
20. Changes were managed through an integrated change control process.					
Summary					

II. CONTRIBUTION TO ORGANIZATION PROFITS

Item	1	2	3	4	5
1. Risks were considered from a customer perspective and identified as opportunities to enhance overall project value.					
2. Opportunities were sought to add value to the project's product or service.					
3. The project was viewed as a key part of the organization's strategic plan.					
4. The project was viewed as important within the organization, with appropriate accountability and authority assigned to the Project Manager throughout the project life cycle.					
5. The project was continually reviewed to ensure that it still supported the organization's strategic goals and that resources were committed and made available as planned.					
6. The relationship of the project to the organization's strategic plan was known so that management responsibilities were identified.					
7. The priority of the project within the project portfolio was known, thereby ensuring effective resource allocation and overall support.					
8. A clear description of the project objectives, in measurable terms, was prepared and made available.					

Item	1	2	3	4	5
9. Stakeholders were identified when the decision was made to pursue the project; thus, there was a high level of shared ownership.					
10. Through the project charter, the project was linked to the ongoing work of the organization.					
11. The business case for the project, including its return on investment, was known and monitored.					
12. A financial database was established to track labor hours, incurred costs, budgets, and cash flow requirements.					
13. Market conditions concerning the project were identified and considered throughout the life cycle.					
14. A gap analysis was conducted to compare the estimated effect of a selected project on the organization's strategic targets to determine its long-term benefits.					
15. A profitability analysis was prepared.					
16. Specific criteria for project selection and continuation were followed.					
17. Project scope, quality, time, and cost targets were established based on maximizing customer satisfaction.					
18. The project was considered valuable as core competencies were enhanced.					
19. Key stakeholders recognized the project's value proposition.					
20. The overall cost did not exceed the delivered value.					
Summary					

III. EFFECTIVE PLANNING

Item	1	2	3	4	5
1. Planning was based on a deliverable-oriented Work Breakdown Structure that served as the framework for the entire project.					
2. Priorities were set so that less important tasks did not dominate more important ones.					
3. Planning recognized organizational constraints.					
4. Assumptions made during the planning process were minimal.					
5. Time was organized and managed productively.					
6. Stakeholders were identified; a Stakeholder Management Plan was prepared to manage stakeholder influence.					
7. Plans were progressively elaborated as additional details became known and then made available.					
8. In preparing the Project Management Plan and the various subsidiary plans, information was gathered from numerous sources; plans were updated and refined based on new information, project execution, and/or approved changes.					

Item	1	2	3	4	5
9. Planning was not conducted in a vacuum, as stakeholders actively participated in the process.					
10. Action was taken to ensure that the project was performed according to the plans.					
11. Throughout the planning process, templates were followed, when applicable, and updated based on actual experience.					
12. Technical, schedule, cost, quality, and performance measurement baselines were established.					
13. Planning was viewed as essential to obtain information about future events in a systematic way and to anticipate needed actions to attain project goals.					
14. Interrelationships and interfaces were identified and known.					
15. Work packages were assigned to specific individuals or organizational units to complete.					
16. Planning was participative, which meant that the team acted in accordance with the plan during the project.					
17. Plans were used as a way to develop strategies and policies and increase a power base.					
18. A Resource Breakdown Structure was prepared and used.					
19. A network schedule was prepared and used that showed the dependencies between tasks.					
20. Quality standards relevant to the project were identified and satisfied.					
Summary					

IV. USEFUL POLICIES, PROCEDURES, AND PROCESSES

Item	1	2	3	4	5
1. Organizational policies, processes, and procedures were reviewed for applicability to the project; tailoring was performed as needed.					
2. Active involvement was the norm in formulating project-specific procedures.					
3. Participation was sought in discussion of the project's mission, scope, and deliverables to ensure understanding of customer requirements.					
4. The importance of processes for interpersonal communication among project team members was stressed.					
5. Changes to team procedures, as defined in the team charter, were made to increase effectiveness.					
6. Changes to the organization's project management methodology were made to increase effectiveness.					
7. Internal and external best practices were identified and considered in the development or refinement of policies, processes, and procedures.					

Item	1	2	3	4	5
8. An effective process was established for conflict resolution within the team, whenever possible.					
9. Changes were suggested to existing policies, processes, and procedures to minimize bureaucracy and maximize effectiveness.					
10. Team-related barriers were identified and removed to improve effectiveness.					
11. Emphasis was placed on guidelines to promote flexibility and innovation in project work.					
12. Agreed-upon performance measurement criteria were established to measure team performance overall and individually.					
13. Win-win strategies were developed to meet both individual and team goals.					
14. Processes were repeated and revised during the project, as required.					
15. Organizational procedures were followed to show when the end of a specific phase in the project was reached.					
16. A process measurement database was established to collect and use data on processes and products.					
17. Process boundaries were established that included the owners and stakeholders involved.					
18. Targets for improved performance were established to guide the process improvement activities.					
19. A process improvement plan was prepared in conjunction with the key stakeholders.					
20. A metrics system was implemented to help maintain control over the status of processes.					
Summary					

V. FOCUS ON PROBLEM SOLVING

Item	1	2	3	4	5
1. Proactive preventive actions were taken, as appropriate.					
2. Corrective actions were taken when needed, following established processes and procedures.					
3. Initiative was taken to identify and resolve any project-related problems.					
4. Issues were identified and tracked to resolution.					
5. Action items were assigned and monitored until completed.					
6. Open communication was fostered to facilitate information sharing and problem/issue discussion.					
7. Achieving consensus was the goal before decisions were made.					

Item	1	2	3	4	5
8. Time was taken to gather and analyze information before making decisions affecting the project.					
9. The most important information was recognized and communicated to others in an expeditious manner.					
10. All stakeholders prepared written communications in an easy-to-read, understandable manner.					
11. Team meetings were not dominated; open-ended questions were asked to encourage information exchange.					
12. When competing requirements and objectives existed, information was gathered, analyzed, and integrated to determine methods of fair resolution.					
13. Team decisions were viewed as more complete than decisions made by a single team member.					
14. Problems were redefined as opportunities.					
15. Agreements were sought on specific actions when conflicts arose among team members.					
16. Creativity was used to resolve differences among team members.					
17. Contingency plans were prepared.					
18. Changes followed a standard process to determine needed corrective actions.					
19. Risks were discussed at team meetings to ensure they were monitored and responses were effective.					
20. Root-cause analysis was conducted to distinguish causes from symptoms.					
Summary					

VI. DEDICATED PERSONAL COMMITMENT

Item	1	2	3	4	5
1. Emphasis was placed on taking initiative in order to complete assigned work on or ahead of schedule.					
2. Requests were completed in a timely manner.					
3. Dependability and reliability were the norm.					
4. Emphasis was placed on continuous improvement of one's own results on assigned tasks.					
5. Responsibility was taken for one's opinions, statements, and points of view.					
6. A self-assessment was performed of one's own strengths and weaknesses.					
7. The focus was on issues, not personalities.					

Item	1	2	3	4	5
8. The competing demands of scope, time, cost, quality, resources, and risks were balanced throughout the project.					
9. The specific targets (scope, time, cost, and quality) that were within each team member's power to change and influence were evident.					
10. Intrinsic motivation was the norm, reducing the need for extrinsic incentives as key motivating factors.					
11. Attainable personal work goals were set.					
12. Work was structured so that discretionary, rather than prescribed, approaches could be followed.					
13. The emphasis was on solving problems quickly; there was individual responsibility for completing assigned tasks, and joint acceptance of responsibility by the project team.					
14. The emphasis was on managing project capacity and capability to deliver expected value.					
15. There was a sense of obligation to others associated with the project.					
16. Critical success factors were identified with objectives determined to best meet priority goals.					
17. Stress was minimized, with an emphasis on understanding one's own work style.					
18. Setbacks were analyzed so that they could be used as possible opportunities.					
19. The emphasis was more on personal change than change in other team members.					
20. Multi-tasking was minimized so that assigned tasks could be completed as planned, and successful results could be fostered.					
Summary					

VII. PROFICIENT TECHNICAL KNOWLEDGE, SKILLS, AND COMPETENCIES

Item	1	2	3	4	5
1. Advice was sought from other subject-matter experts to advance knowledge.					
2. Opinions were sought from peers on work in progress or completed.					
3. Initiative was taken to offer informal and formal assistance to other team members.					
4. Information on new developments that might affect other project assignments was provided to others promptly.					
5. The project's technical goals were met consistently.					
6. Additional information was sought to clarify technical concerns, even from those outside the project.					

Item	1	2	3	4	5
7. The contributions of others were leveraged to the greatest extent possible to increase personal knowledge and skills.					
8. Opportunities were sought to upgrade knowledge and skills continually.					
9. New information and practices were used to improve performance.					
10. The constructive comments of others were used to the maximum extent.					
11. Options were kept open, and alternatives were sought and analyzed in order to obtain desired performance results on technical issues.					
12. Existing paradigms were challenged when conflicts arose so they might be viewed as opportunities rather than as problems to be solved.					
13. New tools and techniques were piloted to facilitate project work.					
14. Innovative solutions were sought to meet the project's goals and objectives.					
15. Standards and practices unique to the specific technical area were followed.					
16. Information was exchanged freely rather than viewing technical expertise as a source of individual power.					
17. Benchmarking was used, as appropriate, to gather new ideas and identify potential alternative methods.					
18. Obtaining applicable technical certifications and participating in technical forums and conferences were encouraged.					
19. Technical performance measurement was used as a key tool and technique in project monitoring and control.					
20. Any deviations were analyzed to help forecast the degree of success in achieving the project's scope objectives.					
Summary					

VIII. FOCUS ON PROJECT PEOPLE

Item	1	2	3	4	5
1. Teamwork and cooperation were encouraged.					
2. Cooperative rather than competitive working relationships were the norm.					
3. The atmosphere was one of friendliness among team members.					
4. Innovative ways to optimize cooperation among team members were used.					
5. The team was united in common actions and rewards.					
6. Team members established a foundation of trust and open communication.					

Item	1	2	3	4	5
7. There was an emphasis on listening to others as a way of expressing understanding.					
8. Empathy was shown toward other team members, especially in the face of competing pressures among project objectives.					
9. Constructive feedback that recognized successes was provided to other team members in a nonthreatening manner; working relationships and project performance were emphasized.					
10. Mentoring and coaching were provided to other team members, as appropriate, to transfer knowledge and best practices.					
11. Openness and flexibility to conflicting opinions were displayed when presenting points of view.					
12. Team members viewed conflicts as a way to reduce "group think" and strengthen team motivation.					
13. The project vision was known to all team members.					
14. The contributions of other team members to another's work were recognized and acknowledged.					
15. Time was set aside to listen to the points of view of other team members and to provide advice and direction, when warranted.					
16. Opportunities were sought to promote long-lasting relationships among team members.					
17. Self-serving motives were not attributed to other team members.					
18. Services and support were volunteered to others during the project.					
19. Project roles, responsibilities, and authority were known to all team members.					
20. Team and individual performance appraisals were conducted.					
Summary					

IX. EMPHASIS ON PROFESSIONAL RESPONSIBILITY

Item	1	2	3	4	5
1. Different perspectives and alternatives were examined concerning issues under discussion.					
2. An appreciation of the views and ideas of others was fostered.					
3. Respect was shown for other team members.					
4. A nonjudgmental attitude was expressed toward the ideas and work of other team members.					
5. A well-developed sense of personal standards and principles guided behavior.					
6. Each team member was viewed as a person of equal worth and value, with reciprocal communication and mutual respect considered the norm.					

Item	1	2	3	4	5
7. There was an awareness of the project's social and cultural issues.					
8. Information was shared with appropriate communities.					
9. Confidentiality was maintained, as appropriate.					
10. Any unethical behavior was identified, and appropriate corrective actions were taken.					
11. Intellectual property was respected.					
12. Legal standards were followed.					
13. Appropriate judgment was exercised to protect the community and project stakeholders.					
14. Personal accusations were not made toward other team members.					
15. There was an awareness of one's own values and ethical standards.					
16. The environment was one where dignity and respect were the norm.					
17. Team members exercised appropriate judgment throughout the project.					
18. Team members recognized the importance of building the capabilities of their colleagues.					
19. Team members used lessons learned to advance the profession of project management in the organization.					
20. The team actively worked to balance the interests of the various project stakeholders.					
Summary					

X. EFFECTIVE USE OF BOTH POWER AND POLITICS

Item	1	2	3	4	5
1. Applicable international, national, regional, and local laws and customs, as well as the political climate, were known and followed.					
2. Team members understood how the project affected the people with a vested interest it in.					
3. Formal and informal communication networks were established with project stakeholders.					
4. Judgment was exercised in determining the fair resolution of project conflicts among team members.					
5. Groups and individuals possessing formal and informal power in areas important to the project were identified.					
6. Proprietary thinking was viewed as destructive, with open exchange of information considered the norm.					
7. Decisions made considered the various tasks, constraints, assumptions, and interfaces of the project.					

Item	1	2	3	4	5
8. Actual situations dictated the type of power to use, with an emphasis on the use of earned or personal power whenever possible.					
9. Effective alliances and networks were built with project stakeholders.					
10. The emphasis was on using power in a positive way as a means to influence others.					
11. Information was viewed as a project resource to be used by all team members.					
12. The political climate was analyzed to determine how best to manage the project and its stakeholders.					
13. Political issues were managed to avoid conflicts and struggles among stakeholders.					
14. Guidelines were developed to help manage political issues affecting the project.					
15. Alternative approaches for dealing with controversial issues were explored.					
16. A collaborative project management environment was fostered.					
17. There was an emphasis, whenever possible, on changing the course of events to overcome resistance.					
18. Conflicts were viewed as a way to promote creative solutions.					
19. Power struggles among stakeholders were minimal or nonexistent.					
20. Meetings were considered constructive and useful ways to spend time and to resolve problems and issues.					
Summary					
TOTAL SUMMARY OF ALL CATEGORIES					

INSTRUMENT 3–G

Collaborative Leadership Instrument

Use this instrument to determine to what extent collaborative behavior was permitted and/or encouraged within the team. The absolute score is not nearly as important as indications of improvement from one assessment to the next.

	Yes	No
During the project's kickoff meeting, do you ensure that other team members contribute to insights concerning		
1. What is our mission?	_____	_____
2. What is our scope statement?	_____	_____
3. Who are our customers?	_____	_____
4. What do our customers value?	_____	_____
5. What are our deliverables?	_____	_____
6. What is our plan?	_____	_____
During other project team meetings, do you encourage team members to		
7. Reach a consensus before a decision is made?	_____	_____
8. Evaluate options objectively based on fact rather than feeling?	_____	_____
9. Feel comfortable with decisions that are reached?	_____	_____
10. Think about project goals and objectives as alternatives are discussed and decisions are made?	_____	_____
11. Take project constraints seriously in order to find ways to best handle them?	_____	_____
12. Limit the number of assumptions that are made, as they will limit team options later in the project?	_____	_____
13. Consider new alternatives and innovative ways to solve problems and resolve issues?	_____	_____
14. Participate fully and offer ideas and suggestions in areas in which they can contribute?	_____	_____
15. Provide information that may challenge the existing plan or procedure in order to suggest opportunities to further the project's goals and objectives?	_____	_____

Adapted from Parviz F. Rad and Ginger Levin, *Achieving Project Management Success Using Virtual Teams* (Boca Raton, FL: J. Ross Publishing). © 2003 by J. Ross Publishing, Inc. Reprinted with permission.

	Yes	**No**
16. Discuss with others any concerns with issues that might impact future decisions that are made?	_____	_____

Do you feel that it is important for you to

17. Set high standards of performance based on your own goals and objectives?	_____	_____
18. Describe the broader implications of the team's decisions and actions?	_____	_____
19. Express confidence in the team's ability to meet or exceed the project's goals and objectives?	_____	_____
20. Specify the importance of each team meeting?	_____	_____
21. Look for different perspectives on the various issues that are under discussion?	_____	_____
22. Emphasize the importance of working together as a team even if team members work in different locations?	_____	_____
23. Help develop an appreciation for the views and ideas of other team members?	_____	_____
24. Seek alternative and innovative ways of accomplishing the project's goals and objectives?	_____	_____
25. Place a high priority on learning and experimenting with new approaches and ideas?	_____	_____

Effectiveness of Team Meetings

Meeting Attributes	1—Significant Improvements Required	2—Some Improvements Required	3—Useful	4—Valuable	5—Extremely Valuable
Clarity of meeting goals					
Clarity of meeting agenda					
Time devoted to each agenda item					
Ability to participate					
Ability to understand another's views					
Ability to interact with other team members					
Materials presented					
Decisions reached					
Action items presented					
Importance of the meeting to overall project work					
Overall Meeting Effectiveness					

INSTRUMENT 3–1

Project Management Duties

This instrument describes job-specific behaviors, knowledge, skills, and abilities needed to be successful in project management positions. It describes expectations of employees holding various project management positions at three different levels (entry, proficient, and master). This information can help identify training and career development opportunities. An organization's executive management can use this information in performance reviews and internal certification to assess each individual's progress.

A general description of each competency is required.

Entry Level	Proficient	Master
These are the prerequisite or minimum things an employee must know and do in the job. An entry-level employee should possess this knowledge, skill, and ability.	These are the core aspects of the job that the employee must perform. An employee in this position should show proficiency in these competencies by performing core requirements.	These are the contributions an employee can bring to the job beyond the core job requirements. An employee who has gained comprehensive knowledge and skills relating to this job should perform these mastery-level aspects.

Each successive level includes the knowledge and skills from the previous levels.

Project Integration Management: Includes the processes and activities needed to identify, define, combine, unify, and coordinate the various processes and project management activities within the Project Management Process Groups (PMBOK® 2004).

PROJECT INTEGRATION MANAGEMENT

Project Team Member	Entry Level	Proficient	Master
Develop the Project Charter			
Develop the Preliminary Project Scope Statement			
Develop the Project Management Plan	• Assists in the review of the preliminary project scope statement and project management methodology in the development of the Project Management Plan	• Supports the team in the development of the Project Management Plan • Uses the project management information system • Reviews historical data about previous projects to use in preparing the Project Management Plan • Maintains the plan as part of the project's documentation management system	• Provides support in developing key sections of the Project Management Plan • Sets up the project management information system for use on the project
Direct and Manage Project Execution	• Performs assigned work, as authorized, in accordance with the Project Management Plan and project procedures • Provides technical input to support project activities • Attends and supports status review meetings • Identifies needed changes • Keeps the Project Manager informed and up to date about progress • Prepares work-related procedures	• Collects project data and reports cost, schedule, technical, and quality progress • Prepares change requests, as directed • Maintains the project management information system	• Forecasts status information to support decision making • Collects and documents lessons learned • Implements approved process improvement activities • Assesses performance of work packages against the Project Management Plan

Project Team Member	Entry Level	Proficient	Master
Monitor and Control Project Work	• Compares work performed against the plan	• Maintains the project management information system • Prepares change requests, as directed • Implements approved changes as they occur	• Provides forecasts to update current cost and schedule information
Integrated Change Control	• Supports the project's change management system • Identifies required changes and analyzes them for technical input	• Maintains the project management information system • Prepares change requests, as directed • Implements approved changes as they occur • Assists in the development of the project's change control system	• Develops the project's change control system • Assists in the development of the configuration management system, as warranted
Close Project	• Provides assistance to the team in terms of preparing final project documentation	• Finalizes documentation for assigned work packages according to the administrative closure procedure • Uses the project management information system to perform both administrative and contract closure procedures	• Ensures that project documentation is complete • Prepares confirmation for formal acceptance by the client

Associate Project Manager	Entry Level	Proficient	Master
Develop the Project Charter			
Develop the Preliminary Project Scope Statement			
Develop the Project Management Plan	• Prepares an initial draft of the Project Management Plan • Determines needed tailoring of the organizational management methodology for the project's plan	• Finalizes the Project Management Plan	• Ensures that the plan includes all actions needed to define, integrate, and coordinate the subsidiary plans into the Project Management Plan

Associate Project Manager	Entry Level	Proficient	Master
Direct and Manage Project Execution	• Performs activities to accomplish project objectives • Provides guidance to the project team, as required, throughout the project • Reviews each deliverable to ensure that requirements are met • Reviews work performance information on the status of project activities and recommends corrective and preventive actions, as required • Provides authorization to team members to begin work on assigned work packages	• Supports the project team selection process • Selects and manages sellers according to procurement management procedures • Manages project resources • Manages project risks and implements response actions • Documents lessons learned • Reviews organizational procedures to ensure compliance with the project • Provides support to status review meetings	• Implements planned methods and standards • Verifies and controls project deliverables • Implements corrective and preventive activities • Leads status review meetings • Identifies issues affecting the project and assigns action items, as appropriate
Monitor and Control Project Work	• Monitors implementation of approved changes when and as they occur	• Uses earned value management to integrate scope, schedule, and resources to measure and report project progress	• Assesses actual performance against the plan to recommend corrective and preventive actions
Integrated Change Control	• Recommends whether formal configuration management procedures should be followed • Reviews change requests and recommends corrective or preventive action	• Implements corrective and preventive actions • Reviews deliverables • Maintains project baselines • Reviews performance reports to assess issues that may cause future problems	• Determines whether formal configuration management is warranted • Evaluates change requests to ascertain trends that may affect project outcomes
Close Project	• Reviews the administrative closure and contract closure procedures for specific applicability to the project	• Monitors the team in performance of administrative and contract closure procedures • Meets with stakeholders to ascertain overall performance against both client and team success factors	• Conducts a final lessons-learned review with team members and other stakeholders • Reviews documentation to ensure it is complete

Project Manager	Entry Level	Proficient	Master
Develop the Project Charter			
Develop the Preliminary Project Scope Statement	• Develops the preliminary project scope statement	• Issues the preliminary project scope statement	
Develop the Project Management Plan	• Issues the Project Management Plan • Determines the project life cycle to follow • Requests expert assistance, as required, in project plan development • Conducts a lessons-learned meeting at the beginning of each project to establish a process and ensure lessons learned are collected and analyzed by all members of the project team	• Ensures that the Project Management Plan will maintain the integrity of the performance measurement baseline	• Reviews and enhances the Project Management Plan
Direct and Manage Project Execution	• Directs performance of project activities • Manages the internal project working environment to ensure work is conducted effectively throughout the project life cycle • Manages the technical and organizational interfaces • Establishes and manages external and internal communications channels • Communicates regularly with stakeholders, both internal and external, on project issues • Leads the team in completing the project • Ensures the team has access to required skills and knowledge	• Maintains awareness of related projects within the organization to ensure that this project is complementary and supportive • Closes each phase of the project according to the administrative closure procedure • Reviews the impact of conflicting requirements on individual areas of the overall project and manages them to achieve project objectives or modifies them accordingly • Collects and analyzes lessons learned	• Reviews all project deliverables • Adapts approved changes into the project's scope, plans, and environment • Establishes and maintains links to manage the alignment between project objectives and the organization's strategic objectives throughout the project life cycle • Reviews all project management functions at key review and approval phases and other milestones

Project Manager	Entry Level	Proficient	Master
Monitor and Control Project Work	• Analyzes earned value information and recommends corrective actions, as needed • Reports progress against baselines to provide a measure of performance throughout all phases of the project life cycle	• Implements corrective and preventive action • Requests the services of experts, as required • Collects and analyzes lessons learned	• Monitors and controls the execution of all planned and scheduled activities in the Project Management Plan to ensure client expectations are met
Integrated Change Control	• Works actively to influence the changes that may affect the project • Reviews approved changes for trends • Documents the complete impact of requested changes • Controls project quality to standards based on quality reports • Approves changes to the project and incorporates them into revised baselines	• Maintains the integrity of baselines by releasing only approved changes for incorporation into the project's products or services, and maintains their related configuration and planning documents • Provides guidance to the team regarding the use of formal configuration management	• Assesses factors that seem to circumvent integrated change control so that only approved changes are implemented • Controls and updates the scope, cost, budget, schedule, and quality requirements based on approved changes by coordinating changes across the project • Identifies, analyzes, and reports lessons learned
Close Project	• Finalizes closeout plans and procedures to ensure final outcomes of project phases have been attained, and overall project objectives have been met • Obtains the services of experts, as required, to support the team in the closing phase • Reviews project files to ensure that final documentation is up to date and ready to be archived	• Formally closes each phase of the project • Transfer's final files for archiving • Analyzes lessons learned throughout the project, but especially in the close project phase	• Formally closes the project • Ensures formal acceptance of the final product, service, or result to the client, including receipt of formal confirmation that requirements were met, and the customer or sponsor officially accepted the deliverables • Recommends changes to the organization's overall project management practice

Project Management Office Staff Member	Entry Level	Proficient	Master
Develop the Project Charter	• Supports management by providing data to make decisions concerning projects to pursue • Supports the development of the organization's project management information system	• Assists in establishing a portfolio management system for project selection and pipeline management • Assists in the development of the organization's project management methodology • Assesses and recommends methods, tools, or models for use in project selection • Collects lessons learned during the project charter process	• Develops a portfolio management system for the organization's projects • Develops the organization's project management methodology • Develops the organization's project management information system • Develops a template for the project charter • Develops project charters • Prepares the business case justifying each project, including return on investment
Develop the Preliminary Project Scope Statement	• Develops a template for the preliminary project scope statement	• Provides support to Project Managers in developing the preliminary project scope statement	
Develop the Project Management Plan	• Supports the team in terms of organizational policies and procedures for project plan development	• Provides support to the project team in developing the Project Management Plan	• Reviews drafts of the Project Management Plan to ensure it complies with organizational policies and procedures
Direct and Manage Project Execution		• Assists the team in the use and maintenance of the project management information system • Provides support to status review meetings • Develops a work authorization system for the organization's projects	• Facilitates status review meetings, as requested
Monitor and Control Project Work	• Supports the team in performance measurement, as required	• Supports the team in the use and maintenance of the project management information system • Assists the team in the use of earned value techniques	• Provides information to support status reporting, progress measurement, and forecasts

Project Management Office Staff Member

	Entry Level	Proficient	Master
Integrated Change Control	• Assists the team in the use of the project's change control system	• Assists the team in the use of configuration management • Assists in the development of an integrated change control system for the organization's projects and in configuration management procedures and guidelines • Assists in the development of the organization's knowledge management system	• Develops an integrated change control system for the organization's projects • Develops guidelines for formal configuration management on the organization's projects • Performs configuration audits, as requested • Develops the organization's knowledge management system
Close Project	• Provides support to the team, as requested, in the use of administrative closure and contract closure procedures	• Assists in the development of the administrative closure and contract closure procedures • Reviews final project documentation to ensure t is complete prior to archiving	• Develops the organization's administrative closure and project closure procedures

Project Management Office Director

	Entry Level	Proficient	Master
Develop the Project Charter	• Enhances the portfolio management system that describes organizational methods for project selection • Issues the organization's project management methodology • Issues guidelines and criteria for tailoring the organization's project management methodology for specific project requirements • Obtains the services of experts, as required, to assess inputs to develop the project charter • Issues a template for the project charter • Supports the preparation of the organization's strategic plan	• Implements the portfolio management system • Implements the organization's project management knowledge system • Consults with experts within and outside the organization, as appropriate, concerning project selection • Updates practices in the project charter process based on lessons learned	• Recommends projects to pursue • Issues project charters • Reviews initiatives to ensure that selected projects satisfy client, sponsor, and other stakeholder needs, wants, and expectations • Updates the organization's knowledge management system based on collected lessons learned

Project Management Office Director	Entry Level	Proficient	Master
	• Establishes criteria for selection of the organization's Project Managers • Identifies and appoints Project Managers and determines each Project Manager's authority level • Identifies internal and external organizational and environmental constraints • Develops the organization's corporate knowledge management system		
Develop the Preliminary Project Scope Statement	• Provides guidance to the Project Manager in the use of the organization's methodology for developing the preliminary project scope statement • Obtains the services of experts, as required, to assist in the development of the preliminary project scope statement	• Mentors the Project Manager, as needed, in developing the preliminary project scope statement • Analyzes lessons learned in developing the preliminary project scope statement	• Updates the organization's knowledge management system based on lessons learned in developing the preliminary project scope statement
Develop the Project Management Plan	• Obtains the services of experts, as required, to assist in the development of the Project Management Plan • Reviews all Project Management Plans to determine the extent to which the organization's project management methodology is followed • Collects lessons learned on the project plan development process	• Mentors the Project Manager in the development of the Project Management Plan • Analyzes lessons learned for changes to the organization's methodology	• Updates the organization's knowledge management system based on lessons learned collected across the organization's projects in project planning
Direct and Manage Project Execution	• Issues the organization's work authorization system • Issues a standard project life cycle for the organization's projects	• Mentors the Project Manager, as needed, in project management execution • Analyzes lessons learned for changes to the organization's methodology	• Updates the organization's knowledge management system based on lessons learned collected across the organization's projects in project execution

Project Management Office Director	Entry Level	Proficient	Master
Monitor and Control Project Work	• Regularly reviews project progress to ensure overall objectives are met • Supports the Project Manager to obtain the services of experts, as required	• Mentors the Project Manager in the monitoring and controlling process, as needed • Analyzes lessons learned for changes to the organization's methodology	• Updates the organization's knowledge management system based on lessons learned collected across the organization's projects in the monitoring and controlling process
Integrated Change Control	• Issues the organization's integrated change control system • Issues guidelines for formal configuration management • Provides guidance to project teams regarding the use of configuration management and obtains services of experts, as required • Ensures the team has access to configuration management tools and techniques	• Determines the organization's procedures regarding integrated change control • Mentors the Project Manager, as needed, in the integrated change control process • Analyzes lessons learned for changes to the organization's methodology	• Determines overall organizational procedures regarding the use of formal configuration management • Updates the organization's knowledge management system based on lessons learned collected across the organization's projects in the monitoring and controlling process • Uses data from the knowledge management system for continuous improvement of project management practices
Close Project	• Issues the organization's administrative closure and contract closure procedures • Reviews overall lessons learned • Suggests experts that can assist the team in the close project phase, as requested	• Mentors the Project Manager, as needed, in the close project phase • Analyzes lessons learned for changes to the organization's methodology	• Updates the organization's knowledge management system based on lessons learned collected across the organization's projects in the monitoring and controlling process • Uses data from the knowledge management system for continuous improvement of project management practices

The Project Management Office Director row also includes at Entry Level: • Supports the Project Manager by obtaining needed resources to support the project • Attends and participates in project status review meetings • Collects lessons learned on the execution process

Chief Project Officer	Entry Level	Proficient	Master
Develop the Project Charter	• Makes project selection decisions and ensures projects reflect the direction set in the organization's strategic plan • Determines the organization's communication requirements for selected projects	• Establishes overall standards for project management policies and procedures • Selects the optimum mix of projects in support of the organization's business strategy • Prepares the organization's strategic plan in terms of projects to pursue	• Serves as the advocate for project management, both internally and externally
Develop the Preliminary Project Scope Statement			
Develop the Project Management Plan	• Reviews project plans to ensure they support the organization's long-term strategy and business values		
Direct and Manage Project Execution	• Establishes financial control procedures • Ensures that deliverables support business objectives • Attends and participates in selected project review meetings	• Promotes a culture of management by projects throughout the organization, where projects are viewed as strategic assets and critical to the organization's success • Ensures that project strategies complement strategic goals • Positions project management as the solution to the organization's problems and as the opportunity for its success	
Monitor and Control Project Work			
Integrated Change Control	• Uses data from the knowledge management system for changes required to overall organizational strategies and policies • Adjusts project priorities in light of changing conditions affecting the organization		

Chief Project Officer	Entry Level	Proficient	Master
Close Project	• Evaluates projects to determine their contribution to the organization's success • Establishes final guidelines for project closure		

Project Scope Management: Includes the processes necessary to ensure that the project includes all the work required, and only the work required, to complete the project successfully (PMBOK® 2004).

PROJECT SCOPE MANAGEMENT

Project Team Member	Entry Level	Proficient	Master
Scope Planning	• Assists in the review of the organization's policies, procedures, and guidelines regarding scope management	• Determines the key policies, procedures, and guidelines that affect the development of the project Scope Management Plan	• Supports the development of the project Scope Management Plan
Scope Definition	• Reviews the preliminary scope statement and suggests needed enhancements • Identifies internal and external stakeholders	• Determines the key policies, procedures, and guidelines that affect development of the scope statement • Reviews approved change requests to determine if the scope statement is affected • Records brainstorming sessions on alternative approaches • Supports the preparation of the stakeholder analysis • Prepares change requests, as directed	• Supports the development of the project scope statement • Uses state-of-the-art techniques to perform product analyses • Supports brainstorming sessions on alternative approaches • Develops a matrix for use in prioritizing requirements among stakeholders and to determine stakeholder interests and influences • Supports the development of the constraints and assumptions list • Supports the development of the configuration management and change control requirements

Project Team Member	Entry Level	Proficient	Master
Create Work Breakdown Structure (WBS)	• Assists in review of WBS templates for use on the project • Prepares entries to the WBS Dictionary for assigned work packages	• Supports the team in developing the WBS • Ensures that each entry in the WBS Dictionary includes a code or account identifier • Maintains the WBS Dictionary	• Determines if a standard template can be used on the project for the WBS • Assists in the decomposition process for the WBS • Finalizes the WBS Dictionary • Prepares change requests if changes are needed to the scope statement as a result of WBS development
Scope Verification		• Assembles data needed for inspections and reviews	• Provides support to inspections and reviews • Prepares change requests, as required, based on changes from the scope verification process
Scope Control	• Supports the team in preparing reports on project work performance	• Prepares reports on project work performance • Reviews the standard scope change control system to see if changes are needed for the project • Prepares scope change control requests, as directed	• Prepares change requests, as directed, that may affect the scope statement, WBS, and WBS Dictionary • Prepares the project's scope change control system • Analyzes scope change control requests

Associate Project Manager	Entry Level	Proficient	Master
Scope Planning	• Determines whether the standard template for the Scope Management Plan needs tailoring to fit the needs of the project	• Drafts the project's Scope Management Plan	• Reviews the project's Scope Management Plan
Scope Definition	• Determines whether the standard template for the scope statement needs tailoring to fit the needs of the project • Conducts brainstorming sessions on alternative approaches • Prepares the stakeholder analysis	• Prepares the project's scope statement • Determines the product analysis techniques to use on the project • Analyzes the results of the stakeholder analysis to ensure that all stakeholders are identified and that needs, wants, and expectations are documented	• Reviews the project's scope statement • Completes the stakeholder analysis • Prioritizes requirements based on the stakeholder analysis • Ensures that project objectives include measurable success criteria

Associate Project Manager	Entry Level	Proficient	Master
			• Identifies needed project approval requirements
	• Identifies what is and is not included within the project • Identifies objectives linked to deliverables, requirements, assumptions, and constraints • Describes the characteristics of the product, service, or result of the project • Lists constraints and assumptions • Defines the initial project organization	• Describes conditions or capabilities to be met by the project deliverables • Describes the level of configuration management and change control to be implemented on the project • Conducts planning meetings with stakeholders to collect and analyze requirements	
Create WBS	• Decides on use of a standard WBS template with appropriate tailoring or leads the team in the WBS decomposition process • Issues the WBS Dictionary	• Prepares the final WBS	• Issues the WBS
Scope Verification	• Arranges for inspections of work and deliverables and analyzes their results • Maintains product documentation	• Determines whether changes are required based on inspections and reviews; if so, recommends corrective action or otherwise processes documentation for acceptance	• Ensures that the scope verification process complements work done in quality control • Implements corrective actions based on inspections and reviews • Obtains final acceptance of completed work and deliverables
Scope Control	• Implements the scope change control system • Integrates scope change control with other control processes • Reviews and analyzes performance reports	• Reviews the effectiveness of the scope change control system periodically and implements improvements, as required • Assesses the magnitude of scope variation to determine causes of variance relative to the baseline and to determine needed corrective actions • Identifies lessons learned	• Implements corrective action, as required, based on variance analysis • Determines whether a formal configuration management system is needed on the project

Project Manager	Entry Level	Proficient	Master
Scope Planning	• Enhances the Scope Management Plan • Arranges for experts to support the team in scope management planning, if requested	• Finalizes and issues the project's Scope Management Plan	• Updates the Scope Management Plan, as required, during the project and ensures that it is consistent with other subsidiary plans in the Project Management Plan
Scope Definition	• Enhances the scope statement • Arranges for experts to support the team in scope definition, if requested • Uses the results of the stakeholder analysis during requirements definition and development	• Finalizes and issues the scope statement • Prepares a plan to work with each stakeholder identified during the stakeholder analysis and assigns resources • Reviews the scope definition process for lessons learned and needed enhancements	• Updates the Scope Management Plan, if required, based on the scope statement • Ensures that the results of the stakeholder analysis demonstrate quantifiable expectations that can lead to project success • Updates the Project Management Plan, as required • Recommends changes to the scope definition process based on lessons learned
Create WBS	• Updates the scope statement, as required, based on WBS development • Updates the Scope Management Plan, as required, based on WBS development	• Establishes the project scope baseline	• Updates the scope baseline, if necessary • Recommends changes to the process for creating the WBS based on lessons learned
Scope Verification	• Reviews the results of inspections and reviews on all project deliverables and analyzes them to determine whether there are overall trends that need monitoring throughout the project • Reviews deliverables to ensure that all were completed satisfactorily	• Recommends changes to the scope verification process based on lessons learned	

Project Manager

	Entry Level	Proficient	Master
Scope Control	• Ensures that scope changes follow the established scope control process • Analyzes the extent of scope creep to determine preventive actions throughout the project and takes corrective actions, as required • Determines whether scope change requests require modifications to the WBS, WBS Dictionary, scope statement, and Scope Management Plan • Manages the impact of scope changes within established schedule, cost, and quality constraints to meet project objectives • Reviews progress and records results to assess the effectiveness of scope management procedures	• Ensures that project scope changes are managed in conjunction with the schedule and cost changes • Prevents unauthorized or incorrect changes from being included in the technical baseline • Controls the impact of scope changes • Establishes a formal configuration management system, if required • Arranges for training and other guidance for team members in configuration management tools and techniques • Updates the scope baseline, scope statement, WBS, and WBS Dictionary, as required, based on scope changes • Collects lessons learned on the project in scope control	• Recommends changes in the scope control process based on lessons learned • Updates the Project Management Plan, as required, based on scope changes • Reissues the scope baseline, as required • Compares project outcomes periodically against defined scope to communicate the achievement of project objectives

Project Management Office Staff Member

	Entry Level	Proficient	Master
Scope Planning	• Supports the team in determining policies, procedures, and guidelines for use in scope planning	• Supports the development of scope management templates	• Supports the development of policies, procedures, and guidelines on scope management • Develops the Scope Management Plan templates
Scope Definition	• Supports the team in determining policies, procedures, and guidelines for use in scope definition	• Supports the development of the scope statement template • Reviews available product analysis techniques and maintains up-to-date information on their enhancements for use on the organization's projects	• Develops the scope statement template • Suggests various product analysis techniques for use within the organization • Facilitates brainstorming sessions on alternative approaches • Provides templates and tools for use in stakeholder analysis

Project Management Office Staff Member

	Entry Level	Proficient	Master
Create WBS	• Provides available templates to the team for use in WBS development	• Assists the team in the development of the WBS • Supports the development of standard WBSs for the organization's projects • Assists the team in the development of the WBS Dictionary	• Facilitates decomposition sessions, if used, in WBS development • Develops standard WBSs for the organization's projects • Defines standard components of the WBS Dictionary
Scope Verification		• Assists the team in inspections and reviews	• Prepares guidelines for inspections and reviews
Scope Control	• Assists the team in preparing performance reports	• Prepares standard formats for team use in performance reports • Assists in the development of a standard scope change control system	• Develops a standard scope change control system • Assists the team in variance analysis • Develops guidelines for configuration management • Reviews available tools and techniques for use in configuration management

Project Management Office Director

	Entry Level	Proficient	Master
Scope Planning	• Issues the Scope Management Plan template • Reviews each project's Scope Management Plan	• Mentors the Project Manager, as required, in scope planning • Obtains the services of experts to assist the Project Manager and team in scope planning	• Develops policies, procedures, and guidelines on scope management • Updates standard Scope Management Plan templates based on use on the organization's projects • Recommends scope management policy changes based on best practices and lessons learned

Project Management Office Director	Entry Level	Proficient	Master
Scope Definition	• Issues the scope statement template • Reviews each project's scope statement • Determines appropriate product analysis techniques to use on various types of the organization's projects • Issues standard approaches and tools to use to conduct a stakeholder analysis	• Mentors the Project Manager, as required, in scope definition • Obtains the services of experts to assist the Project Manager and team in scope definition • Reviews the outcomes of stakeholder analysis conducted on projects to determine whether expectations are quantifiable and can lead to successful project completion • Collects lessons learned in the scope definition process for future enhancements	• Updates standard scope statement templates based on use in the organization's projects • Monitors the use of experts for assistance in scope definition to determine if staff recruitments and/or training initiatives are warranted
Create WBS	• Issues WBS templates • Issues standards for the WBS Dictionary • Reviews the project scope baseline for completeness	• Mentors the Project Manager, as required, in the process of creating the WBS • Issues standards for updates to the scope baseline • Collects lessons learned in the WBS development process for future enhancements	• Updates standard WBS templates based on use in the organization's projects
Scope Verification	• Issues guidelines for inspections and reviews • Collects lessons learned in the scope verification process for future enhancements	• Mentors the Project Manager, as required, in the scope verification process	
Scope Control	• Establishes project scope metrics • Analyzes scope changes across projects to determine ways to best minimize scope creep and to assess the effectiveness of the scope control process	• Mentors the Project Manager, as required, in the scope control process • Ensures that configuration management tools and techniques are state-of-the-art, and prototypes new developments on selected projects before full-scale implementation	• Updates the organization's project management methodology based on lessons learned across projects in scope control

Project Management Office Director

	Entry Level	Proficient	Master
	• Issues standard formats for performance reports • Issues the standard scope change control system • Assesses the magnitude of scope variation across projects to determine causes of variance relative to the baseline • Issues standards for the use of formal configuration management on the organization's projects		

Chief Project Officer

	Entry Level	Proficient	Master
Scope Planning	• Issues policies, procedures, and guidelines on scope management		
Scope Definition	• Evaluates the perceived value and overall impact of the project on clients and end users		
Create WBS			
Scope Verification			
Scope Control			

Project Time Management: Includes the processes required to accomplish timely completion of the project (PMBOK® 2004).

PROJECT TIME MANAGEMENT

Project Team Member	Entry Level	Proficient	Master
Activity Definition	• Assists the team in reviews of the available project management information system and schedule software tools • Assists the team in reviews of the organization's lessons-learned database	• Assists the team in reviews of the scope statement to focus on assumptions and constraints • Reviews the WBS and WBS Dictionary • Reviews the Project Management Plan	• Assists in the development of the activity list by decomposing assigned work packages • Assists in documenting activity attributes • Prepares change requests, as needed, throughout the project for other changes to the WBS and scope statement • Updates the activity attributes, as needed, throughout the project
Activity Sequencing	• Assists the team in reviews of documents for data that may affect activity sequencing	• Assists the team in reviews of the organization's templates for use in activity sequencing • Assists in the preparation of the network diagram using project management software	• Prepares the network diagram • Assists in the determination of the types of dependencies on the project • Assists in determining whether leads and lags are required • Updates the activity list and activity attributes, as directed, during the project • Prepares change requests, as directed, during the project
Activity Resource Estimating	• Assists the team in reviews of historical information to assist in the estimating process	• Assists the team in reviews of the organization's policies regarding staffing and the rental or purchase of supplies and equipment • Prepares the resource calendar • Provides information on resource requirements for assigned work packages • Uses software in the resource estimating process	• Prepares the Resource Breakdown Structure • Prepares initial estimates of required resources • Prepares change requests that affect other areas of the project, as directed • Updates the activity attributes, if required

Project Team Member	Entry Level	Proficient	Master
Activity Duration Estimating	• Assists the team in reviews of historical information to use in the activity duration estimating process • Assists the team in reviews of constraints and assumptions from the project scope statement	• Provides information on duration estimates for assigned work packages • Uses project management software in the activity duration estimating process • Reviews commercially available software for applicability • Maintains the composite resource calendar	• Documents data and assumptions that support duration estimates for each activity duration estimate • Reviews activity resource requirements in conjunction with the preparation of activity duration estimates • Reviews the risk register for information that affects activity durations • Reviews the activity cost estimates as duration estimates are prepared
Schedule Development	• Assists the team in reviews of historical information to use in the schedule development process • Assists the team in reviews of constraints and assumptions from the project scope statement • Maintains the project calendar	• Uses project management software for schedule development • Supports the team in the preparation of the project schedule • Supports the team in the use of schedule compression approaches • Prepares change requests, as directed, if the schedule development process notes needed changes in other aspects of the project	• Reviews the risk register to identify risk response plans needed to support schedule development • Suggests needed imposed dates on activity starts and finishes • Prepares the initial project schedule • Uses schedule compression approaches • Prepares supporting data for the schedule • Updates activity attributes, as required • Updates the project calendar • Supports the preparation of the Schedule Management Plan
Schedule Control	• Assists the team in preparing schedule progress reports • Reviews templates for use in schedule reporting	• Selects a template to use in schedule reporting • Prepares schedule progress reports • Provides assistance in establishing a schedule change control system • Uses earned value analysis for schedule performance measurement • Uses project management software to track schedule variances and to forecast the effects of schedule changes	• Develops a schedule control system for the project • Provides data on the schedule variance (SV) and the schedule performance index (SPI) • Assists in the analysis of the SV and SPI • Contributes toward the analysis of options and forecasts the impact of changes to the schedule • Prepares change requests, as directed, after analysis of schedule performance

Associate Project Manager	Entry Level	Proficient	Master
Activity Definition	• Develops the activity list so that project objectives can be met • Develops activity attributes	• Develops the list of key milestones • Identifies in the activity attributes the multiple attributes associated with each schedule activity	• Issues the activity list and activity attributes • Issues the list of key milestones • Determines if any changes are required to the scope statement and the WBS
Activity Sequencing	• Issues the network diagram • Determines the mandatory, discretionary, and external dependencies that should be included • Determines the use of leads and lags • Prepares the summary narrative to accompany the network diagram and to describe the basic approach that was used in its development	• Reviews the network diagram and suggests enhancements, as required • Determines if changes are needed to the activity list and activity attributes, as appropriate, and requests that change requests be prepared • Uses rolling-wave planning throughout the project and updates the network, as needed	• Collects lessons learned in the development of the network diagram for future projects
Activity Resource Estimating	• Coordinates work in activity resource estimating with work under way in cost estimating • Identifies project deliverables and needed resources	• Enhances the Resource Breakdown Structure • Determines when resources will be required and the specific quantities needed	• Reviews the resources that have been identified, the needed quantities, and the basis for the estimates • Establishes the resource calendar • Collects lessons learned in the resource estimating process
Activity Duration Estimating	• Provides additional detail to the duration estimates throughout the project	• Prepares the activity duration estimates • Prepares needed updates to activity attributes	• Collects lessons learned in the activity duration estimating process • Develops estimates of needed contingencies or reserves
Schedule Development	• Works with stakeholders, including the client, to determine major milestones • Reviews proposed imposed dates for concurrence • Compiles the schedule data and information into the schedule model for the project	• Reviews the network for points of path convergence that can be identified and used in schedule compression analysis • Provides additional resources and guidance, as needed, to the team for schedule development	• Develops the final project schedule • Updates the project schedule, as required, and notifies stakeholders of modifications • Recommends when a new target schedule is warranted • Assesses the schedule for various "what if" situations and adjusts it accordingly

Associate Team Member	Entry Level	Proficient	Master
	• Prepares the Schedule Management Plan	• Applies project and resource calendars to schedule activities • Determines the format to use to present the schedule	• Uses Monte Carlo analysis, as appropriate • Adjusts leads and lags, as required, to develop a viable project schedule • Updates resource requirements as a result of schedule development
Schedule Control	• Approves approaches for standard schedule reports • Implements the schedule change control system • Reviews performance reports for schedule issues • Uses performance measurement techniques to assess the magnitude of schedule variations • Implements mechanisms to measure, record, and report progress of activities according to the agreed-upon Schedule Management Plan and Project Management Plan	• Reviews SV and SPI data to assess whether corrective action is required	• Documents and communicates SV and SPI values to project stakeholders as appropriate • Implements corrective actions, as required • Collects lessons learned in schedule control • Recommends corrective actions based on variance analysis and SV and SPI data

Project Manager	Entry Level	Proficient	Master
Activity Definition	• Refines the activity list throughout the project • Uses rolling-wave planning in the activity definition process • Ensures that the activity list is used in the schedule • Develops lessons learned in the activity definition process	• Enhances the activity list with a focus on planning the schedule objectives so that project objectives can be met • Determines planning packages	• Determines management control points • Determines whether changes are required in other areas of the project based on development of the activity lists • Develops lessons learned in the activity definition process
Activity Sequencing	• Develops lessons learned in the preparation of the network diagram	• Provides guidance, including training, as required, to enhance team members' expertise in activity sequencing	• Determines whether changes are warranted in other areas of the project based on the activity sequencing process • Develops lessons learned in the activity sequencing process

Project Manager	Entry Level	Proficient	Master
Activity Resource Estimating	• Determines desired resources throughout the organization for use on the project and the need for contracting to augment the team • Ensures that resources are available outside the project team, as required • Issues the activity resource requirements • Updates the activity attributes • Issues the Resource Breakdown Structure • Issues the project calendar	• Provides guidance, including training, as required, to enhance team member expertise in estimating resources • Obtains needed resources through staff acquisition or procurement • Obtains experts, as needed, to assist in the activity resource estimating process	• Determines whether changes are warranted in other areas of the project as a result of the resource estimating process • Develops lessons learned in the resource estimating process
Activity Duration Estimating	• Determines the activity estimating approach to use on the project • Determines the need for additional resources to support the activity duration estimating process • Issues the activity duration estimates • Updates the activity attributes • Determines the need for contingency reserves or buffers and documents that need with other related data and assumptions	• Provides guidance, including training, as required, to enhance team member expertise in activity duration estimating • Obtains the services of experts, as required, to assist in the activity duration estimating process • Tracks the use of contingency reserves or buffers throughout the project to assess the accuracy of the estimate and to evaluate lessons learned	• Determines whether changes are warranted in other areas of the project as a result of the activity duration estimating process • Develops lessons learned in the activity duration estimating process
Schedule Development	• Determines the schedule methodology for use on the project • Issues the preliminary and final project schedules • Determines the need for resource reallocation • Determines if changes are required as a result of the schedule development process that affect other aspects of the project and issues change requests; refines the schedule as needed throughout the project	• Addresses schedule activities that must be performed to meet specific delivery dates or situations where shared or critical resources are available only at certain times or in limited quantities and arranges for the required support • Updates the Schedule Management Plan and Project Management Plan, as required	• Addresses resource reallocation requirements across other projects underway in the organization • Issues the schedule baseline • Reviews progress throughout the life cycle and implements schedule changes to ensure consistency with changing scope, objectives, and constraints relative to time and resource availability

Project Manager	Entry Level	Proficient	Master
	• Issues the Schedule Management Plan • Formalizes agreement to the schedule, as appropriate, and communicates it to stakeholders as described in the Communications Management Plan		
Schedule Control	• Ensures that the schedule change control system is part of the project's integrated change control system • Analyzes the magnitude of schedule performance variation and implements corrective or preventive actions • Reports schedule progress to stakeholders as defined in the Communications Management Plan • Informs stakeholders of authorized changes and schedule revisions	• Requests changes in the review of performance measurements and variance analysis • Initiates and manages responses to perceived, potential, or actual schedule changes to achieve project objectives • Makes decisions on suggested changes to the schedule baseline • Prevents unauthorized or incorrect changes from being included in the schedule baseline	• Updates the schedule baseline • Re-baselines the schedule, as required • Updates the Project Management Plan as required • Reviews project outcomes to determine the effectiveness of time management activities and suggests changes to the organization's project management practice, as appropriate

Project Management Office Staff Member	Entry Level	Proficient	Master
Activity Definition	• Assists the team in the review of activity definition–related policies, procedures, and guidelines	• Assists the team in the use of scheduling software • Assists the team in the review of standard templates to use in activity definition on the project	• Develops activity definition–related policies, procedures, and guidelines • Develops templates for activity definition on the organization's projects
Activity Sequencing	• Assists the team in the review of policies and procedures affecting activity sequencing	• Assists the team in the use of scheduling software • Assists the team in the review of standard templates that are available for the organization's network diagrams	• Develops templates for network diagrams • Assists the team in the review of dependencies

Project Management Office Staff Member	Entry Level	Proficient	Master
Activity Resource Estimating	• Assists the team in the development and maintenance of the resource calendar	• Assists the team in the use of estimating software • Assists the team in the development of the Resource Breakdown Structure	• Assists the team on available resources throughout the organization that could support the project • Analyzes patterns of resource usage for trends • Prepares standard templates for Resource Breakdown Structures for use on the organization's projects • Uses project management software to help organize resource pools, define availability, and maintain information on resource rates • Forecasts resource requirements for the organization's projects
Activity Duration Estimating	• Assists the team in the development and maintenance of the composite resource calendar	• Assists the team in the use of software for duration estimates	• Assists the team in tools and techniques to use for activity duration estimates • Provides data on the use of different duration estimating methodologies within the organization to establish guidelines and policies for use on future projects
Schedule Development	• Assists the team on when to use imposed dates in schedule development	• Assists the team in the use of software for schedule development • Establishes standard formats to present the schedule	• Assists the team in the use of either the critical path or critical chain method • Assists the team in the use of schedule compression approaches • Assists the team in the use of Monte Carlo analysis • Prepares a template for the Schedule Management Plan • Maintains currency of the latest developments in project management software to determine whether changes are warranted to the organization's standard scheduling software

Project Management Office Staff Member	Entry Level	Proficient	Master
Schedule Control	• Assists the team in the use of standard schedule reporting templates	• Develops standard templates for schedule reports	• Develops a standard format for a schedule change control system

Project Management Office Director	Entry Level	Proficient	Master
Activity Definition	• Issues activity planning–related policies, procedures, and guidelines • Issues templates for activity definition on the types of the organization's projects and ensures that they can be used to identify typical schedule milestones • Provides experts, as requested, to support the project team in this process	• Based on lessons learned, updates activity definition–related policies, procedures, and guidelines • Mentors the Project Manager, as needed, in the activity definition process	
Activity Sequencing	• Issues network diagram templates • Ensures that up-to-date software is available to support the team • Determines the network diagramming method to use throughout organization	• Mentors the Project Manager, as needed, in the activity sequencing process • Based on lessons learned, updates the activity sequencing templates • Decides whether different software should be used for scheduling in the organization's projects and, if so, uses pilot projects to assess effectiveness before full-scale implementation	• Determines whether changes are required to the standard methodology to develop network diagrams in the organization

Project Management Office Director	Entry Level	Proficient	Master
Activity Resource Estimating	• Provides experts, as requested, to support the team in assessing resource-related issues • Provides assistance in alternatives analysis • Ensures that published estimating data are available to guide the team • Ensures that up-to-date software is available to assist the team • Reviews the various projects under way in the organization for dependencies among them that might affect resource use • Issues the Resource Breakdown Structure templates	• Mentors the Project Manager, as needed, in the activity resource estimating process • Decides whether different software should be used for estimating and, if so, uses pilot projects to assess effectiveness before full-scale implementation • Reviews the process for lessons learned to enhance the organization's project management methodology and knowledge management system • Provides information about the potential availability of resources	• Determines whether the organization should obtain additional resources with key areas of expertise to support future projects
Activity Duration Estimating	• Provides experts, as requested, to support the team in assessing duration estimating issues • Provides guidance in the use of different estimating approaches • Ensures that up-to-date software is available to support the team • Reviews projects, on request, to determine if contingency reserves or buffers are warranted	• Mentors the Project Manager, as needed, in the duration estimating process • Decides whether different software should be used for duration estimating and, if so, uses pilot projects to assess effectiveness before full-scale implementation • Determines desired duration estimating methods for different types of the organization's projects	• Reviews the organization's projects to determine whether duration methodologies are consistent or require revisions • Establishes policies for the use of different duration estimating methodologies on different types of the organization's projects
Schedule Development	• Establishes standards for use of the critical path method or critical chain in schedule development • Establishes standards for resource leveling approaches • Establishes standards for the use of schedule compression techniques • Issues a template for the Schedule Management Plan	• Mentors the Project Manager, as needed, in the schedule development process • Reviews resource use across projects to determine whether critical resources are required at key points and arranges for needed support • Decides whether different software should be used for duration estimating in the organization's projects and, if so, uses pilot projects to assess effectiveness before full-scale implementation	• Establishes policies for use of the critical path and critical chain scheduling approaches on the organization's projects • Determines whether changes are required to schedule development methods • Analyzes lessons learned in schedule development for improvements to the project management practice

Project Management Office Director	Entry Level	Proficient	Master
Schedule Control	• Issues templates for the standard schedule reports • Issues templates for the standard schedule control system • Reviews lessons learned for changes to the organization's project management methodology in project time management	• Establishes metrics for project time management	• Determines whether changes are required to schedule control methods • Analyzes lessons learned in schedule control for improvements to the project management practice

Chief Project Officer	Entry Level	Proficient	Master
Activity Definition			
Activity Sequencing			
Activity Resource Estimating	• Establishes policies regarding staffing and the rental or purchase of supplies and equipment		
Activity Duration Estimating			
Schedule Development			
Schedule Control			

Project Cost Management: Includes the processes involved in planning, estimating, budgeting, and controlling costs so that the project can be completed within the approved budget (PMBOK® 2004).

PROJECT COST MANAGEMENT

Project Team Member	Entry Level	Proficient	Master
Cost Estimating	• Reviews the project's scope statement for information about project requirements for consideration in cost estimating • Reviews the WBS and WBS Dictionary for information about each deliverable	• Reviews the Schedule Management Plan and Staffing Management Plan for information to support cost estimating • Reviews information on risk responses for use in cost estimating • Provides data to support the cost estimating process	• Supports the cost estimating process • Uses project management software in support of cost estimating
Cost Budgeting		• Reviews available data for use in the cost budgeting process	• Supports the development of the budget • Maps costs against time for inclusion in the project cash flow
Cost Control	• Supports the team in gathering data for cost reports	• Supports the team in the review of work performance information pertaining to the status and cost of project activities • Prepares and submits change requests, as directed • Analyzes change requests submitted by others for cost implications • Monitors expenditures against approved plans and the project's budget	• Establishes the project's cost control system • Uses earned value analysis techniques in performance measurement and forecasts • Provides information to support performance reviews • Uses project management software to monitor and forecast the effects of changes or variances

Associate Project Manager	Entry Level	Proficient	Master
Cost Estimating	• Reviews available estimating approaches for applicability to the project • Assigns the project's cost estimates to the correct accounting category • Uses computerized tools to assist in cost estimating • Supports the preparation of the Cost Management Plan • Considers the extent to which risk is included in the cost estimates	• Prepares the Cost Management Plan • Recommends specific tools and techniques to use in cost estimating • Supports the preparation of cost estimates	• Evaluates the information requirements of different stakeholders and how stakeholders want to measure costs and at what times • Issues the Cost Management Plan • Prepares cost estimates for the resources needed to complete each schedule activity
Cost Budgeting	• Allocates overall cost estimates to individual activities • Assigns costs to the time period when they will be incurred	• Prepares change requests that involve other aspects of the project based on the cost budgeting process • Ensures that agreed-upon financial management processes and procedures are implemented	• Determines whether it is necessary to update the Cost Management Plan
Cost Control	• Ensures that requested changes are agreed upon by key stakeholders • Monitors performance to detect and understand variances from the plan • Prepares variance and trend analyses • Reviews performance reports for issues on cost performance • Integrates cost control with other control processes • Establishes control account plans • Maintains the project's cost management system • Identifies lessons learned	• Defines the formats for the various cost reports • Records appropriate changes against the cost baseline • Ensures that incorrect, inappropriate, or unapproved changes are not included in the reported cost or resource use • Analyzes information through earned value for project performance measurement • Participates in performance reviews • Recommends changes for increasing or decreasing the budget • Provides assistance in the review of project outcomes to determine the effectiveness of initial and subsequent cost management approaches	• Ensures that potential cost overruns do not exceed the authorized funding periodically and in total for the project • Manages changes when and as they occur • Acts to bring expected cost overruns within acceptable limits • Informs stakeholders of approved changes • Conducts performance reviews • Selects cost analysis methods and tools for use in identifying variations, evaluating options, and recommending actions • Communicates performance information to stakeholders • Implements corrective action in terms of adjusting schedule activity budgets to balance cost variances

Project Manager	Entry Level	Proficient	Master
Cost Estimating	• Refines cost estimates throughout the project as additional data are obtained • Updates the Cost Management Plan based on requested and approved changes • Uses the Cost Management Plan to establish precision levels and define units used in measurements • Estimates required contingency allowances or reserves • Ensures that the cost of quality is included in cost estimating • Describes the constraints and assumptions associated with the cost estimates	• Collects and analyzes lessons learned from the cost estimating process • Mentors others on the team in the cost estimating process • Establishes requirements for the Cost Management Plan	• Ensures that the cost estimate through the control account is linked to the organization's accounting system • Reviews the cost estimates for changes to the Cost Management Plan • Reviews the cost estimates for changes that may impact the Project Management Plan
Cost Budgeting	• Establishes the project's cost baseline • Updates the Cost Management Plan	• Establishes the contingency reserve • Derives project funding requirements • Establishes a spending plan or cash flow forecast • Conducts analyses of changing financial conditions and the effect on project objectives periodically over the project life cycle	• Authorizes changes to the budget and contingency reserves • Reconciles expenditures of funds with funding limits set by the client or by the organization
Cost Control	• Establishes variance thresholds for costs at designated times over the duration of the project to show the agreed amount of variation • Manages cost contingencies or reserves • Determines how cost variances will be managed on the project • Prevents unauthorized or incorrect changes from being included in the cost baseline • Acts to bring expected costs within acceptable limits	• Selects the specific earned value rule to determine the estimate to complete • Establishes earned value criteria (0–100, 50–50, 25–75, etc.) for use on the project • Updates and issues revised cost estimates based on cost information and informs stakeholders of authorized changes • Forecasts estimates of completion • Documents lessons learned, including the root causes of variances • Evaluates options and responses to cost variations and takes action to maintain control throughout the project life cycle	• Issues budget updates and revises the cost baseline • Updates the Project Management Plan, as needed, based on cost control initiatives • Analyzes lessons learned in the cost control process • Ensures that the project's cost objectives are achieved

Project Team Member	**Entry Level**	**Proficient**	**Master**
	• Ensures that controllable and uncontrollable costs are estimated and budgeted separately		

Project Management Office Staff Member	**Entry Level**	**Proficient**	**Master**
Cost Estimating	• Provides descriptions of the cost management processes	• Provides information concerning available products in the marketplace for use in cost estimating • Assesses commercial databases for applicability for cost/rate information on the organization's projects • Provides information on resource rates • Maintains commercially available data for use in cost estimating	• Provides information to support return on investment, discounted cash flow, and investment payback analysis on projects • Prepares a template for the Cost Management Plan • Recommends the use of commercial databases • Develops cost estimating templates for use by the project team • Assists the team in the use of parametric models and in computerized tools to support cost estimating
Cost Budgeting			
Cost Control	• Assists the team in reviews of work performance information for cost control	• Assists the team in the use of earned value analysis • Provides support in the use of computerized tools for cost management	• Designs a cost control system for use on the organization's projects • Collects lessons learned on projects in cost control for the knowledge management system

Project Management Office Director	Entry Level	Proficient	Master
Cost Estimating	• Predicts and analyzes the prospective financial performance of the project's product • Analyzes return on investment, discounted cash flow analysis, and investment payback analysis • Issues the Cost Management Plan template • Establishes guidelines as to when specific types of cost estimates should be prepared on projects • Ensures that resources are available and provides needed guidance in the development of project cost estimates • Ensures that cost estimates are complete prior to preparing detailed budget requests and authorizing work • Determines the need for enhanced software to assist in cost estimating	• Establishes a life-cycle costing system for the organization • Mentors the Project Manager, as required, in cost estimating • Predicts and analyzes prospective financial performance of the project's product • Considers the cost of project decisions on the cost of using the project's product	• Evaluates the effectiveness of the life-cycle costing system in terms of improved decision making, reduced cost and execution time, and improved quality and performance of project deliverables • Develops overall cost strategies for the organization's projects
Cost Budgeting	• Provides guidance in establishing the project's cost baseline • Approves the project's budget	• Mentors the Project Manager, as needed, in cost budgeting • Identifies and resolves budget discrepancies	• Establishes cost targets for projects
Cost Control	• Develops the organization's cost management system • Ensures that resources are available to support project cost control • Evaluates lessons learned in cost control in terms of use of earned value, variance, and trend analysis • Determines the need for enhanced project management software to assist in cost control	• Mentors the Project Manager in cost control • Recommends improvements in cost control practices	• Establishes and analyzes metrics for project cost management • Analyzes lessons learned in cost management for improvements to the organization's project management practice

Project Management Office Director

	Entry Level	Proficient	Master
	• Reviews and analyzes project outcomes to determine the effectiveness of the organization's cost management system		

Chief Project Officer

	Entry Level	Proficient	Master
Cost Estimating	• Establishes the organization's cost estimating policies	• Determines the pricing strategy for the project's product	
Cost Budgeting			
Cost Control			

Project Quality Management: Includes all the activities of the performing organization that determine quality policies, objectives, and responsibilities so that the project will satisfy the needs for which it was undertaken (PMBOK® 2004).

PROJECT QUALITY MANAGEMENT

Project Team Member	Entry Level	Proficient	Master
Quality Planning	• Performs rudimentary analysis of the scope statement and other documents for quality requirements • Provides data to support quality planning	• Assists in the development of the Quality Management Plan • Contributes to cost-benefit analysis	• Assists in cost-benefit analysis • Contributes to the development of the Quality Management Plan
Perform Quality Assurance	• Reviews quality planning and control tools and techniques for applicability to quality assurance	• Assists the team in the review of work performance information for inputs to quality assurance	• Assists the team in the use of quality planning and control tools and techniques for quality assurance
Perform Quality Control	• Reviews the Quality Management Plan, metrics, and checklists for use in quality control	• Assesses approved change requests and deliverables • Reviews work performance information, including technical performance information, as an input to quality control	• Assists the team in the use of quality control tools and techniques • Prepares a defect log

Associate Project Manager	Entry Level	Proficient	Master
Quality Planning	• Prepares the preliminary cost-benefit analysis • Contributes to the draft Quality Management Plan • Develops quality requirements in consultation with stakeholders	• Assesses acceptance criteria for quality requirements • Drafts the Quality Management Plan • Reviews the organization's quality policy for applicability to the project • Reviews quality checklists • Ensures that agreed-upon quality requirements are included in the Project Management Plan and used as the basis for performance measurement	• Refines the cost-benefit analysis • Designs experiments to support quality planning • Finalizes the Quality Management Plan, including the project's quality policy • Contributes to the development of the Process Improvement Plan • Develops quality metrics • Updates the Project Management Plan, as needed • Identifies project quality criteria and communicates them to project stakeholders • Maintains the project's quality management system

Associate Project Manager	Entry Level	Proficient	Master
Perform Quality Assurance	• Reviews quality control measurements for use in quality assurance • Reviews implemented change requests, corrective actions, preventive actions, and defect repairs for use in quality assurance • Provides assistance in the ongoing review of project outcomes to determine the effectiveness of quality management activities • Identifies causes of unsatisfactory results in consultation with stakeholders to determine needed process changes	• Uses quality planning and control techniques in quality assurance • Reviews approved change requests as inputs to quality assurance • Ensures that work is undertaken according to agreed-upon quality standards • Refines the quality management system as a result of work completed and quality audit recommendations	• Requests quality audits • Proposes the use of process analysis • Recommends corrective actions • Recommends updated quality standards • Documents the results of activities and performance to determine compliance with quality standards • Reviews processes periodically to determine if changes are required • Documents lessons learned and recommends improvements
Perform Quality Control	• Uses quality control tools and techniques • Recommends preventive and corrective actions	• Analyzes quality control activities before they are fed back to the quality assurance process • Requests changes as a result of preventive and corrective actions	• Implements preventive and corrective actions • Validates and implements recommended defect repair

Project Manager	Entry Level	Proficient	Master
Quality Planning	• Refines the Quality Management Plan, as needed • Identifies other possible quality planning tools for use on the project • Prepares an assessment of the cost of quality • Prepares a draft process improvement plan • Prepares draft quality metrics	• Issues the Quality Management Plan • Finalizes the Process Improvement Plan • Finalizes the quality metrics • Completes the quality checklist	• Issues the Process Improvement Plan • Issues the quality baseline
Perform Quality Assurance	• Uses process analysis as a quality assurance tool and technique • Reviews the results of quality audits and recommends changes	• Implements corrective actions • Implements requested changes	• Updates the Project Management Plan • Updates the project's quality standards

Project Manager	Entry Level	Proficient	Master
Perform Quality Control	• Ensures that corrective and preventive actions have been implemented • Ensures that change requests follow standard processes • Updates the quality baseline, as required	• Validates the correctness of deliverables • Updates the Project Management Plan, as required	

Project Management Office Staff Member	Entry Level	Proficient	Master
Quality Planning	• Assists the team in reviewing organizational quality policies, procedures, guidelines, and historical databases and lessons learned • Provides data to support quality planning	• Assists the team in conducting cost-benefit analyses	• Contributes to the development of the Quality Management Plan • Assists the team in the use of quality planning tools • Drafts a standard Quality Management Plan template
Perform Quality Assurance	• Assists the team in the possible use of various quality planning and quality control techniques for quality assurance	• Assists the team in the review of quality control measurements	• Assists the team in the review of work performance information • Drafts standards for process analysis • Drafts standards for quality audits
Perform Quality Control	• Assists the team in the review of the Quality Management Plan, metrics, checklists, and policies and procedures	• Assists the team in the use of quality control techniques	• Assists the team in the review of work performance information • Reviews completed checklists for lessons learned • Reviews the use of quality control tools and techniques for lessons learned

Project Management Office Director	Entry Level	Proficient	Master
Quality Planning	• Finalizes the Quality Management Plan template • Drafts a Process Improvement Plan template • Provides guidelines on establishing a quality baseline	• Issues the Quality Management Plan template • Finalizes the Process Improvement Plan template • Drafts quality metrics for use throughout the organization • Finalizes guidelines on establishing a quality baseline • Mentors Project Managers in quality planning	• Issues the Process Improvement Plan template • Implements standard quality metrics • Issues guidelines on establishing a quality baseline • Participates in benchmarking forums
Perform Quality Assurance	• Finalizes and issues standards for quality audits • Finalizes and issues standards for process analysis • Requests quality audits and obtains resources to perform them • Establishes standards for quality management systems on projects to enable both effective management and communication of quality issues and outcomes	• Mentors Project Managers in quality assurance • Recommends quality improvement initiatives • Recommends changes to increase process and procedure effectiveness	• Implements quality improvement initiatives • Implements changes to policies and procedures • Updates the organization's quality standards and processes
Perform Quality Control	• Establishes standard tools and techniques for quality control • Provides guidance on when to update the quality baseline	• Mentors Project Managers in quality control • Reviews and changes policies, processes, and procedures in light of the use of quality control tools and techniques and lessons learned	

Chief Project Officer	Entry Level	Proficient	Master
Quality Planning	• Participates in external and internal benchmarking forums • Ensures that project quality policies support other organizational quality initiatives (e.g., ISO, Malcolm Baldrige)	• Determines whether changes are required to the organization's quality policy and strategic initiatives • Establishes communities of practice in quality management and project management	• Implements needed changes in the organization's quality policy
Perform Quality Assurance	• Uses the results of quality audits and project quality assurance initiatives for overall organizational improvements and policy changes		
Perform Quality Control			

Project Human Resource Management: Includes the processes that organize and manage the project team (PMBOK® 2004).

PROJECT HUMAN RESOURCE MANAGEMENT

Project Team Member	Entry Level	Proficient	Master
Human Resource Planning	• Reviews checklists for use in human resource planning • Reviews activity resource requirements as input to the Staffing Management Plan • Maintains the organizational chart	• Suggests templates for use in human resource planning • Maintains the Resource Breakdown Structure and uses it in tracking project costs • Maintains the Resource Assignment Matrix	• Provides assistance in identifying key constraints • Provides assistance in the development of the Staffing Management Plan • Provides assistance in the development of the project's Resource Breakdown Structure • Prepares a Responsibility Assignment Matrix • Updates and maintains the resource histogram as part of the Staffing Management Plan
Acquire Project Team		• Prepares and maintains a project team directory	• Provide data on policies, guidelines, and procedures concerning staff acquisition
Develop Project Team	• Prepares an individual development plan		
Manage Project Team	• Prepares a team newsletter • Prepares a team bulletin board • Provides input to team member performance appraisals • Assists in the development of the team charter	• Establishes a team Web site	• Suggests methods for reward and recognition, such as recognition dinners, certificates of appraisals, and other organization perquisites • Maintains an issue resolution log concerning obstacles confronting the team and tracks how they are resolved

Associate Project Manager	Entry Level	Proficient	Master
Human Resource Planning	• Determines the key organizations and departments that will be involved in the project and assesses their working relationships • Provides assistance in the development of the Organizational Breakdown Structure • Prepares the project organization chart • Determines key staff acquisition issues to address in the Staffing Management Plan	• Determines the needed disciplines and specialty areas for the project • Evaluates candidates' resumes • Identifies constraints that may limit the team's effectiveness • Prepares the project's Resource Breakdown Structure	• Issues the Staffing Management Plan • Determines team roles and responsibilities and issues the Resource Assignment Matrix • Prepares the project's Organizational Breakdown Structure
Acquire Project Team	• Reviews resource requirements for individual tasks to determine whether the project staffing levels are appropriate • Ensures that staff are assigned according to the Staffing Management Plan	• Evaluates staff assignments to determine if other resources are required	• Negotiates for project team member assignments • Updates the Staffing Management Plan, as needed
Develop Project Team	• Suggests team-building activities • Holds a kick-off meeting • Establishes a "war" room or a "team" room	• Identifies overall training needs for the project team • Prepares the team charter working with the team	• Works with each team member to prepare an individual development plan • Issues the team charter
Manage Project Team	• Tracks team member performance • Uses organizational policies, procedures, and systems to reward team members • Maintains regular and frequent contact with each team member • Promotes open communication and proactive use of conflicts to avoid group think • Processes change requests concerning staffing issues	• Provides input to team performance appraisals • Resolves or escalates conflicts among team members	• Appraises team member performance using the performance appraisal system as well as the individual development plan • Recommends corrective and preventive actions concerning potential or emerging human resource issues • Updates the Project Management Plan, as required

Project Manager	Entry Level	Proficient	Master
Human Resource Planning	• Analyzes project interfaces • Assesses the level of trust and respect in place in terms of working relationships • Determines methods to release staff members on the project without compromising overall team morale • Prepares a plan for recognition and rewards	• Identifies any unique challenges as the project moves from one life-cycle phase to another in terms of staffing requirements • Determines the impact of contractual agreements with unions or other groups	• Assesses the individual goals and agendas of project stakeholders • Determines which groups and people have informal power in areas important to the project • Networks with key stakeholders throughout the project • Evaluates the overall effectiveness of the Staffing Management Plan for updates to the knowledge management system
Acquire Project Team	• Provides mentoring in terms of negotiations for project team members and assists, as requested, in the negotiation process • Prepares documents and justifications for needed contracts to augment the project team in specific areas of expertise	• Implements policies and procedures for work on the virtual team, including expectations and processes for conflict resolution and collaborative leadership	• Evaluates acquisition activities for lessons learned • Ensures that the project organization and structure optimize the alignment of individual and group competencies
Develop Project Team	• Establishes a core project management team, as required • Works to improve the skills and competencies of project team members • Uses teamwork to improve feelings of trust and cohesiveness among team members • Ensures that ongoing training of project team members is identified, planned, and implemented • Ensures that each individual's responsibilities, authority, and performance measurement criteria are agreed upon	• Ensures that team development is part of every team meeting • Establishes a team-based reward and recognition system and measures performance against agreed-upon criteria • Takes action to overcome shortfalls in performance and encourage career progression • Makes recognition and reward decisions	• Assesses the effectiveness of strategies for both co-located and virtual teams • Evaluates team development initiatives for lessons learned • Actively promotes team development strategies • Promotes continuous improvement of the project team for overall project effectiveness

Project Manager

	Entry Level	Proficient	Master
Manage Project Team	• Updates the Staffing Management Plan • Identifies and resolves intra-organizational, inter-project, and intra-project conflicts and manages them to promote a positive working environment	• Provides suggestions on conflict resolution approaches for difficult situations • Updates the organization's staffing pool database • Identifies internal and external influences on individual and team performance and morale; takes corrective or preventive action, as required, to reduce the impact on project effectiveness	• Assesses the effectiveness for lessons learned concerning the team charter, conflict resolution approaches, procedures for virtual teams, issues and solutions documented in the issue log, and needed special skills or competencies for future projects

Project Management Office Staff Member

	Entry Level	Proficient	Master
Human Resource Planning	• Assists the project team in the analysis of staffing requirements in areas such as activity resource requirements, quality assurance, risk management, and procurement	• Prepares a template for a project organization chart • Prepares templates for the Resource Breakdown Structure and the Organizational Breakdown Structure • Prepares templates for the Resource Assignment Matrix • Prepares a training plan for the project based on analysis of needed areas of expertise and to help team members achieve needed certifications that would help the project	• Defines standard project roles and responsibilities • Provides data on economic conditions that could restrict staffing levels • Prepares standard job descriptions for project management positions • Prepares a standard conflict management approach • Prepares a template for project performance appraisals • Provides information on new approaches in organizational theory • Prepares a template for a plan for recognition and rewards
Acquire Project Team		• Provides data to the Project Manager on policies, guidelines, and procedures affecting staff acquisition	• Prepares a template for a project team charter
Develop Project Team			• Facilitates team development initiatives at the request of the Project Manager • Establishes guidelines for a team performance appraisal system • Establishes guidelines for team recognition and rewards

Project Management Office Staff Member	Entry Level	Proficient	Master
Manage Project Team			• Develops guidelines to track the performance of team members • Develops a format for an issue log for tracking and resolving obstacles confronting the team • Provides input into policies and procedures for interpersonal communication and conflict resolution to promote a positive working environment

Project Management Office Director	Entry Level	Proficient	Master
Human Resource Planning	• Determines standard project roles and responsibilities • Issues job descriptions • Issues standard templates for organization charts, performance appraisals, and conflict management approaches • Ensures that the Staffing Management Plan complies with regulations, contracts, and other human resource policies • Establishes requirements for the Staffing Management Plan • Prepares a project management competency model	• Updates job descriptions based on lessons learned • Establishes a project management career path • Updates templates based on new approaches in organizational theory • Mentors the Project Manager, as required, in human resource planning • Issues a standard format for a plan for recognition and rewards	• Establishes concentrated networking approaches for use on projects • Establishes criteria for recognition and rewards • Assesses the effectiveness of various project organizational structures
Acquire Project Team	• Ensures that guidance is available concerning negotiation approaches and the use of contracts to supplement the project team in other areas of expertise	• Mentors the Project Manager, as required, in negotiation techniques for staff acquisition	• Updates negotiation techniques based on effectiveness

Project Management Office Director

	Entry Level	Proficient	Master
Develop Project Team	• Develops a standard project management curriculum that includes interpersonal skills training • Develops processes and procedures for work in the virtual environment • Issues guidelines for a team performance appraisal system • Issues guidelines for team recognition and rewards	• Mentors the Project Manager, as required, in team development activities	• Evaluates team development approaches for lessons learned and enhancements • Evaluates the effectiveness of the team performance appraisal process • Promotes a system of continuous improvement in terms of project management competencies throughout the organization
Manage Project Team	• Reviews lessons learned on each project in terms of team management for applicability on future organization projects • Conducts performance appraisals of Project Managers and Project Management Office staff members	• Mentors the Project Manager, as needed, in team management activities	• Revises policies and procedures for team management based on lessons learned

Chief Project Officer

	Entry Level	Proficient	Master
Human Resource Planning	• Assesses overall human resource policies and procedures for effectiveness • Establishes project organizational structures	• Implements changes in human resource policies to increase effectiveness	
Acquire Project Team	• Establishes recruitment practices for project management • Establishes incentives for staff assignments in project management		
Develop Project Team	• Establishes a budget for project management training that includes direct and indirect costs	• Ensures that the organization's reward and recognition system supports a team-based reward and recognition system on projects	• Ensures that virtual teams are considered a strategic asset to the organization
Manage Project Team	• Assists in influencing others, as required, to contribute toward project success		

Project Communications Management: Includes the processes required to ensure timely and appropriate generation, collection, distribution, storage, retrieval, and ultimate disposition of project information (PMBOK® 2004)

PROJECT COMMUNICATIONS MANAGEMENT

Project Team Member	Entry Level	Proficient	Master
Communications Planning	• Reviews data from earlier projects concerning communications issues	• Analyzes the usefulness of lessons learned and historical information • Reviews the project scope statement	• Assists in the development of the Communications Management Plan • Conducts a stakeholder analysis of information needs
Information Distribution	• Assists in the identification of information distribution methods • Supports records management	• Supports the determination of information gathering and retrieval requirements • Supports the preparation of informal and formal project reports	• Sets up appropriate electronic tools for use on the project, as required, according to the Communications Management Plan • Maintains project records in the agreed-upon formats
Performance Reporting	• Assists the team in collecting information on deliverable status and change requests, and uses information presentation software	• Supports the preparation of project reports • Provides information to assist in status review meetings • Seeks assistance, as required, in reporting initiatives	• Prepares project performance reports and ensures they are written and distributed according to the Communications Management Plan • Supports status review meetings with the client
Manage Stakeholders	• Gathers information on stakeholder requirements and expectations	• Assists the team in the review of stakeholder requirements and expectations • Provides data and support to the issue and action item log	• Establishes an issue and action item log and maintains it during the project • Provides assistance in the ongoing review of project activities to determine the effectiveness of communications

Associate Project Manager	Entry Level	Proficient	Master
Communications Planning	• Supports the development of the Communications Management Plan • Analyzes stakeholder requirements • Identifies assumptions and constraints	• Prepares the communications requirements analysis with input from stakeholders • Identifies potential communications channels • Identifies internal and external communications needs • Determines the communications technologies to use on the project	• Assesses the urgency of the need for information • Evaluates the project environment • Evaluates the availability of technology • Establishes a schedule to show when each type of communication will be produced • Establishes a distribution structure for project information
Information Distribution	• Ensures that information is distributed according to the Communications Management Plan • Provides information to stakeholders about resolved issues, approved changes, and general project status • Responds to unexpected requests for information • Prepares a project newsletter • Maintains project records • Manages the generation, gathering, analysis, and storage of information	• Establishes the information-gathering and retrieval system • Documents lessons learned • Ensures that records management is up to date • Contacts stakeholders for feedback • Tracks unexpected requests for information to determine if updates to the Communications Management Plan are needed • Ensures that agreed-upon communications networks are in place with stakeholders	• Supports the development of a lessons-learned process on the project • Participates in lessons-learned meetings • Updates the Communications Management Plan, as required, based on analysis of unexpected requests for information • Monitors information distribution system problems and takes corrective action, as required
Performance Reporting	• Suggests needed tailoring of the organization's standard performance reporting process • Participates in status review meetings • Suggests formats for the time and cost reporting systems • Prepares change requests as a result of the analysis of project performance, as necessary	• Reviews the standard process for collecting baseline data and distributing performance information to stakeholders for use in the project and tailors it accordingly • Issues some performance reports • Establishes time and cost reporting systems • Ensures that information presentation tools are available	• Issues performance reports • Conducts status review meetings

Associate Project Manager	Entry Level	Proficient	Master
Manage Stakeholders	• Communicates with selected stakeholders as stated in the Communications Management Plan • Reports any problems that require resolution	• Addresses and resolves issues with stakeholders on the project • Maintains customer relationships within established guidelines to ensure clarity of objectives and reduce conflicts	• Ensures that each issue or action item is assigned and resolved • Suggests changes in terms of stakeholder management based on lessons learned

Project Manager	Entry Level	Proficient	Master
Communications Planning	• Issues the Communications Management Plan • Ensures that a system is in place appropriate to the project needs in terms of methodologies used to transfer information • Ensures that each team member is aware of his or her responsibilities in information distribution • Determines the information and communications needs of each stakeholder	• Updates and refines the Communications Management Plan as the project progresses • Enhances the communications technologies in use on the project, as required, for greater effectiveness • Ensures that the communications systems are compatible with the expertise of the project team and arranges for training and other guidance, as appropriate	• Updates and refines the Project Management Plan as a result of development and use of the Communications Management Plan • Reviews overall project communications management strategies • Suggests changes to standard templates and methodologies for communications planning to enhance effectiveness
Information Distribution	• Establishes a lessons-learned process for the project • Conducts lessons-learned meetings • Uses the lessons learned as updates to the Risk Management Plan • Prepares and conducts project presentations • Prepares and issues project reports • Establishes formal and informal communications networks between the project team and the client and other stakeholders and manages them to ensure effective communications • Identifies any perceived or actual problems and takes corrective actions	• Ensures that team members have appropriate training and other guidance in terms of enhancing communications skills and using technologies on the project • Evaluates project records and reports • Ensures that lessons learned lead to overall product and service improvements • Ensures that the generation, gathering, analysis, and distribution of information are managed to improve decision-making processes and overall communications effectiveness	• Ensures that lessons learned become part of the organization's knowledge management system • Evaluates team member performance in terms of improved business skills • Ensures that the information distribution system in place is such that the quality, validity, timeliness, and integrity of information and distribution are maintained • Ensures that information validation processes are developed to ensure consistent quality and accuracy of data • Contacts stakeholders for suggested improvements

Project Manager	Entry Level	Proficient	Master
Performance Reporting	• Prepares formal project reports • Conducts project presentations • Prepares forecasts of project progress • Implements corrective action to bring future performance in line with the plan • Ensures that the team has the needed guidance and training in use of information presentation tools	• Analyzes forecasts of project progress and reissues them, as required • Provides mentoring to the Project Manager, as required, in performance reporting	• Updates the lessons-learned process based on results in performance reporting • Suggests needed enhancements to the process, including methods for improvement in presentations and reports
Manage Stakeholders	• Uses the issue and action item log to ensure that all issues are resolved • Approves change requests in terms of changes in the Staffing Management Plan to reflect changes to how communications with stakeholders will occur • Uses communication methods for each stakeholder, as stated in the Communications Management Plan	• Ensures that all stakeholder concerns are addressed • Updates the Project Management Plan if there are changes to the Communications Management Plan • Implements corrective actions	• Communicates on a regular basis with key project stakeholders throughout the life of the project • Assumes complete responsibility for stakeholder management on the project • Addresses issues with stakeholders proactively, as required • Updates the lessons-learned process • Manages client relationships to ensure clarity of understanding and minimize conflicts throughout the project

Project Management Office Staff Member	Entry Level	Proficient	Master
Communications Planning	• Provides input to the project team in terms of available historical information and lessons learned	• Provides information to the project team in terms of available communication technologies • Develops a standard approach to communications requirements analysis • Develops a standard approach to assessing technology requirements	• Assists the team in conducting a stakeholder analysis as part of the communications requirements analysis • Develops a template for the Communications Management Plan • Establishes a glossary of common terms used on different types of projects

Project Management Office Staff Member	Entry Level	Proficient	Master
Information Distribution	• Supports the team in obtaining information on available electronic tools for use in communications on the project • Assists the team in the preparation of project reports and presentations	• Assists the team in methods for establishing an information-gathering and retrieval system • Assists the team in records management	• Establishes a lessons-learned process for use on the organization's projects • Facilitates the project team's lessons-learned meetings, as requested
Performance Reporting	• Assists the team in reviewing deliverables and change requests • Assists the team in preparing performance reports and data for status review meetings	• Establishes a format for standard status review meetings • Establishes a format for time and cost reporting systems • Collects lessons learned on each project for the knowledge management system	• Establishes a standard process to collect baseline data and distribute it to stakeholders on the organization's projects • Reviews lessons-learned documentation on specific projects to suggest needed changes to the performance reporting process
Manage Stakeholders	• Assists the team in reviewing the Communications Management Plan in approaches to use for each identified stakeholder	• Assists the team in use of the issue and action item log	• Establishes a standard format for the issue and action item log

Project Management Office Director	Entry Level	Proficient	Master
Communications Planning	• Issues templates for the development of the Communications Management Plan and for the communications requirements and technology analyses • Resolves issues, as appropriate, if they are escalated by the Project Manager • Provides guidance in updating and refining the Communications Management Plan, as requested	• Mentors the Project Manager, as required, in communications planning	• Assesses the Communications Management Plan templates, the templates for the requirements and technology analyses, and the glossary of terms for further refinements

Project Management Office Director	Entry Level	Proficient	Master
Information Distribution	• Establishes a standard format for a lessons-learned process within the organization • Ensures that the lessons learned on each project are analyzed to determine if the process needs refinement • Contacts stakeholders periodically to determine satisfaction with the information distribution process • Ensures that training and other guidance are available in enhancing the communications skills of Project Managers and team members • Sets standards for communications technology methods to distribute information	• Ensures that the lessons learned on each project become part of the organization's knowledge management system • Mentors the Project Manager, as required, in terms of information distribution methods and approaches and in conducting lessons-learned meetings • Evaluates technologies used to determine whether enhancements are required • Conducts pilot projects to introduce new technologies for the organization's projects	• Evaluates lessons learned for possible updates to organizational policies, processes, and procedures • Determines standard technologies for use in information distribution on the organization's projects
Performance Reporting	• Issues the standard process for use in gathering baseline data and providing performance information to stakeholders, with guidance on tailoring to meet the needs of specific projects • Ensures that project performance reports provide information on scope, schedule, cost, and quality as well as risk and procurement status • Contacts clients, as appropriate, concerning the effectiveness of status review meetings for overall changes to the process • Attends project presentations	• Mentors the Project Manager, as required, in the performance reporting process • Suggests changes to improve the effectiveness of the performance reporting process • Conducts independent project performance reviews following the standard organizational process	• Evaluates lessons learned to determine needed enhancements to the performance reporting process

Project Management Office Director

	Entry Level	Proficient	Master
Manage Stakeholders	• Evaluates the issue and action item logs for overall lessons learned in stakeholder management and updates the process, as required • Assists in negotiations with key stakeholders, as requested by the Project Manager	• Mentors the Project Manager, as requested, in stakeholder management • Suggests changes to the stakeholder management process	• Evaluates lessons learned to determine needed enhancement • Contacts stakeholders, as requested by the Project Manager

Chief Project Officer

	Entry Level	Proficient	Master
Communications Planning	• Ensures that funding is available for appropriate communications technologies for the organization's projects		
Information Distribution	• Updates organizational policies, processes, and procedures based on lessons learned		
Performance Reporting			
Manage Stakeholders	• Contacts key stakeholders as required to determine overall satisfaction with the project		

Project Risk Management: Includes the processes concerned with conducting risk management planning, identification, analysis, response planning, and monitoring and control of a project; most of these processes are updated throughout the project (PMBOK® 2004).

PROJECT RISK MANAGEMENT

Project Team Member	Entry Level	Proficient	Master
Risk Management Planning	• Reviews organizational risk management approaches and definition of terms	• Reviews policy statements and other documents to determine risk tolerance • Supports risk management planning meetings	• Participates in the risk management planning meetings and analysis as a recorder • Assists in the preparation of the Risk Management Plan
Risk Identification	• Reviews project documentation for potential risks • Supports risk brainstorming sessions as a recorder • Supports the preparation of cause-and-effect analysis, flowcharts, and influence diagrams	• Suggests risks based on documentation reviews • Participates in risk brainstorming sessions • Prepares interview guides for use in risk interviews • Participates in SWOT (strengths, weaknesses, opportunities, threats) analysis	• Assesses the possible impact on the project's requirements based on documentation reviews of risks • Suggests approaches to risk brainstorming sessions, such as use of a Risk Breakdown Structure • Participates in risk interviews, as requested • Participates in assumptions analysis • Sets up a structure for the risk register
Qualitative Risk Analysis	• Assembles data from past projects and the lessons-learned database for use in the qualitative risk analysis process	• Establishes a watch list for monitoring low-priority risks • Maintains the risk register	• Contributes to the prioritization of risks • Updates the risk register, as directed, based on the qualitative risk analysis • Provides support to the development of the risk probability and impact assessment and the probability and impact matrix by preparing supporting detail
Quantitative Risk Analysis	• Assembles data from past projects and the lessons-learned database for use in the quantitative risk analysis process	• Maintains the risk register	• Provides support in the development of questions for interviews to help quantify the probability and impact of risks on project objectives • Documents the results of risk interviews

Project Team Member	Entry Level	Proficient	Master
Risk Response Planning	• Assembles data for use in risk response planning	• Maintains the risk register	• Assists in the information-gathering process to determine the most appropriate risk or opportunity response
Risk Monitoring and Control	• Assembles data for use in risk monitoring and control	• Maintains the risk register • Participates in discussions of risks at status meetings	• Assists in risk reassessments • Assists in variance and trend analysis

Associate Project Manager	Entry Level	Proficient	Master
Risk Management Planning	• Participates in the risk management planning meetings • Supports the preparation of the Risk Breakdown Structure • Determines whether categories used on other projects for risks might be applicable to this project • Contributes to the preparation of the Risk Management Plan	• Takes an active role in the risk management planning process • Develops risk cost elements and schedule activities • Prepares the risk probability and impact matrix • Determines the risk register format • Reviews work on the Risk Management Plan and adds to it, as appropriate	• Leads the risk management planning meeting • Determines the need to tailor existing templates for the risk categories and probability impact matrix • Enhances the Risk Management Plan
Risk Identification	• Reviews the scope statement, and Schedule, Cost, and Quality Management Plans for potential risks • Identifies stakeholders who might be candidates for risk interviews • Conducts interviews with selected stakeholders • Leads brainstorming sessions • Participates in root cause identification analysis	• Leads risk interviews with stakeholders • Leads SWOT analysis • Develops risk checklists	• Leads the assumption analysis • Leads the preparation of cause-and-effect diagrams, flowcharts, and influence diagrams • Suggests use of the Delphi technique and recommends potential participants
Qualitative Risk Analysis	• Supports the development of the risk probability and impact assessment • Based on the qualitative analysis, categorizes project risks by sources of risk	• Suggests risks that require additional attention and response as a result of the qualitative risk analysis • Supports the development of the risk urgency assessment	• Leads the development of the risk probability and impact assessment • Leads the development of the probability and impact matrix

Associate Project Manager	Entry Level	Proficient	Master
		• Supports the development of the risk data quality assessment • Determines the risk score	• Leads the development of the risk urgency assessment • Leads the development of the risk data quality assessment • Analyzes trends in qualitative risk results
Quantitative Risk Analysis	• Supports the risk interview process	• Conducts risk interviews • Provides support in the use of modeling techniques for quantitative risk analysis	• Provides data to identify realistic and achievable cost, schedule, or scope targets, given the project risks • Provides data for decision making as to the best outcome if some conditions are uncertain • Uses modeling techniques for quantitative risk analysis
Risk Response Planning	• Serves as a risk owner, as appropriate	• Supports the determination of the appropriate risk response • Provides data to consider in the development of risk triggers	• Determines the appropriate risk response based on available data • Prepares fallback plans • Develops risk triggers
Risk Monitoring and Control	• Implements contingency plans and workarounds • Supports the risk reassessment process • Analyzes trends in the project's execution for use in risk monitoring and control • Supports reserve analysis	• Leads the risk reassessment process • Leads status meetings in which risk is an agenda item • Supports technical performance measurement to forecast degrees of success in achieving the project's scope objectives	• Suggests changes to the Project Management Plan and Risk Management Plan based on implementing contingency plans or workarounds • Recommends corrective and preventive actions • Prepares change requests • Contributes to the ongoing review of project outcomes to determine the effectiveness of risk management activities • Reports issues and responses for consideration in revisions to the organization's risk management approach

Project Manager	Entry Level	Proficient	Master
Risk Management Planning	• Reviews the Risk Management Plan • Determines the level of tailoring required on existing templates • Determines the frequency with which risk management will be performed on the project • Finalizes the Risk Breakdown Structure	• Issues the Risk Management Plan and communicates it to the client and other stakeholders • Determines lead and support roles and responsibilities on the project for risk management • Establishes a risk management system to enable effective management and communication of risk events, responses, and results to stakeholders • Assigns resources and estimates costs involved in risk management and includes them in the cost baseline • Determines how risk activities will be recorded and tracked	• Determines the need to audit risk management processes on the project • Determines the need to revise stakeholder tolerances for risk and works with project stakeholders accordingly • Suggests changes to the organization's standard templates for risk management • Determines how the outcomes of risk management will be communicated during the project to the client and other stakeholders
Risk Identification	• Selects risk experts to participate in Delphi analysis and reviews the results of the analysis • Selects people to participate in risk interviews • Prepares a list of identified risks	• Describes each identified risk in terms of its root causes and uncertain project assumptions • Updates risk categories, as required • Identifies, documents, and analyzes potential/actual risk events	• Updates the Risk Management Plan and the Project Management Plan, as needed • Determines how often risk identification should be performed on the project • Suggests new categories to use as a result of the risk identification process • Determines whether the Risk Breakdown Structure requires updating
Qualitative Risk Analysis	• Leads the development of a risk data quality assessment • Analyzes the results of the risk probability and impact assessment • Prioritizes those risks for further quantitative analysis and response based on their risk rating • Selects experts to participate in the risk probability and impact assessment	• Selects risk analysis methods and tools for use on the project • Determines, through the use of risk categories, common root causes of risks in the project to help improve the effectiveness of the risk responses • Assesses the risks in terms of priority and places those deemed of low significance on a watch list for continued monitoring	• Analyzes the results of the qualitative risk analysis for trends to determine if overall project performance is improving or deteriorating • Identifies, as a result of the qualitative risk analysis, risks that require immediate and urgent responses • Focuses attention on items of highest significance to the project • Determines the need for additional qualitative risk analysis on the project

Project Manager	Entry Level	Proficient	Master
Quantitative Risk Analysis	• Analyzes the results of the quantitative risk analysis to determine the probability of achieving the cost and time objectives • Determines the risks that are most likely to impact the critical path	• Describes the basis for the assessed probability and impact for those risks determined to be important to the project • Serves as an expert in the risk probability and impact assessment • Determines whether quantitative risk analysis is needed • Estimates potential project schedule and cost outcomes as a result of the quantitative risk analysis • Prioritizes the risks that pose the greatest threat or provide the greatest opportunity to the project	• Determines the need for additional quantitative risk analysis on the project • Analyzes the results of quantitative risk analysis for trends that may lead to conclusions about risk responses
Risk Response Planning	• Selects the appropriate risk response to achieve the project objectives • Assigns risk owners • Identifies contingent response strategies • Addresses residual risks • Prepares contingency plans and triggers for their execution	• Manages risks according to the Risk Management Plan • Addresses risks by priority and adds resources and activities into the budget, schedule, and Project Management Plan, as required • Calculates needed contingency reserves	• Enters into risk-related contractual agreements, as needed • Updates the Project Management Plan as a result of selected risk responses
Risk Monitoring and Control	• Leads reserve analysis • Leads technical performance measurement activities • Requests risk audits and analyzes their results • Monitors internal and external risks to project outcomes and initiates remedial actions	• Ensures that resources are available for risk audits • Implements corrective and preventive actions • Modifies project objectives, if necessary, based on risk monitoring and control • Identifies risk issues and recommends improvements for application in future projects	• Updates the Project Management Plan as a result of risk monitoring and control activities • Assesses the effectiveness of the risk management system in light of the project outcomes

Project Management Office Staff Member	Entry Level	Proficient	Master
Risk Management Planning	• Provides input to a common definition of risk management terms • Reviews policy statements to obtain insights on risk tolerances	• Reviews authority levels for decision making on risk in the organization • Provides input to the standard templates for the Risk Management Plan, Risk Breakdown Structure, risk categories, and probability and impact matrix • Ensures that the level, type, and visibility of risk management are appropriate for the risk and the importance of the project to the organization	• Develops standard templates for the Risk Management Plan, Risk Breakdown Structure, risk categories, and probability/impact matrix • Develops a standard terminology for risk management practices • Develops a risk management methodology for use on the organization's projects • Facilitates the risk probability and impact assessment process, as requested by the Project Manager • Recommends standard software for project risk management
Risk Identification	• Assists the team in documentation reviews, especially from previous project files • Assists the team in developing risk interview guides	• Assists the team in the use of commercial databases and studies, including the results of benchmarking forums • Assists the team in performing SWOT analysis • Assists the team in the use of cause-and-effect diagrams, flowcharts, and influence diagrams	• Facilitates the brainstorming sessions • Facilitates the Delphi process • Assists the team in setting up the project's risk register • Assists the team in analyzing the root causes of risks • Assists the team in performing assumption analysis
Qualitative Risk Analysis		• Assists the team in developing the probability and impact matrix • Assists the team in the development of criteria for a watch list for risks that should be monitored further • Assists the team in updating the risk register	• Categorizes the organization's projects to assist in the use of qualitative risk analysis techniques • Suggests risk rating rules for use in the probability and impact matrix • Assists the team in determining the overall rating for each risk and opportunity • Assists the team in the overall analysis of trends in the results of the qualitative analysis

Project Management Office Staff Member

	Entry Level	Proficient	Master
Quantitative Risk Analysis		• Assists the team in updating the risk register • Assists the team in documenting the results of risk interviews	• Assists the team in the use of quantitative risk analysis modeling techniques
Risk Response Planning		• Provides assistance to the team in updating the risk register	• Assists the team in the review and analysis of data in selecting the risk response
Risk Monitoring and Control	• Collects data on the actual cost of risk responses and the use of contingency reserves	• Maintains databases on risk lessons learned • Assists the team in updating the risk register	• Facilitates status meetings in which risks are discussed, as requested • Suggests changes to the templates for the Risk Management Plan, including the probability and impact matrix and the risk register, based on lessons learned

Project Management Office Director

	Entry Level	Proficient	Master
Risk Management Planning	• Issues templates for the Risk Management Plan, Risk Breakdown Structure, risk categories, and probability/impact matrix • Issues a glossary of standard terms for use in the organization regarding risk management • Selects standard software for project risk management • Assigns resources to assist the project team in risk management initiatives • Reviews and approves the Risk Management Plan for each project • Issues the organization's risk management methodology	• Determines the standard frequency for risk management activities on the organization's projects by category • Determines the number of risk audits and risk reviews that will be held • Mentors the Project Manager, as needed, in risk management planning	• Suggests changes to the organization's risk management policies, including the authority levels for risk management decisions • Participates in risk reviews • Assesses the risk audits for overall lessons learned in the organization's risk management methodology • Analyzes the risk data for inclusion in the knowledge management system • Ensures that funds are available for projects to identify and analyze risks

Project Management Office Director	Entry Level	Proficient	Master
Risk Identification	• Provides standard risk identification checklists to the Project Manager and team • Provides templates for the risk register to the Project Manager and team • Suggests updates to the organization's list of risk categories • Participates in Delphi analysis	• Assesses data from the organization's projects to determine if changes are needed to the standard risk categories and the risk checklist • Recommends risk identification techniques for use by Project Managers • Determines the root causes of risks affecting the organization's projects • Assesses the effectiveness of the standard template for the risk register • Mentors the Project Manager, as needed, in risk identification	• Determines the frequency of risk identification
Qualitative Risk Analysis	• Provides standard definitions of the levels of probability and impact for use throughout the organization • Evaluates the quality of available information on project risks to determine the assessment of the risk's importance to projects • Provides guidance in developing indicators of priority in risk urgency assessment • Develops a standard risk probability and impact matrix and defines standard terms for low-, moderate-, or high-priority risks	• Mentors the Project Manager, as needed, in qualitative risk analysis techniques • Determines the combinations of probability and impact that result in classifying a risk as high, moderate, or low as risk rating rules	• Assesses the overall effectiveness of the qualitative risk analysis process in terms of its ability to improve overall project performance and focus on high-priority risks

Project Management Office Director	Entry Level	Proficient	Master
Quantitative Risk Analysis	• Provides standard tools and guidance to the Project Manager and team on quantitative risk analysis and modeling techniques to use • Provides guidance to the Project Manager and team on whether quantitative risk analysis should be repeated • Serves as an expert, as appropriate, in a possible risk interview	• Mentors the Project Manager, as needed, in quantitative risk analysis	• Assesses the overall effectiveness of the quantitative risk analysis process in terms of its ability to quantify the possible outcomes for the organization's projects and their probabilities and to assess the likelihood of achieving project objectives
Risk Response Planning	• Provides guidance to the Project Manager in evaluating risk responses in terms of the significance of the risk and in determining whether the response is cost effective • Provides guidance to the Project Manager in calculating the amount of contingency reserve needed	• Reviews responses selected for lessons learned for future projects • Establishes standards for selecting certain types of responses • Mentors the Project Manager in risk response planning • Establishes standards for risk-related contractual agreements	• Assesses the results of the process for changes in terms of contingency reserves of time and cost according to the organization's risk tolerances
Risk Monitoring and Control	• Ensures that resources are available for periodic risk audits	• Mentors the Project Manager, as needed, in risk monitoring and controls	• Assesses results and lessons learned, including data on the actual cost of risk monitoring and control activities versus their benefit, for changes in the organization's overall approach to project risk management and changes to risk management templates

Chief Project Officer	Entry Level	Proficient	Master
Risk Management Planning	• Ensures that sufficient resources (people, dollars, and time) are available for risk management in the organization to establish a risk management capability in tools, techniques, and training • Provides funding for ongoing maintenance of the risk management capability and to continue training initiatives • Conducts assessments of needed changes in risk management practices in the organization to increase overall project management maturity and to verify process effectiveness • Ensures that risks are viewed as opportunities for organizational transformation • Promotes and establishes a culture of open communication on project risks	• Establishes the organization's risk management policies, including the authority levels for decision making • Prepares policy statements concerning risk management practices	• Enhances risk management policies to support transformation and innovation initiatives
Risk Identification	• Serves as an expert on a Delphi committee or as an expert for risk interviews, as appropriate		
Qualitative Risk Analysis			
Quantitative Risk Analysis			
Risk Response Planning	• Sets policies for the use of contingency reserves for time and cost • Sets policies for the use of risk-related contractual agreements		
Risk Monitoring and Control	• Assesses the results of risk management initiatives to identify any trends that could lead to overall business development opportunities		

Project Procurement Management: Includes the processes to purchase or acquire the products, services, or results needed from outside the project team to perform the work (PMBOK® 2004).

PROJECT PROCUREMENT MANAGEMENT

Project Team Member	Entry Level	Proficient	Master
Plan Purchases and Acquisitions	• Performs rudimentary analysis of procurement documents • Provides data to support procurement planning	• Performs detailed analysis of procurement documents • Assists in the development of the Procurement Management Plan	• Contributes to the development of the Procurement Management Plan
Plan Contracting	• Assists in the review of procurement document requirements	• Reviews procurement document requirements	• Validates procurement document requirements
Request Seller Responses	• Gathers information on potential contractors	• Performs intermediate evaluation techniques	
Solicit Sellers			• Contributes to the contractor selection process
Contract Administration	• Provides nominal tracking and monitoring	• Provides minimal tracking and monitoring	• Performs detailed tracking and monitoring
Contract Closure	• Reviews documents for completeness	• Validates documents for completeness	• Ensures document completeness

Associate Project Manager	Entry Level	Proficient	Master
Plan Purchases and Acquisitions	• Assists with the make-or-buy analysis evaluation	• Performs the make-or-buy analysis	• Reviews the make-or-buy analysis
Plan Contracting	• Reviews existing project documents • Gathers information for use in the development of evaluation criteria	• Suggests the format of the procurement document • Contributes to the development of evaluation criteria	• Provides procurement documents to the procurement department • Finalizes the evaluation criteria
Request Seller Responses		• Provides input to the bidder's conference	• Participates in the bidder's conference

Associate Project Manager	Entry Level	Proficient	Master
Solicit Sellers	• Assists in the development of weighting systems and screening systems	• Develops weighting and screening systems • Develops the Contract Management Plan	• Participates in proposal reviews • Finalizes the Contract Management Plan
Contract Administration	• Assesses the standard change management system for use on the project • Provides input for review sessions with contractors	• Suggests tailoring, as required, to the change management system • Reviews and monitors contractor performance	• Implements the contract change management system • Holds formal reviews with contractors • Updates the Procurement Management Plan and Contract Management Plan, as required • Takes corrective action, as needed
Contract Closure	• Updates contract documentation • Suggests lessons learned	• Prepares documents for archiving • Submits lessons learned	• Submits documents to archives • Finalizes lessons learned for the knowledge management system

Project Manager	Entry Level	Proficient	Master
Plan Purchases and Acquisitions	• Reviews procurement guidelines and regulations • Provides input to assumptions and constraints • Prepares the draft Procurement Management Plan • Provides recommendation on types of contracts to use • Finalizes the make-or-buy analysis	• Recommends the type of contract to be used • Works with the procurement department on requirements • Prepares the Procurement Management Plan • Discusses the Procurement Management Plan with stakeholders	• Works with stakeholders to ensure that the Procurement Management Plan will meet objectives
Plan Contracting	• Reviews and suggests standard forms for use • Suggests procurement documents for use • Prepares evaluation criteria	• Assesses evaluation criteria used for evaluation and modifies them, as required	• Ensures that planned approaches are consistent with those used on other project procurements

Project Manager	Entry Level	Proficient	Master
Request Seller Responses	• Participates in the bidder's conference, if appropriate • Reviews the procurement document package finalized by procurement department • Conducts site visits, if required	• Conducts the bidder's conference, if appropriate • Signs off on the procurement document package	
Select Sellers	• Implements the selection criteria • Evaluates the proposals • Updates the Procurement Management Plan • Develops a seller rating system	• Makes final decisions in conjunction with the procurement department • Prepares the negotiating sequence for selected sellers • Participates in the negotiation process • Updates the Procurement Management Plan	• Evaluates the effectiveness of proposal evaluation techniques • Conducts the negotiation process working with the procurement department
Contract Administration	• Ensures that products/services are received to facilitate payment • Conducts performance reviews • Integrates the contract change control system with the integrated project change control system • Proposes contract amendments, as required • Implements the Contract Management Plan	• Leads performance reviews with contractors • Implements corrective and preventive actions as required	• Plans to ensure a common approach to achieve project objectives • Reviews progress to analyze variances and ensure that agreed-upon changes are implemented
Contract Closure	• Requests a procurement audit • Ensures that the contractor receives formal acceptance	• Reviews the findings of the procurement audit for lessons learned	• Implements lessons learned on current and future contracts

Project Management Office Staff Member	**Entry Level**	**Proficient**	**Master**
Plan Purchases and Acquisitions	• Provides data on marketplace conditions to Project Managers • Ensures that project managers have required information on policies, procedures, and guidelines, especially in terms of possible project constraints • Prepares guidelines for the use of different contract types, in conjunction with the procurement department	• Assists the team in the preparation of the Procurement Management Plan and in the development of the make-or-buy analysis	• Provides advice concerning the possible need to update the Project Management Plan and project scope statement
Plan Contracting	• Ensures that project teams have access to the required standard forms	• Assists the teams in the development of procurement documents	• Assists the team in the use of evaluation criteria
Request Seller Responses	• Ensures that project teams have access to the qualified seller lists	• Assists the team in placing advertisements, as required	• Assists the team in the bidder's conference, as necessary • Reviews the procurement document package to ensure that it is in compliance with organizational procedures
Select Sellers	• Develops proposed approaches for standard weighting and screening systems • Develops contract negotiating guidelines	• Reviews approaches for weighting and screening systems • Reviews contract negotiation guidelines • Develops approaches for a seller rating system • Develops a template for a Contract Management Plan	• Reviews approaches for a seller rating system • Develops proposal evaluation techniques • Supports proposal evaluation, as requested

Project Management Office Staff Member	Entry Level	Proficient	Master
Contract Administration	• Assists the team in contract administration tasks • Ensures that project teams are aware of organizational policies regarding payment systems	• Provides input to the development of a contract change management system • Assists in an ongoing review of project outcomes to ensure the effectiveness of contract administration activities	• Develops a records management system as part of the project management information system (PMIS) • Provides support in the conduct of buyer reviews of contractor performance • Develops guidelines for use by the project teams in reviews of contractor performance • Develops a contract change management system
Contract Closure	• Assists the team in completing the required contract documentation, including the indexed, final contract file	• Assists the team in documenting lessons learned	• Analyzes lessons learned and proposes recommendations • Reviews the results of procurement audits • Assists the team in reviewing contract closure activities to ensure the quality of final documentation

Project Management Office Director	Entry Level	Proficient	Master
Plan Purchases and Acquisitions	• Reviews the Procurement Management Plan for conformance to organizational policies and suggests needed changes • Ensures that the Procurement Management Plan supports the Project Management Plan	• Develops techniques for the make-or-buy analysis • Issues the template for the Procurement Management Plan • Requests expert involvement, as required • Mentors the Project Manager in procurement planning	• Supplies resources to the Project Manager to assist in the process, as required • Provides techniques for use in the make-or-buy analysis • Distributes the format for the Procurement Management Plan
Plan Contracting	• Ensures that standard forms are useful and provides updates, as required • Proposes standard evaluation criteria for use as guidelines for the organization's different types of procurements	• Updates standard forms, as required • Issues evaluation criteria templates	

Project Management Office Director	Entry Level	Proficient	Master
Request Seller Responses	• Provides guidance in the conduct of the bidder's conference	• Mentors Project Managers in the plan contracting process • Assesses needed changes to standard procurement document packages	• Assesses and implements needed changes in the use of the bidder's conference • Implements needed changes to standard procurement document packages
Select Sellers	• Supports the negotiation process • Implements guidelines for the weighting system, screening system, seller rating system, and proposal evaluation techniques • Issues the template for the Contract Management Plan	• Mentors the Project Manager in the select seller process negotiation tactics and procedures • Determines whether changes are needed, and implements them accordingly, in the template for the Procurement Management Plan • Provides additional resources to the project team, as required	• Acquires the services of experts, as necessary, to assist in proposal evaluation • Updates tools and techniques and negotiating guidelines based on lessons learned
Contract Administration	• Implements the contract change management system • Implements guidelines for the PMIS to include contractor records management • Supports the Project Manager if there are contested changes, claims, and disputes	• Reviews experiences to determine whether changes are required to guidelines, templates (Procurement Management and Contract Management Plans), processes, and the contract change management system • Mentors the Project Manager in contract administration	• Ensures that contract administration lessons learned are part of the organization's knowledge management system • Establishes guidelines for the use of partnering
Contract Closure	• Based on lessons learned, implements proposed changes to policies, procedures, and guidelines	• Mentors the Project Manager in contract closure	

Chief Project Officer	Entry Level	Proficient	Master
Plan Purchases and Acquisitions	• Assists in obtaining support from the procurement department, as required • Reviews and suggests modifications to organizational policies involving procurement and contracting	• Implements new or revised organizational procurement policies	
Plan Contracting	• Ensures that experts are available, as required, to assist project teams in this process		
Request Seller Responses			
Solicit Sellers	• Ensures that experts are available to assist project teams in proposal evaluation	• Implements changes in negotiation policies and procedures	
Contract Administration	• Promotes the use of an enterprise PMIS that includes information and communications technologies to enhance contract administration	• Ensures that the organization is on the cutting edge in enterprise systems that include a contract administration component • Supports partnering initiatives in major contractual endeavors	• Revises policies, as appropriate, concerning enterprise information systems and partnering with major contractors
Contract Closure		• Ensures that lessons learned are incorporated into the organization's knowledge management system	

INSTRUMENT 3–J

Knowledge and Competency Requirements by Project Position

Project Management Position

Process	Project Team Member	Associate Project Manager	Project Manager	Project Management Office (PMO) Staff Member	Director, PMO	Chief Project Officer
Develop Project Charter			Initiating processes Organizational project management policies and procedures Stakeholder identification techniques Stakeholder expectations	Initiating processes Business needs documentation Measurement of the project's value Enterprise environmental factors analysis Market conditions analysis Organizational project management policies and procedures Benefit-measurement methods Mathematical modeling Template development	Organizational project management policies and procedures Project evaluation methodologies Project requirements and objectives Portfolio analysis Decision-making processes Assumption analysis techniques Constraint identification techniques Level of authority Alternatives analysis Resource skills and categories	Decision-making processes Strategic planning Policy analysis Portfolio management Economic value added Transformation strategies Innovation strategies Corporate culture International and political environment Functional business areas

Adapted from Parviz F. Rad and Ginger Levin, *The Advanced Project Management Office* (Boca Raton, FL: CRC Press). © 2002. Reproduced by permission of Routledge/Taylor & Francis Group, LLC.

Project Management Position

Process	Project Team Member	Associate Project Manager	Project Manager	Project Management Office (PMO) Staff Member	Director, PMO	Chief Project Officer
Develop Preliminary Scope Statement			Requirements analysis methods Cost estimating approaches Constraint identification techniques Assumptions identification techniques Communications techniques	Product analysis Project objectives analysis Project management methodology contents Project management software Template development	Organizational project management policies and procedures Project requirements and objectives Communications techniques Project management strategies	Strategic planning Portfolio management Financial management Social-economic-environmental sustainability Decision-making processes
Develop Project Management Plan	Planning processes Project life cycle Contents of a project management plan	Project management software Existing project documents Documentation management Configuration management Planning processes Project life cycle Contents of a project management plan	Planning methodologies Contents of a project management plan Planning processes Project management methodology contents Assumption identification techniques Constraint identification techniques Communications techniques Management reviews Tactical planning	Planning processes Enterprise environmental factors analysis Project life cycle Project management software Project management methodology contents Template development	Organizational project management policies and procedures Project management methodologies and tools Planning methodologies Internal project environment Organizational policies Project management strategies Establishing metrics Social-economic-environmental sustainability	Planning strategies External project environment Policy development Strategic planning Portfolio management Social-economic-environmental sustainability

Project Management Position

Process	Project Team Member	Associate Project Manager	Project Manager	Project Management Office (PMO) Staff Member	Director, PMO	Chief Project Officer
Direct and Manage Project Execution	Executing processes	Executing processes	Executing processes	Executing processes	Organizational policies	Establishing direction
	Product-specific technical requirements	Project management software	Problem solving	Project management software	Problem-solving techniques	Internationalization
	Phase-end requirements	Earned value analysis	Decision-making techniques	Methods analysis	Decision-making techniques	Policy analysis
	Change request analysis	Tracking performance against a plan	Implementing corrective and preventive actions		Internationalization	Program evaluation
	Tracking performance against a plan	Technical skills and application	Issue analysis and evaluation		Meeting management techniques	Portfolio management
	Methods to prepare and analyze change requests	Lessons-learned analysis	Workload balancing techniques		Knowledge management	Influencing the organization
	Project management software		Resource management			
	Preparing meeting agendas and taking minutes of meetings		Motivational techniques			
			Communications techniques			
			Management/ leadership principles and techniques			
			Meeting management techniques			

Project Management Position

Process	Project Team Member	Associate Project Manager	Project Manager	Project Management Office (PMO) Staff Member	Director, PMO	Chief Project Officer
Monitor and Control Project Work	Monitoring and controlling processes Tracking and monitoring techniques Change request analysis Project management software Data collection techniques	Monitoring and controlling processes Risk analysis techniques Forecasting Earned value management techniques Work performance analysis	Monitoring and controlling processes Risk analysis techniques Performance assessment techniques Earned value management techniques	Monitoring and controlling processes Project management software Earned value management techniques	Controlling processes Program evaluation Knowledge management	Decision-making processes Strategic planning Portfolio management
Integrated Change Control	Monitoring and controlling processes Tracking and monitoring techniques Data collection techniques Methods to prepare and analyze change requests Reporting changes Project management software	Monitoring and controlling processes Configuration management software Defect repair analysis Documentation management Analysis of change requests Tracking and monitoring Integration methodologies	Monitoring and controlling processes Gathering, assessing, and integrating information Earned value management Change management techniques Lessons-learned analysis Configuration management	Monitoring and controlling processes Configuration management software Knowledge management approaches	Gathering, assessing, and integrating information Knowledge management Integration techniques	Decision-making processes Portfolio management

Project Management Position

Process	Project Team Member	Associate Project Manager	Project Manager	Project Management Office (PMO) Staff Member	Director, PMO	Chief Project Officer
Close Project	Closing processes Existing project documents	Closing processes Existing project documents Project management methodologies Archiving methodologies	Closing processes Customer requirements Acceptance procedures Formal acceptance documentation Resource redeployment planning Lessons-learned documentation	Closing processes Archiving methodologies Project management methodologies Lessons-learned database Enterprise environmental factors analysis	Organizational project management policies and procedures Acceptance procedures Knowledge management Program evaluation techniques	
Scope Planning	Planning processes Existing project documents	Planning processes Existing project documents Change management methodologies Scope Management Plan templates	Methods to establish quantifiable criteria Planning methodologies Meeting management techniques Stakeholder expectations Change request process	Benefit/cost analysis techniques Market conditions analysis Lessons-learned database Template development	Planning methodologies Personnel policies Establishing metrics Knowledge management	Organizational influences Strategic planning Economic value added Transformation analysis Innovation analysis

Project Management Position

Process	Project Team Member	Associate Project Manager	Project Manager	Project Management Office (PMO) Staff Member	Director, PMO	Chief Project Officer
Scope Definition	Existing project documents Product analysis techniques [systems engineering, value engineering, value analysis, function analysis, Quality Function Deployment (QFD)] Change request analysis	Existing project documents Documentation management Benefit-cost analysis techniques Configuration management techniques	New product development methodologies Stakeholder analysis techniques Acceptance criteria Alternatives identification Constraint identification Alternatives analysis Boundary definitions Approval requirements	Product analysis techniques (systems engineering, value engineering, value analysis, function analysis, QFD) Template development	Communications techniques Acceptance requirements Knowledge management	
Create WBS	Purpose and uses of a WBS Purpose and uses of a WBS Dictionary	Purpose and uses of a WBS Purpose and uses of a WBS Dictionary	WBS development and decomposition techniques Purpose and uses of a WBS Purpose and uses of a WBS Dictionary Baseline analysis anc identification	WBS decomposition techniques Purpose and uses of a WBS Purpose and uses of a WBS Dictionary Template development	Knowledge management	

Project Management Position

Process	Project Team Member	Associate Project Manager	Project Manager	Project Management Office (PMO) Staff Member	Director, PMO	Chief Project Officer
Scope Verification	Inspection techniques	Inspection techniques Documentation management	Acceptance processes Authorization procedures	Inspection techniques	Acceptance processes Approving authorities	
Scope Control	Tracking and monitoring techniques Data collection techniques Methods to prepare and analyze change requests Reporting changes	Performance measurement techniques Configuration management procedures Variance analysis techniques Change requests	Change management techniques Lessons-learned analysis Performance measurement technique Corrective and preventive actions Performance reviews	Performance measurement techniques Configuration management procedures Lessons-learned database	Control thresholds Knowledge management Integration techniques	
Activity Definition	Existing project documents Purpose of the activity list	Existing project documents Activity list templates Control accounts Planning packages Activity attributes Decomposition techniques	Decomposition techniques Purpose of the activity list Planning processes Rolling wave planning Constraint identification Assumptions analysis	Existing project documents Activity attribute definition Template development	Planning policies Knowledge management	

Project Management Position

Process	Project Team Member	Associate Project Manager	Project Manager	Project Management Office (PMO) Staff Member	Director, PMO	Chief Project Officer
		Project management information system Purpose of the activity list		Planning processes and procedures Project management software		
Activity Sequencing	Existing project documents Product characteristics Change request analysis Types of dependencies	Precedence Diagramming Method (PDM) techniques Dependency identification and analysis Network templates	Integrating and sequencing activities and tasks Assumption identification techniques Constraint identification techniques	PDM and ADM diagramming techniques Project management software	Knowledge management	
Activity Resource Estimating	Existing project documents Identifying resource requirements	Project management software	Resource estimating techniques Negotiation techniques	Project management software	Knowledge management Mentoring Organizational policies	Policy development

Project Management Position

Process	Project Team Member	Associate Project Manager	Project Manager	Project Management Office (PMO) Staff Member	Director, PMO	Chief Project Officer
Activity Duration Estimating	Existing project documents Risk identification methods Bottom-up estimating approach	Computerized estimating tools and techniques	Estimating techniques Assumption identification techniques Constraint identification techniques Resource identification techniques	Computerized estimating tools and techniques	Knowledge management	
Schedule Development	Project activity characteristics Existing project documents Project and resource calendars Project management software	Resource leveling techniques Critical Path Method (CPM) and Program Evaluation and Review Technique (PERT) Crashing and fast tracking Project management software Schedule milestones Schedule model data	Planning methodologies Presentation techniques (Gantt, milestone, network) Constraint identification techniques Assumption identification techniques Resource management Baseline analysis and identification	Resource leveling techniques CPM and PERT Crashing and fast tracking Critical chain Simulation (Monte Carlo) Project management software Template development	Establishing metrics Resource management Knowledge management	

Project Management Position

Process	Project Team Member	Associate Project Manager	Project Manager	Project Management Office (PMO) Staff Member	Director, PMO	Chief Project Officer
Schedule Control	Tracking and monitoring techniques Data collection techniques Methods to prepare and analyze change requests Reporting changes	Performance measurement techniques Earned value management techniques Project management software Variance analysis techniques Integration methodologies	Change management techniques Forecasting Lessons-learned analysis Performance measurement techniques Corrective and preventive actions Performance reviews Variance management	Earned value management techniques Change control methodologies Project management software Lessons-learned database	Control thresholds Knowledge management Earned value management methodologies Integration techniques	
Cost Estimating	Product requirements Existing project documents Bottom-up cost estimating approach Risk identification techniques Gathering quotes and required data	Computerized estimating tools and techniques Market analysis Lessons-learned analysis	Planning methodologies Costing alternatives Reserve analysis Estimating methodologies Activity cost estimates	Return on investment, payback analysis, discounted cash flow analysis Market analysis Estimating publications Computerized estimating tools and techniques Parametric modeling Template development	Life-cycle costing Value engineering Costing alternatives Precision levels Organizational policies Knowledge management	Marketing policies Cost estimating policies

Project Management Position

Process	Project Team Member	Associate Project Manager	Project Manager	Project Management Office (PMO) Staff Member	Director, PMO	Chief Project Officer
Cost Budgeting	Existing project documents Tracking and monitoring techniques	Budgeting controllable and uncontrollable costs Cost allocation Cost aggregation Funding requirements	Budget management techniques Cost allocation Funds reconciliation Baseline analysis and identification	Tracking and monitoring techniques	Organizational policies Knowledge management	
Cost Control	Tracking and monitoring techniques Data collection techniques Methods to prepare and analyze change requests Reporting changes	Performance measurement techniques Earned value management techniques Project management software Variance analysis techniques Integration methodologies	Change management techniques Forecasting Lessons-learned analysis Performance measurement techniques Corrective and preventive actions Performance reviews Variance management	Earned value management techniques Project management software Change control methodologies Lessons-learned databases	Control thresholds Integration techniques Earned value methodologies Performance reviews Knowledge management	

Project Management Position

Process	Project Team Member	Associate Project Manager	Project Manager	Project Management Office (PMO) Staff Member	Director, PMO	Chief Project Officer
Quality Planning	Existing project documents Statistics QFD Product requirements Flowcharting Quality checklists Standards and regulations	Statistics Standards and regulations Benefit-cost analysis Designing experiments Cost-of-quality analysis	Planning methodologies Assessing applicable standards Threshold analysis Process improvement planning Quality management planning Baseline analysis and identification Establishing metrics	Statistics QFD Designing experiments Cost of quality templates and categories Quality checklist templates Lessons-learned database	Establishing metrics Precision and accuracy thresholds Customer satisfaction surveys Continuous improvement methodologies Continuous improvement targets Benchmarking Knowledge management	Industry standards Policy development
Quality Assurance	Existing project documents Tracking and monitoring Methods to prepare and analyze change requests	Industry product and service standards Quality control measures	Quality assurance standards and techniques Lessons-learned analysis Process analysis techniques	Industry product and service standards Auditing practices and procedures Interviewing techniques	Quality assurance standards and techniques Continuous process improvement methodologies Quality auditing Process analysis techniques Corrective action recommendations Knowledge management	Policy development and evaluation Quality roles and responsibilities

Project Management Position

Process	Project Team Member	Associate Project Manager	Project Manager	Project Management Office (PMO) Staff Member	Director, PMO	Chief Project Officer
Quality Control	Statistics Data collection techniques Inspections Flowcharting Diagramming techniques Checklists Methods to prepare and analyze change requests	Control limits Statistical sampling Trend analysis Pareto analysis Defect repair review Tracking and monitoring Inspections	Adjusting processes Acceptance decisions Preventive and corrective actions	Control limits Statistical sampling Trend analysis Inspections Checklist development	Organization-specific checklists Procedures for managing, and benefiting from, historical data Adjusting processes	
Human Resource Planning	Existing project documents Organization charts	Responsibility Assignment Matrix Regulatory compliance Organizational Breakdown Structure Resource Breakdown Structure	Resource estimating techniques Workload balancing techniques Organizational policies and procedures Competency analysis Planning methodologies Project interfaces Networking skills	Template development Economic condition analysis Position descriptions Job analysis	Organizational policies and procedures Organizational theory Establishing metrics Project interfaces Competency analysis Recognition and reward criteria Release criteria Networking skills	Organizational theory Human resource management policies Organizational behavior Collective bargaining agreements Standards and regulations

Project Management Position

Process	Project Team Member	Associate Project Manager	Project Manager	Project Management Office (PMO) Staff Member	Director, PMO	Chief Project Officer
			Constraint identification techniques Assumption identification techniques Staffing planning Stakeholder analysis techniques Training needs analysis		Knowledge management	
Staff Acquisition	Existing project documents Project team directory	Documentation management Roles and responsibilities analysis	Negotiation techniques Resource sources and availability Human resource management policies	Template development	Human resource management policies Virtual team policies and procedures Competency analysis Negotiation techniques Mentoring	Policy development

Project Management Position

Process	Project Team Member	Associate Project Manager	Project Manager	Project Management Office (PMO) Staff Member	Director, PMO	Chief Project Officer
Develop Project Team	Self-assessment Professional responsibility	Self-assessment Professional responsibility Team charter	Professional responsibility Facilitation techniques Team-building methods and techniques Motivational techniques Conflict resolution techniques Recognition options Stress management Self-assessment Appreciation of cultural differences Performance assessments Meeting management techniques	Professional responsibility Facilitation techniques Self-assessment Template development	Professional responsibility Self-assessment Stress management Appreciation of cultural differences Policy analysis (reward and recognition) Mentoring Performance assessment approaches Knowledge management	Policy development (reward and recognition) Professional responsibility Aligning people

Project Management Position

Process	Project Team Member	Associate Project Manager	Project Manager	Project Management Office (PMO) Staff Member	Director, PMO	Chief Project Officer
Manage Project Team	Professional responsibility Existing project documents	Professional responsibility Performance reporting Issue log maintenance Team charter Lessons-learned analysis	Professional responsibility Conflict resolution techniques Stress management Matrix management Recognition events Appreciation of cultural differences Preventive and corrective action approaches Meeting managemen: techniques	Professional responsibility Team procedure development Issue log template Lessons-learned database	Professional responsibility Stress management Appreciation of cultural differences Preventive and corrective action approaches Mentoring Knowledge management	
Communications Planning	Requirements analysis methodologies Existing project documents Stakeholder analysis	Technology analysis Information transfer approaches Stakeholder responsibility relationships	Communications management concepts Planning methodologies Constraint identification techniques Assumption identification techniques Stakeholder analysis	Template development Requirements analysis methodologies Technology analysis Glossary development Lessons-learned database	Establishing metrics Planning methodologies Escalation processes Conflict management Knowledge management	Policy development

Project Management Position

Process	Project Team Member	Associate Project Manager	Project Manager	Project Management Office (PMO) Staff Member	Director, PMO	Chief Project Officer
Information Distribution	Report preparation Project management software Methods to prepare and analyze change requests	Retrieval systems Distribution methodologies Documentation management Project reporting Project presentations Stakeholder feedback analysis	Communications management tools and techniques Professional responsibility Communications skills Stakeholder management Reporting techniques Product and service improvements Presentation techniques Lessons-learned meetings Meeting management	Distribution methodologies Conferencing tools Collaborative work management tools Lessons-learned database	Mentoring Business skills Knowledge management	Policy development

Project Management Position

Process	Project Team Member	Associate Project Manager	Project Manager	Project Management Office (PMO) Staff Member	Director, PMO	Chief Project Officer
Performance Reporting	Existing project documents Data collection techniques Methods to prepare and analyze change requests Time reporting system	Performance measurement techniques Reporting (production and requirements) Information-gathering techniques Information-compilation techniques Resource utilization Earned value management techniques Trend analysis Documentation management	Presentation techniques Reporting techniques Performance measurement techniques Meeting management techniques Corrective and preventive actions	Earned value management techniques Forecasting Performance measurement techniques	Review standards and frequency Program evaluation methodologies Mentoring Integration methodologies	
Manage Stakeholders	Existing project documents	Stakeholder analysis Communications methodologies Issue log Lessons-learned analysis	Stakeholder management Meeting management Communications skills Negotiation techniques	Template development Lessons-learned database	Communications skills Negotiation techniques Knowledge management	Organizational politics Corporate culture

Project Management Position

Process	Project Team Member	Associate Project Manager	Project Manager	Project Management Office (PMO) Staff Member	Director, PMO	Chief Project Officer
Risk Management Planning	Existing project documents Project life cycle	Meeting management Project life cycle Project management methodologies Risk Breakdown Structure Probability and impact analysis	Assumption identification techniques Constraint identification techniques Risk management concepts Facilitation techniques Budgeting techniques Planning methodologies Role and responsibility definition Meeting management	Template development Risk categories Facilitation techniques	Establishing metrics Knowledge management Risk management methodology Mentoring	Corporate culture Policy development Decision level authorities Risk tolerance analysis
Risk Identification	Interviewing techniques Existing project documents Document analysis techniques Brainstorming	Existing project documents Information-gathering techniques Root cause analysis Facilitation techniques Diagramming techniques Risk register	Assumptions analysis Constraint identification Establishing warning indications Document analysis techniques	Facilitation techniques Diagramming techniques Template development	Knowledge management	

Project Management Position

Process	Project Team Member	Associate Project Manager	Project Manager	Project Management Office (PMO) Staff Member	Director, PMO	Chief Project Officer
Qualitative Risk Analysis	Existing project documents Risk watch list	Probability/impact analysis Data reliability analysis	Assumptions identification techniques Assumptions testing methodologies Priority ranking approaches Trend analysis Prioritization approaches	Data precision analysis Probability/impact analysis Lessons-learned database	Trend analysis Probability and impact level definition Information quality evaluation Urgency evaluation methodologies	
Quantitative Risk Analysis	Interviewing techniques	Sensitivity analysis Decision tree analysis Expected monetary value analysis Modeling and simulation analysis Probabilistic analysis Interviewing techniques	Trend analysis Probability assessments Prioritization approaches	Simulation (Monte Carlo) Interviewing techniques Decision tree analysis Sensitivity analysis	Trend analysis	

Project Management Position

Process	Project Team Member	Associate Project Manager	Project Manager	Project Management Office (PMO) Staff Member	Director, PMO	Chief Project Officer
Risk Response Planning	Existing project documents Risk watch list	Strategy analysis Trigger development Requirements analysis Risk register	Workload management Planning methodologies Response strategy analysis Strategy selection Budget management Contractual approaches Reserve analysis	Lessons-learned database	Knowledge management Risk strategy development	Policy development
Risk Monitoring and Control	Tracking and monitoring Methods to prepare and analyze change requests Performance reporting	Earned value analysis Tracking and monitoring Variance and trend analysis Data management	Change management techniques Alternative analysis Assumptions analysis Reserve analysis Meeting management Lessons-learned database Performance reviews	Auditing techniques Interviewing techniques Earned value analysis Lessons-learned database	Trend analysis Knowledge management Establishing metrics Review methodologies Integration methodologies	

Project Management Position

Process	Project Team Member	Associate Project Manager	Project Manager	Project Management Office (PMO) Staff Member	Director, PMO	Chief Project Officer
Plan Purchases and Acquisitions	Product analysis	Make-or-buy analysis techniques	Procurement guidelines and regulations	Marketing research and analysis	Establishing metrics	Policy development
	Procurement documents requirements	Risk analysis techniques	Professional responsibility	Contract type assessment	Roles and responsibilities assessments	Organizational culture
	Existing project documents	Contract type information and assessment	Planning methodologies	Template development	Estimating methodologies	Procurement guidelines
		Scheduling methodologies	Assumptions identification techniques		Coordination techniques	
		Contract statement of work	Constraints identification techniques			
			Types of contracts			
			Supply chain management			
			Make-or-buy analysis techniques			
			Coordination techniques			
			Integration methodologies			

Project Management Position

Process	Project Team Member	Associate Project Manager	Project Manager	Project Management Office (PMO) Staff Member	Director, PMO	Chief Project Officer
Plan Contracting	Existing project documents Procurement document requirements	Existing project documents Procurement document requirements Criteria analysis	Types of contracts Criteria analysis Financial analysis Production analysis Estimating approaches	Standard forms	Types of contracts Life-cycle costing techniques	Intellectual property guidelines
Request Seller Responses			Meeting management techniques Procurement documents		Meeting management techniques	Organizational policies
Select Sellers	Evaluation techniques Existing project documents	Evaluation methodologies Lessons learned analysis	Evaluation methodologies Negotiation techniques Contractual agreement requirements Terms and conditions requirements Workload management Legal requirements	Template development Rating system templates Lessons-learned database	Negotiation techniques Estimating approaches Knowledge management Legal requirements	

Project Management Position

Process	Project Team Member	Associate Project Manager	Project Manager	Project Management Office (PMO) Staff Member	Director, PMO	Chief Project Officer
Contract Administration	Tracking and monitoring Existing project documents Methods to prepare and analyze change requests Records management	Payment analysis techniques Performance assessments Change management techniques Inspections Documentation management	Administration of contracts Managing multiple providers Meeting management Auditing methodologies Performance assessments Claims analysis Legal requirements	Template development Information technology Lessons-learned databases	Administration of contracts Legal requirements Knowledge management	
Contract Closure	Closing processes Document review	Closing processes Documentation management Auditing methodologies	Closing procedures Claims analysis Acceptance procedures Legal requirements Lessons-learned analysis	Closing processes Auditing methodologies Lessons-learned databases	Closing processes Legal requirements Knowledge management	

INSTRUMENT 3–K

Team Maturity Checklist

The checklist provides no Level 0 entry and no questions for Level 1, with the hope that project teams will aspire to higher levels of maturity.

LEVEL 1—INITIAL

If the team responds in the affirmative to fewer than 75% of the questions listed for Level 2, then the team (and the organization hosting the team) must take immediate, drastic measures to improve the management and success of the projects conducted by formalized teams.

LEVEL 2—DEVELOPED

The project team is operating as a Level 2 team if the response to at least 75% of the following questions is "Yes."

Level 2: Enterprise Attributes

- Has the organization prepared and issued an organizational policy statement that addresses the use of formalized project teams?
- Have Project Managers received training in team-building activities specific to project management?
- Have project team members received training in the technologies to be used on the project?
- When a team member's work on a project is complete, or when the project is complete, is the reassignment process a smooth one?

Level 2: People Attributes

- Has the team established a system of regular communication among its members, which includes standards for availability and responsiveness?
- Has the team prepared a procedure to identify issues and escalate them to the next level of management if the issues cannot be resolved within the team?

- If the team members cannot resolve conflicts, have they prepared a procedure that describes how to escalate them to the Project Manager or project sponsor?
- Has the team prepared a procedure that prioritizes information so that communication is facilitated and team members do not have a sense of information overload?
- Do team members suggest ideas for improving the effectiveness of their work on the team on a regular basis?

Level 2: Things Attributes

- Are project team members involved in the overall project planning process?
- Has the team prepared a team charter that describes items such as
  - Team purpose?
  - Project objectives?
  - Any special factors?
  - Scope of work?
  - Roles and responsibilities?
  - Project time frame?
  - Project deliverables?
  - Operating procedures?
  Have team members and the Project Manager signed off on this charter?
- Has the team prepared a Responsibility Assignment Matrix? Does each member of the team have a copy of it?
- Has the Project Manager, with input from the team, prepared a Resource Breakdown Structure? Does each member of the team have a copy?
- Has a project organization chart been prepared?
- Has a project team directory been prepared?
- Does each team member participate in determining the time required for his or her assigned work packages and associated activities?
- Does each team member agree to his or her specific commitments in the assigned work packages in support of the overall project?
- Does the team have a process for making new team members quickly feel like they are part of the team? Can they easily learn processes and procedures to follow?
- Has the team prepared a system for regular status and progress reporting and project reviews?
- Can team members access the team's information and data in a Web-based "team room" at any time or in a "war room" if the team is co-located?
- Have team members established performance criteria for both individual and overall team performance on the project?
- Do team members periodically review their progress on the project and make any required changes?
- Do team members collect data throughout the project and make these data available for use within the organization, both on current and future projects?
- Do team members routinely document lessons learned?

LEVEL 3—ENHANCED

If the team answers "Yes" to all the preceding questions, then it is a Level 2 team in terms of maturity. Responses to the questions below determine whether the team can be considered to be at Level 3. If the team answers "No," "Don't Know," or "Does Not Apply" to more than 25% of these questions, then these items represent areas for improvement.

Level 3: Enterprise Attributes

- Have team members received training in the practices to follow when they are assigned to work on a project?
- Has the organization officially recognized the desirability of project teams as part of its overall strategy for continued success?
- Do people in the organization volunteer for assignments as Project Managers and team members?
- Are Project Managers of complex, long-term projects assigned on a full-time basis, without responsibility for managing other projects and without functional responsibilities?
- Is funding available to train project team members on the policies, processes, and procedures to follow in their work on the project?
- Is funding available for project team-building activities?
- Does the organization have a policy that supports open communication in all directions without fear of reprisal?
- Are people available with expertise in managing and working on teams to mentor, coach, and provide consultation, as appropriate?
- Have team members received training in self-management and self-motivation?
- Have team members received training in skills for effective communication and in use of the selected technologies and tools?

Level 3: People Attributes

- Does the team conduct a team orientation session to determine the communication technologies and protocols that will be used on the project?
- Has the team established decision-making processes so it is clear when individual decisions can be made, when coordinated decisions are required, and when a consensus decision among team members is required?
- Have team members established personal goals for the project that complement and support the overall project goals?
- Have team members participated in a self-assessment of their own individual personality styles and motivational approaches to enhance communication and understanding?
- When new members join the team, is it easy for them to feel they are part of the team and its culture?
- Has the team prepared a plan to address any needed training for its members?
- Has the team established a schedule for regular communication among team members?

Level 3: Things Attributes

- Does the organization have a standard template for a team charter, which the team can tailor to meet the unique requirements of the specific project?
- Have team members signed the team charter to indicate their support and commitment to it?
- Does the organization have standard templates specifically designed for areas such as requirements definition, stakeholder identification, stakeholder management, preparation of estimates, preparation of schedules, risk identification and analysis, progress monitoring, and change management?
- Is the team organized so that its members are assigned to the specific tasks in their areas of expertise at the time required in the project life cycle?

- Are common tools in terms of software applications and hardware platforms available?
- Has the team established specific standards for language and nomenclature of project management processes so there is a common understanding of the terms to be used?
- Has the team adopted a 360° performance evaluation system to evaluate team member performance collectively?
- Has each team member prepared an individual development plan?
- Are individual accomplishments and team accomplishments recognized?
- Are individual performance objectives established that complement team performance objectives?
- Does management provide regular feedback on team and individual performance?
- Are metrics of team performance collected and analyzed on a regular basis throughout the project?
- Does the team periodically discuss ways to improve team performance throughout the project, and are the indicated corrective actions taken?
- Does each team member collect data on lessons learned and best practices throughout the project on a systematic basis according to a prescribed procedure?
- Are the organization's standard templates and processes for work on a team periodically reviewed and enhanced based on lessons learned by team members?

LEVEL 4—ADVANCED

If the team answers "Yes" to all the preceding questions, then it is a Level 3 team in terms of maturity. The questions below assess whether the team can be considered a Level 4 team. If the answers to more than 25% of these questions are "No," "Don't Know," or "Does Not Apply," then these responses indicate specific areas for improvement.

Level 4: Enterprise Attributes

- Is it evident to people in the organization that teams are the preferred organizational structure for many projects?
- Is the project team considered a key component of organizational strategy?
- Do the organization's vision and mission officially recognize the use of teams?
- Do Project Managers and team members participate in project selection activities and other long-term organizational planning processes, as appropriate?
- Is there emphasis throughout the organization on recognition for creativity and innovation in project work?
- Is there emphasis on continuous development of teams through overall reviews of organizational policies and processes?

Level 4: People Attributes

- Has a team member been officially designated as a relationship manager to facilitate and encourage team-building activities?
- Do team members collectively determine ways to provide mutual support and modify workload and assignments, as required, so that there is equal participation in project activities in support of the overall project goals and objectives?
- Do team members follow and practice collaborative leadership on a routine basis?

- Do team members work to formally establish mentoring relationships among themselves to model and encourage supportive behavior?
- Are numerous face-to-face meetings considered unnecessary because of the open communication that exists on the team?
- Do team members work to ensure that everyone participates equally in team meetings and discussion forums?
- Do team members openly communicate on ways to enhance both individual and overall team performance?
- Do team members want to sustain the relationships they have built with others on the team after the project is complete?

Level 4: Things Attributes

- Does the Project Manager periodically assess the overall performance of the team from a process perspective to determine areas in which future support is warranted?
- Do team members undertake interdependent tasks?
- Do team members regularly monitor the effectiveness of the procedures that are in use?
- Do team members regularly review processes developed, including task and working relationships, to enhance the quality of their work?

LEVEL 5—LEADER

If the answers to all the previous questions, and the majority of the following questions, are affirmative, then the team has achieved the distinction of being at Level 5.

Level 5: Enterprise Attributes

- Does the organization regularly participate in benchmarking forums and learning communities to identify areas in which teams can be even more successful?
- Is the team recognized as a strategic resource for organizational success?

Level 5: People Attributes

- Do team members collectively acknowledge any similarities and differences and develop a plan in order to take advantage of the different insights and contributions that are possible on the project?
- Does the team discuss and resolve any problems in team dynamics within the project team, avoiding the need for escalation to higher levels of management?
- Is there an emphasis among team members on ensuring the confidentiality of team issues and concerns?
- Is the team atmosphere one in which learning, creativity, innovation, information sharing, and a sense of community are the norm?
- Does the team as an entity and team members as individuals promote professional responsibility in its practices?
- Do team members focus on continuous improvement of methods to develop both personal as well as team competence?
- Does the team seek out opportunities for further work to foster customer collaboration throughout the project?

Level 5: Things Attributes

- Is continuous improvement to the team charter encouraged at all levels in the organization?
- Do team members regularly conduct evaluations of team operating processes and performance in all elements critical to project and team success, from both client and team views?
- Are individual and team accomplishments acknowledged and celebrated throughout the project?
- Are knowledge profiles established and maintained?
- Are team members encouraged to submit suggestions for enhancements or changes to policies and procedures?
- Is feedback regarding the implementation of suggestions provided on a timely basis?

Team Success Factors

Use this instrument to determine the team's sophistication and success in handling the various project management knowledge areas, as they impact the successful delivery of the project's product.

This form helps develop a summary for each knowledge area, as well as for the total project effort. Successive assessments should reflect an increase in at least one of these knowledge areas.

Knowledge Area	1—Strongly Disagree	2—Disagree	3—Neutral	4—Agree	5—Strongly Agree
MANAGEMENT OF THINGS ISSUES					
Scope					
1. Project requirements were defined succinctly and remained fairly constant from the beginning of the project.					
2. The project's concept was translated into business terms.					
3. A market study was conducted prior to project planning.					
4. Technical goals remained stable throughout the project.					
5. The team considered the project technically challenging.					
6. Project assumptions and constraints were identified and documented.					
7. A deliverable-oriented project Work Breakdown Structure (WBS) was developed and used for project planning, execution, and control.					

	1—Strongly Disagree	2—Disagree	3—Neutral	4—Agree	5—Strongly Agree
8. A detailed product description was prepared and used to document the product characteristics.					
9. A project scope statement and Scope Management Plan were prepared and used to make project decisions and confirm understandings among stakeholders concerning project scope.					
10. The customer formally accepted the project scope.					
Scope Summary					
Cost					
1. The project met or exceeded sales expectations.					
2. The project met or exceeded volume expectations.					
3. The project met or exceeded return on investment expectations.					
4. The project came in at or below the cost estimate.					
5. The project was completed within or under the original project budget.					
6. In general, adequate funding was available for the project.					
7. Cost performance was monitored throughout the project.					
8. Cost estimates were prepared after budgetary approval was provided but before project execution.					
9. Causes of variance (in terms of cost performance) were analyzed to determine whether corrective action was warranted.					
10. Budget updates were not required because scope changes were minimal.					
Cost Summary					
Quality					
1. The project met or exceeded technical performance expectations.					
2. Accomplishment of technical goals was considered primary, even if it created compromises in terms of cost or schedule.					

	1—Strongly Disagree	2—Disagree	3—Neutral	4—Agree	5—Strongly Agree
3. Project performance was evaluated regularly to ensure that quality standards were met.					
4. Project results were monitored to identify ways to eliminate any causes of unsatisfactory performance.					
5. Rework was minimal.					
6. The cost of preventing mistakes was much less than the cost required for correcting them.					
7. The product or service satisfied real needs.					
8. The team emphasized planning for quality rather than inspecting to see if standards were met.					
9. Quality audits were conducted to identify lessons learned to improve project performance.					
10. Actions were taken to increase product effectiveness to provide added benefits to customers and other stakeholders.					
Quality Summary					
Schedule					
1. The project was completed in less time than expected according to the original schedule.					
2. Schedule performance was monitored throughout the project.					
3. Causes of variance were analyzed to determine whether corrective action was required.					
4. Re-baselining was not necessary since schedule delays were not severe.					
5. Schedule updates did not necessitate adjustments to other aspects of the project.					
6. The specific activities required to produce the project deliverables were identified.					
7. Discretionary dependencies were minimal so that later scheduling options were not affected adversely.					

	1—Strongly Disagree	2—Disagree	3—Neutral	4—Agree	5—Strongly Agree
8. Duration estimates considered the quality of input data and were refined throughout the project as additional data became available.					
9. Imposed dates were few and did not serve as limiting constraints in terms of the project schedule.					
10. Project and resource calendars were synchronized so that schedule efficiency was achieved.					
Schedule Summary					
Contract					
1. Contract terms and conditions did not hinder project execution.					
2. Statements of work clearly identified objectives and described the scope of work to be performed.					
3. Project team members and individuals in the contracting unit had specified responsibilities that were known to them.					
4. Contract completion and final acceptance criteria were defined and explicit.					
5. Partnering agreements were established with contractors and subcontractors to focus all parties on the project's goals.					
6. Make-or-buy analyses were conducted with an emphasis on balancing least-cost and project-specific considerations.					
7. Clear lines of responsibility were established with contractors and subcontractors.					
8. The procurement process was streamlined so timely decisions were made on project issues.					
9. Decisions concerning the number and scope of contracts were made in terms of impact on the project organization, management systems, and necessary interfaces.					
10. Decisions on the type of contract used did not hamper the project team in managing and monitoring contract performance and in project execution.					
Contract Summary					

	1—Strongly Disagree	2—Disagree	3—Neutral	4—Agree	5—Strongly Agree
Integration					
1. The project provided a platform for future opportunities.					
2. The project met or exceeded executive management expectations.					
3. The project added to the company's overall credibility with its customers.					
4. The project was considered important to the success of the organization.					
5. The project's priority within the organization remained unchanged during the time of project performance.					
6. There was an integrated Project Management Plan.					
7. An integrated change control system was established and used.					
8. The various elements of the project were properly coordinated.					
9. Tradeoffs among competing objectives were made to ensure that stakeholder expectations were met or exceeded.					
10. The work of the project was integrated with other efforts under way in the performing organization.					
Integration Summary					
Reporting					
1. Mechanisms were in place to track the project's progress.					
2. Mechanisms were in place to track the project's costs.					
3. Stage-gate decision points were established for the project.					
4. Project review sessions were routinely conducted, and results were distributed to team members.					
5. Actual progress was regularly compared with plans.					
6. A stakeholder analysis was conducted to determine information needs.					

	1—Strongly Disagree	2—Disagree	3—Neutral	4—Agree	5—Strongly Agree
7. Performance reports were distributed to project stakeholders as planned and as requested.					
8. All team members considered project reporting a routine activity.					
9. Project results were compared over time to see if performance was truly improving.					
10. Performance reports provided information required by stakeholders.					
Reporting Summary					
Risk					
1. Throughout the project, "what-if" analyses were conducted.					
2. The project's overall risk in terms of its objectives was known.					
3. Project risks were identified and analyzed.					
4. Periodic project risk audits were conducted to assess overall risk management effectiveness.					
5. Project risks were an agenda item at project reviews.					
6. Use of workaround plans as a risk response was minimal.					
7. A risk database was established and used to provide lessons learned for continuous improvement.					
8. Project risk owners were appointed for each identified risk; they were responsible for analyzing, tracking, and monitoring assigned risks. Their responsibilities were known throughout the team.					
9. Contingency plans were prepared for identified risks that arose during the project.					
10. Risks to the project were accepted when they were in balance with possible opportunities that were afforded by taking the risk.					
Risk Summary					
MANAGEMENT OF THINGS ISSUES SUMMARY					

	1—Strongly Disagree	2—Disagree	3—Neutral	4—Agree	5—Strongly Agree
MANAGEMENT OF PEOPLE ISSUES					
Team-Building Activities					
1. A dedicated "team room" existed for project activities.					
2. Action items from team meetings were recorded and tracked to completion.					
3. Results and early deliverables were shared within the team.					
4. A project kickoff meeting was held.					
5. Team members generally understood each person's role and expected contributions to the team.					
6. Team members had job descriptions that were available and shared throughout the team.					
7. The team established an orientation process for new team members in terms of the team's operating procedures and communication protocols.					
8. There was a supportive culture within the team.					
9. Team members identified with the project's goals.					
10. The team functioned through collaborative leadership.					
Team-Building Activities Summary					
Skills and Experience					
1. The team had the right composition with the requisite skills represented.					
2. The team had the right experience so that a critical mass of experienced people was available on the team.					
3. Team members felt that assigned tasks were in concert with their specific skills and expertise.					
4. Team members supported continuous improvement in terms of personal as well as overall team skills.					
5. Team members provided ideas, suggestions, and best practices to others to further the expertise of the entire team.					
6. A Resource Breakdown Structure was prepared.					

	1—Strongly Disagree	2—Disagree	3—Neutral	4—Agree	5—Strongly Agree
7. A Responsibility Assignment Matrix was prepared.					
8. A project team directory was prepared.					
9. A seamless process was in place for when team members joined or left the project.					
10. The specific resources and quantities necessary were determined as part of overall project planning.					
Skills and Experience Summary					
Conflict Management					
1. During project planning, possible conflicts were considered and discussed.					
2. Team members acknowledged conflict when it existed.					
3. Team members worked to resolve conflict, as required.					
4. There were no interpersonal or other issues that prevented the team from working together effectively.					
5. Team members generated alternative solutions to overcome problems encountered on the projects.					
6. Team members assessed the advantages and disadvantages of different approaches before selecting an alternative to implement.					
7. There were few conflicts in terms of project performance evaluation and rewards among team members.					
8. Team members knew the process to follow if conflicts had to be escalated outside the team in order to be resolved.					
9. A collaborative, win-win solution was obtained whenever conflicts did arise.					
10. The focus was on issues rather than on positions whenever conflicts occurred.					
Conflict Management Summary					
Team Spirit					
1. The team performed as a team, demonstrating interest and enthusiasm during team activities.					

	1—Strongly Disagree	2—Disagree	3—Neutral	4—Agree	5—Strongly Agree
2. The team had a common sense of purpose, values, and goals.					
3. Team members supported the project's vision and worked together supporting a unified goal.					
4. Team spirit and team norms were considered important throughout the project.					
5. Team members encouraged the exchange of diverse perspectives and different points of view.					
6. Team members acknowledged the contributions made by other team members.					
7. Team members assisted others on the team by sharing knowledge and information.					
8. Team members were trustworthy.					
9. Team members were considerate of others' feelings and were friendly.					
10. Because the team felt that project success was paramount, team members were motivated to participate.					
Team Spirit Summary					
Processes and Procedures					
1. The team followed a similar project management process to the organization's standard methodology for this project.					
2. The team consistently followed its Project Management Plan with measurable milestones.					
3. Team members identified technical problems throughout the project so they could collectively resolve them.					
4. The team spent time together establishing a process for its management and decision making.					
5. The team had the authority and discretion to make the decisions that impacted the project.					
6. The team established a project management information system and used it consistently.					

	1—Strongly Disagree	2—Disagree	3—Neutral	4—Agree	5—Strongly Agree
7. The project team knew the activities that had slack in the schedule so they could best allocate their time and ensure that tasks on the critical path were completed as planned.					
8. The team assessed its processes and procedures on a periodic basis to determine if changes were needed to increase effectiveness.					
9. Individual performance was evaluated in a 360°-type fashion.					
10. Team goals were established as performance incentives and evaluation criteria, and the link between performance and rewards was clear.					
Processes and Procedures Summary					
Leadership					
1. The team had an effective leader.					
2. The leader continually worked to build the team.					
3. The leader provided direction to the team.					
4. The leader was visible to the customer.					
5. The leader had the formal authority necessary to complete the project.					
6. The leader was involved in specifying project goals.					
7. Project goals were clear to everyone on the team.					
8. The project had an executive champion or sponsor who was accessible when needed.					
9. At team meetings, management made encouraging remarks or provided constructive criticism, if needed.					
10. Management provided guidance to the team when requested, allowing autonomy at other times when help was not solicited.					
Leadership Summary					
Communications					
1. Team members defined communications channels at the start of the project.					

	1—Strongly Disagree	2—Disagree	3—Neutral	4—Agree	5—Strongly Agree
2. E-mail protocols were followed throughout the project.					
3. Insightful discussions frequently occurred at team meetings, so meetings were viewed as productive.					
4. Data concerning the project were easily accessible by all team members.					
5. During the project, the team used a common vocabulary in project discussions.					
6. Team members informally communicated with one another throughout the project.					
7. Points of contact were established for various issues on the project so that team members and the client knew whom to contact.					
8. When changes were made affecting the project, they were communicated to all team members.					
9. The project team actively participated in project reviews, and results were shared among all team members.					
10. Team members consistently demonstrated effective listening skills.					
Communications Summary					
Customer					
1. The team had good chemistry with its counterparts in the customer's organization.					
2. The team recognized and understood the customer's specific needs, wants, and requirements.					
3. Because of the team's relationship with the customer, the customer's preferences did not change significantly during the project.					
4. Because of the close interaction between the project team and the customer, the customer did not require extensive training in use of the new product once the project was completed.					

	1—Strongly Disagree	2—Disagree	3—Neutral	4—Agree	5—Strongly Agree
5. Products were submitted to the customer for testing and review prior to actual delivery, and customer reactions to prototypes and concepts were sought and encouraged.					
6. Team members showed curiosity about understanding the customer's needs and requirements.					
7. Customers were considered to be active team members.					
8. The team actively worked to uncover and correct any product problem areas that could cause customer dissatisfaction.					
9. The team worked to understand how the customer viewed the solution and engaged in joint planning to understand customer needs and requirements as well as any project limitations so there were no misunderstandings as to what the project was and was not to perform.					
10. The team worked to integrate points of view from diverse stakeholders, including potential conflicts of interest and assessment of competing alternatives.					
Customer Summary					
Vendor					
1. Vendors were considered active team members.					
2. Vendors submitted products or delivered services on time, within budget, and according to specifications.					
3. A standard process for contract change control was used.					
4. Vendors worked with the project team to set up an issue resolution process, including processes for escalating problems.					
5. There was a clear definition of roles and responsibilities between the project team and vendors.					
6. Project performance commitments of both parties (buyer and vendor) were documented after contract award.					
7. Mutual goals and objectives were prepared and agreed to by the buyer and vendors in order to promote clarity and avoid the need for later scope changes.					

	1—Strongly Disagree	2—Disagree	3—Neutral	4—Agree	5—Strongly Agree
8. Project risks were shared between buyer and vendors.					
9. Joint reviews of project progress were conducted according to agreed-upon evaluation criteria.					
10. Open, honest communication was the norm between the buyer and vendors.					
Vendor Summary					
MANAGEMENT OF PEOPLE ISSUES SUMMARY					

CHAPTER 4

Enterprise Metrics

Organizational metrics measure or infer the attributes of the enterprise as a whole. They deal with both the structure and the environment of projects, particularly as influenced by policies and procedures.

Organizational metrics indicate whether the environment is project-friendly, which, in turn, reflects friendliness toward project people and project things. Traditional organizational metrics also deal with the business objectives of projects and the all-important return on investment, which views the success of projects—and the success of the organization—from the pragmatic vantage point of stockholders. Enterprise metrics also show whether an organization is gaining a competitive advantage by achieving its strategic plan.

To acquire and sustain a competitive advantage, organizations must be informed about all aspects of projects and the organization as a whole. Critical information includes the current state, as well as the future direction, of the enterprise and the industry.

As organizations move toward a management-by-projects concept, the project management practice will continue to mature. Until the early 1990s, only a few organizations implemented metrics systems as an integral part of their business processes. Since then, however, project management has been recognized as a critical and competitive tool of world-class companies that are achieving desired business performance (Thamhain 1996).

Thus, a metric can be established to determine whether the effort associated with improvements in project management practice is increasing, decreasing, or staying about the same. This metric would quantify whether the culture of project management is permeating the organization and whether project management processes are effective. (Instruments 4-A, 4-B, and 4-C)

If a formalized maturity evaluation is conducted, the results will further establish a baseline for improvement in the success rate of projects. In essence, metrics should be regarded as enablers of enterprise project management maturity.

Ideally, metrics systems should be viewed as tools by which the enterprise can evaluate overall performance thoroughly and objectively in order to identify continuous improvement opportunities (Neuendorf 2002). However, traditional business metrics do not take into account the full spectrum of the requirements and perspectives of projects. Very few metrics address the formalized manner for transforming business requirements and management perspectives into project objectives. To that end, some organizations have established tools and procedures to determine what worked well and what did not in recent projects.

Ultimately, projects translate the organization's strategic vision into action toward a positive competitive advantage. Likewise, project failures can thwart achievement of leadership in class. In one case, for example, stock value dropped 1.75% upon the negative news of projects (Ward 2002).

Sometimes, even if the metrics system is aligned with company strategy, reporting of performance information is fragmented and isolated within specialty areas. Unfortunately, this pattern of reporting leads to mixed results on overall performance. For example, the quality department may measure and report quality attributes at a certain time period, the finance department may collect and report the values of cost attributes at a different time period, and operations may report daily on project delivery metrics.

In other cases, the metrics designed to measure the performance of the units within the functional areas might not support the overall intended organizational strategy. Activities that are cross-functional may not be evaluated in an integrated fashion, primarily because links may not be in place between project performance and operational performance. Part of the reason for this disparity could be the absence of a consistent performance monitoring system for the organization's overall project environment.

The cost of failures resulting from the lack of appropriate guidelines far outweighs the efforts required to establish those guidelines. Therefore, if an organization has not fully matured in the project management discipline, then a significant amount of effort, organizationally and within the project, might have to be allocated to developing the unified procedures to manage the project. As the organization matures, the total expenditures for project management infrastructure will decrease while the proportion of proactive functions will be maximized (see Figures 4–1 and 4–2).

Figure 4-1
Project Management Office Effectiveness

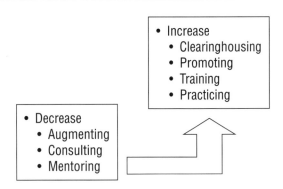

Figure 4-2
Project Management Office Effectiveness and Maturity

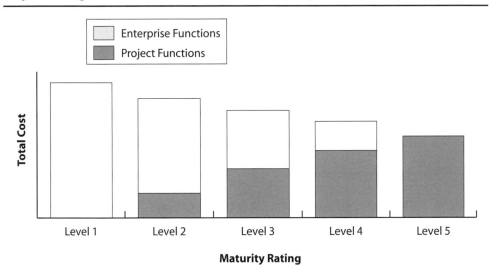

Organizations at higher maturity levels encourage their clients to become actively involved in specifying performance metrics and in setting quality goals. A customized metrics system that is established for the enterprise might be characterized as one that is:

- Driven by business goals

- Consistent across the organization

- Adaptable to specific user needs

- Focused on collecting data as directly as possible

- Compliant with operational data collection policies

- Supported by all affected parties, including the client.

PROJECT MANAGEMENT MATURITY

A formalized assessment of the organization's current project management capabilities yields a detailed description of organizational strengths and weaknesses in project management. Further, the observations made using a metrics system provide the impetus for establishing uniform, enhanced project management practices within the organization.

Continuous improvement procedures provide a quantified baseline for maximizing the benefits from experience on one project into the next. A formalized metrics-based assessment provides the foundation for improvements and guidance for advancement (see Figure 4–3). From this vantage point, portions of the metrics system can be used to determine the current and targeted sophistication of the processes and procedures of the project management activities of the entire organization.

Figure 4-3
Enterprise Project Management Maturity

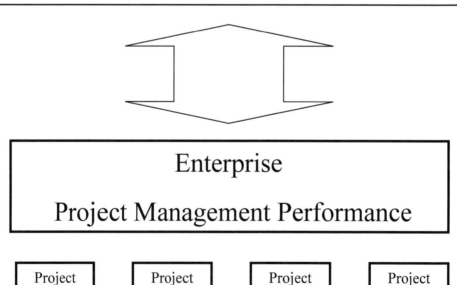

A suite of metrics can be used to determine the existence of realistic, effective project management policies and procedures. A serious distinction should be made between having unused procedures on the shelf and using existing procedures on a regular basis. The metrics associated with a maturity model can be used to signal how often and how regularly project personnel follow established procedures, which, in turn, will shed light on the effectiveness of prevailing project management policies and procedures.

The literature (Pennypacker and Grant 2003) shows that most organizations, even those that consider themselves project-oriented, tend to rank at the lower end of the scale (see Figure 4–4). Thus, there is room for improvement in most organizations. With greater project management maturity, an organization will experience direct and tangible improvements in delivery efficiency, as well as a better market positioning and higher profits. (Instrument 4–D)

Maturity Ranking Scale

An established maturity ranking scale provides plateaus for purposes of continuous improvement of organizational project management capabilities. The indicators of the maturity model highlight the sophistication of key practices in the organization, particularly those in need of improvement. An added advantage of using a standardized scale is that its normal-

Figure 4-4
Maturity Demographics

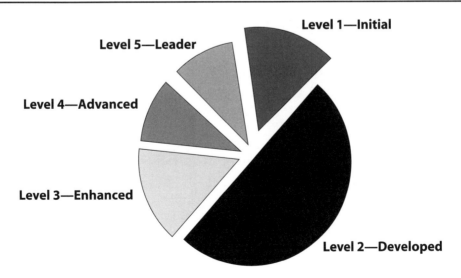

Level 1—Initial
Level 5—Leader
Level 4—Advanced
Level 3—Enhanced
Level 2—Developed

ized capability indicators enable industrywide comparison of project management sophistication. Favorable rankings often provide a point of pride, while less favorable results frequently serve as a source of motivation.

Higher maturity levels signify more effective project procedures, better quality deliverables, lower project costs, and higher project team morale. Organizations at higher levels of maturity have achieved the desired balance among cost-schedule-quality, which ultimately translates into improved profits. In such organizations, there is an objective, quantitative basis for measuring quality and analyzing problems.

With these sophisticated tools, organizations achieve the expected results for cost, schedule, functionality, and quality on most, if not all, projects. Other features of mature organizations include clearly defined roles and responsibilities and the expectation of client satisfaction as the norm.

At higher levels of maturity, metrics evolve with organizational process enhancements until the target process is fully mature and until the process performs at a consistently high level of effectiveness and efficiency. Interestingly, in mature organizations changes to processes are typically small and infrequent. Moreover, in these organizations policies and procedures are not permitted to become counter-productive to the manner in which the project is managed.

Finally, mature organizations establish an environment in which success is expected on every project. This environment can only be created by encouraging project professionals to use innovative practice techniques in support of their responsibilities.

By contrast, lower maturity levels are found in organizations that encourage fixing problems in the field instead of doing it right the first time. In these environments, it is entirely possible that project personnel will repeat the same error in multiple projects or even multiple times in the same project. A low maturity ranking also could be symptomatic of unnecessary or redundant procedures, which, in turn, usually indicate an organization with a history of misdirected improvement efforts.

In immature organizations, there is no rational basis for judging product quality since processes are improvised, quality-directed activities are often curtailed or eliminated, and there is no methodical basis for diagnosing and correcting problems. In these organizations, when a project has an imposed date, functionality and quality are often compromised to meet the schedule. Project managers are like firefighters who react to the current emergency.

Maturity Level Descriptions

Metrics can be grouped by the various maturity levels of the model.

Initial Level

At Level 1, metrics focus on the things aspects of the project, not the people aspects. Some forms are available for some specific processes, but typically there is no guidance on how to use them. Because managers must invent their own practices, processes depend on each project manager's personal orientation, experience, and people skills. At this level, over the life of the project, various team members use miscellaneous project management tools sporadically.

Developed Level

At Level 2, most projects use metrics and follow procedures for some project elements. The organization emphasizes effective project performance, and there is sporadic use of best practices. Relatively meaningful metrics emphasizing things issues are sometimes specified, documented, and repeated.

Evolved Level

At Level 3, best practices, and their accompanying metrics, are integrated into organizational policies, and team members receive training in these best practices. Procedures and metrics reflect indications of widespread consistency. There also is a culture of a common practice, because a general trust exists in the common practice. While it is recognized that the same practice may be conducted differently in different areas to reflect unique circumstances and situations, an organization-wide structure exists for these practices. Finally, project progress data are routinely collected, analyzed, and archived.

Advanced Level

At Level 4, organizational performance is viewed as being interwoven with project performance. Project performance is characterized and analyzed on numerous projects. Corrective actions are prescribed across the organization based on data analysis within specific knowledge areas and pre-established success factors. Performance assessment relies on quantitative data, and project planning data and project performance data are readily available. The organization focuses on continuously improving and aligning personal, workgroup, and organizational capabilities. Equally important, the organization empowers its competent people to conduct continuous improvement in their work processes and to propose organizational changes that support those successful improvements.

Leader Level

At Level 5, the organization regularly evaluates the latest practices with sophisticated metrics, participates in benchmarking forums and learning communities, and uses widespread performance data to forge future improvements. Further, improvement actions are readily identified and quantified. Improvements are either modifications to existing procedures or entirely new procedures. Carefully collected data are used to isolate problems and recommend corrective action in a seamless fashion. Change management is a consistent organizational process.

FOCUS OF ORGANIZATIONAL METRICS

For purposes of identification and elucidation, project management metrics can be grouped into five categories: performance, stability, compliance, capability, and improvement (Florac, Park, and Carleton 1997). Given that these categories are somewhat broad, some overlap exists; consequently, they are not mutually exclusive.

While a relationship exists between maturity levels and these categories, it is not linear, direct, or precise. Metrics in these categories include indices and models that characterize project management maturity from Level 2 through Level 5; Level 1 is not addressed as it signifies a near absence of metrics and/or success.

Figure 4–5 presents a stylized depiction of this relationship. Notably, the metrics categories loosely relate to the three focus areas of things, people, and enterprise. The performance category relates to things, while the compliance and stability categories relate to people. Finally, the capability and improvement categories relate to enterprise issues. The depiction of the relationship allows a better understanding—and a more efficient characterization—of the metrics present at various levels of operational sophistication. (Instrument 4-E)

Performance Metrics

Performance metrics can be regarded as efficiency measures. They focus on the attributes of quality, quantity, cost, and time. These metrics gather

Figure 4-5
Metrics Category and Focus

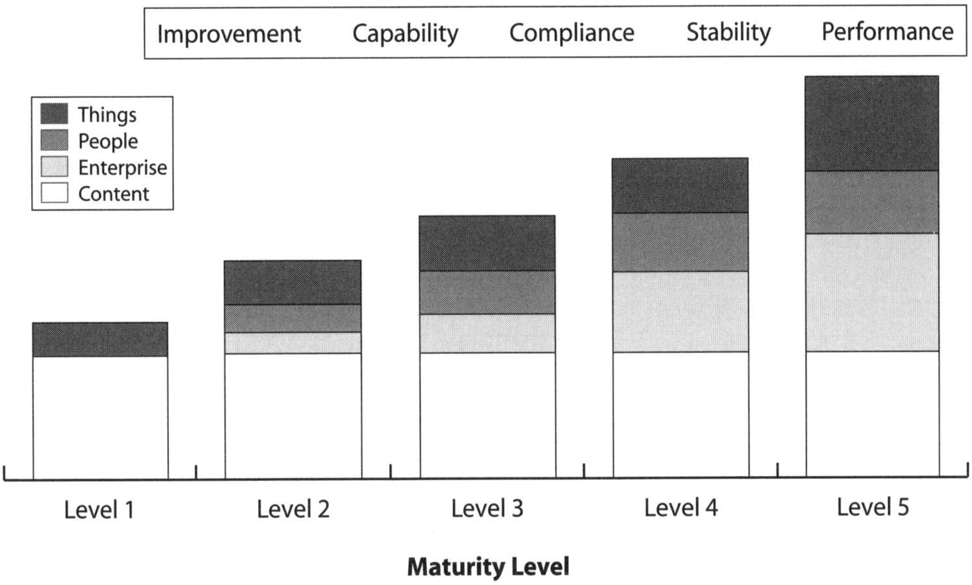

| Improvement | Capability | Compliance | Stability | Performance |

Legend:
- Things
- People
- Enterprise
- Content

Maturity Level: Level 1, Level 2, Level 3, Level 4, Level 5

Maturity Level

specific factual information about project performance, such as the ability to deliver products and services within the client's requirements for quality, timeliness, and cost. Performance metrics also provide the baselines for comparison as the organization works toward establishing repeatable project management practices. If the values of performance metrics vary erratically and unpredictably over time, then the project management process is not in control.

Performance measurement is a process of quantifying the effectiveness and efficiency of purposeful action (Neely et al. 1996). Performance metrics allow the determination of whether internal and external requirements are being met. In addition, Kaplan and Norton (1992) state that performance measurement is a tool for implementing the organization's strategy in order to: translate strategy into concrete objectives, communicate the objectives to the organization's employees, and focus and guide efforts as objectives are reached.

Stability Metrics

Stability metrics focus on the ability to complete projects according to plan consistently. They provide quantitative diagnosis of the shortcomings and respond to the need to improve the processes used for project management.

Stability of project management performance is central to each organization's ability to produce products and deliver services according to plan and to improve processes for even better, more competitive products and services. For example, if people in the organization are using the project management methodology, but products and services still are not meeting the client's requirements, then the methodology must be improved to reduce the variance. (Rad and Levin 2002)

For project management to be stable and predictable, it must be used consistently throughout the organization. To that end, data need to be collected and made available as to how the organization specifies the outcome of projects, the procedures for successful completion, and the resource profile for the project.

Compliance Metrics

Within the context of projects, compliance means that the project management standards of knowledge and practice exist, and that project personnel follow them. Compliance metrics assess project team adherence to the processes and the appropriateness of those processes. They also address the competency and appropriateness of the project team and the sophistication of project management tools. Project management processes that are clearly defined, effectively supported, faithfully executed, continuously reinforced, and diligently maintained are indicative of higher project management maturity and repeatable occasions of project success.

Through an understanding of how well projects are performed throughout the organization, compliance metrics can serve as the basis for improving project management processes. However, project personnel must be aware of, trained in, and given the tools that are needed for the most successful execution of these processes, and the methodology must be executed as defined. For example, even though an organization may have a Project Management Office (PMO), the latest project management software, a suite of approved methodologies, a cadre of project mentors, a project management training program, and a clearly defined career path, there is no guarantee that people in the organization will actually use the available project management concepts, tools, and techniques. (Rad and Levin 2002)

Capability Metrics

Capability metrics allow the project manager to see whether project performance has satisfied client requirements and whether project results meet the intended business needs. The performance variances need to fall within ranges that have been specified for business success. Then, analysis of performance data identifies areas where the process can be improved in order to provide better support for business objectives. Capability metrics should be effective in identifying minute elements of performance so that each project will achieve its intended success factors.

Proven effectiveness of the project management process can easily instill confidence in current and potential clients. However, capability metrics might need improvements to satisfy competitive pressures or to comply with client needs.

Improvement Metrics

Improvement metrics assess how project management can help move the organization to a level of greater profits. They determine if project management is working successfully throughout the organization and if any changes introduced have been effective ones. Improvement metrics typically are considered harder to collect (e.g., the importance of project management tools and techniques on overall profitability of the organization, whether successful implementation of a new product leads to new markets and new facilities). To promote improvements, the project team must understand both the business goals and strategies of the organization and the priorities, risks, and issues associated with them. (Rad and Levin 2002)

PROJECT MANAGEMENT OFFICE

A formalized PMO should be commissioned to perform the functions dealing with development and dissemination of recommended project management guidelines. The PMO should be the cornerstone and focal point of the enterprise's project management initiatives. Thus, the PMO should be directly and actively involved in the development of project management policies and procedures as a means of improving project delivery throughout the organization (see Figure 4–6).

Figure 4-6
Functions of the Project Management Office

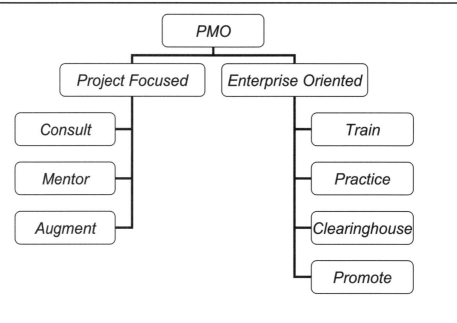

The effectiveness of the PMO should be evaluated by the degree to which the organization's portfolio of projects is successful in terms of responsiveness, cost, and duration. (Instrument 4–F) Therefore, once a PMO is fully installed, it is reasonable to expect that the success rate of projects will increase. Hopefully, metrics will show that more projects are being completed successfully, and with fewer overruns.

At an operational level, PMO effectiveness can be measured by evaluating how the overall cost of maintaining a PMO decreases with time and/or how the organization achieves a higher maturity level. The reduction in effort will come primarily from a significantly reduced project-oriented effort, that is, augmenting, consulting, or mentoring.

The enterprise-oriented efforts, which are usually nonexistent in immature organizations, will reach their peak of effectiveness once the organization has reached a full maturity level. Notably, the cost of maintaining an operational peak for enterprise-oriented functions in a mature organization is far less than maintaining an operational peak for project-oriented functions in an immature one (see Figure 4–7).

Figure 4-7
Project Management Office Costs and Activities

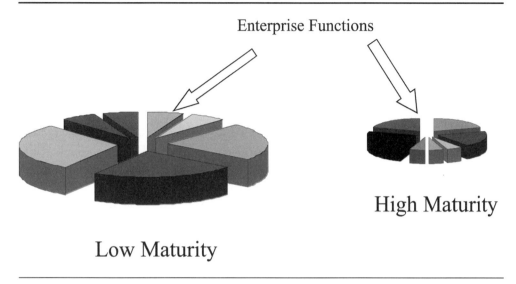

Enterprise Functions

High Maturity

Low Maturity

Looking at the full spectrum of PMO functions, most metrics are interwoven with most of those functions. The full suite of PMO-related metrics includes success of projects, maturity of the organization, competency of personnel, and general employee morale. However, some metrics are PMO-specific in that they determine the effectiveness of the PMO in increasing organizational sophistication in managing projects.

The PMO metrics should also measure the performance of each of its major functions in the project-specific group and in the enterprise-oriented group. These metrics would address the effectiveness of the PMO in carrying out its overall organizational functions, and ultimately, PMO contributions to the profit/loss position of the organization. In that vein, the contributions of all projects to the profit base can be quantified to highlight market deliveries that are earlier than anticipated, hopefully with less cost.

Other indirect metrics for effectiveness of the PMO might include net profit, shareholder value, and increasing asset base. The expectation is for gradual increases in enterprise-oriented functions and significant decreases in project-specific duties, while success rates of projects continue to climb.

It is fair to say that PMO metrics are mostly project metrics; if most of the projects are successful, then, by extension, the PMO is successful. (Instrument 4-G) The usefulness and effectiveness of the PMO could be assessed by indices for the existence, and ease of use, of a standard project management methodology. (Instrument 4-H)

Another index for PMO effectiveness could be a quantification of the timeliness of incorporating changes to the organizational project management methodology as the methodology is being continually improved. The following items could be included in such an assessment:

- Progress against goals for improving project management capabilities

- Enhancements to the project management methodologies and models that are in use

- Benefit of project results to the organization

- Integration of a standard project management information system with the organization's financial, accounting, and human resource systems

- Incorporation of lessons learned into the project management methodology (Instrument 4-I)

- Improvement in project predictability (Instrument 4-J)

- Comparative performance relative to other organizations that are considered to be best in class

- Impact of improvement proposals on the organization's project management competencies

- Effectiveness of the PMO in implementing suggested improvements

- Timeliness in transferring technological innovations into normal practices throughout the organization

- Effort associated with implementing new technological innovations

- Continuous increases in project management competencies

- Impact of a team-based performance incentive system on the organization's profitability.

WORK BREAKDOWN STRUCTURE/RESOURCE BREAKDOWN STRUCTURE TEMPLATES FOR THE ENTERPRISE

Managers have a long history of dividing anticipated project work into smaller and smaller parcels and presenting the resulting schemas graphically. This "breaking down" of the work facilitates a more efficient management of organizational matters in many ways.

Within a project, a Work Breakdown Structure (WBS) provides a framework of common reference for all project elements, for specific tasks within the project, and ultimately for better schedules and better estimates. A WBS facilitates the process of integrating project plans for time, resources, and quality. An effective WBS encourages a systematic planning process, reduces the possibility of omission of key project elements, and simplifies the project by dividing it into manageable units. If the WBS is used as the common skeleton for the schedule, estimate, and quality, it will facilitate communication among the professionals implementing the project.

Each WBS is unique to the project for which it was created; however, if the PMO maintains historical copies of all WBSs on file, they can be used for reference, best practices, and training (see Figure 4–8). Rather than developing a WBS for each project, sometimes it is helpful to develop a general WBS for a family of projects or a common portfolio of projects. Then, when developing the WBS for a new project, only the applicable segments are selected and modified. This practice is appropriate in organizations that conduct projects that are somewhat similar but not identical.

Figure 4-8
Organizational Work Breakdown Structure Modules

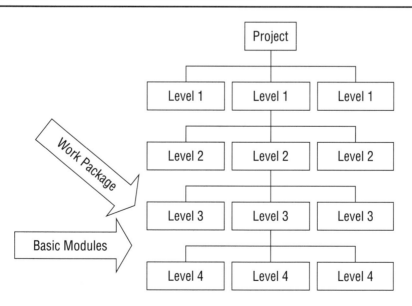

The managerial philosophy of breaking down work also applies to resources. For completeness, in-house resources that are needed for the project should be enumerated in a methodical manner, at the earliest opportunity, through the creation of a Resource Breakdown Structure (RBS). The RBS is a logical, useful classification of the resources necessary to accomplish the project objectives. The RBS facilitates resource assignment and project scheduling in similar projects that use roughly the same mixture of resources.

Rather than developing a new RBS for each project, it is sometimes more efficient to develop an overall RBS for a family of projects. As each new project is planned, only those portions of the common RBS that apply to the project are selected and used. A project RBS is different from all other human resource or budgeting classification methods in that it reflects applicability to project management as compared to cost accounting or personnel evaluations. An RBS is essentially a catalog of all the resources that are, or should be, available to the project.

The practice of formalizing the resource pool falls at the interface between general management and project management. The RBS has its analog in the well-known WBS. In the few organizations that currently use variations of the RBS, project managers can plan the project with greater assurance of the reliability of the resource data (i.e., the project manager can depend on this structure to determine the amount of resources at hand, and their estimated costs, in order to capitalize on organizational memory with respect to project resources).

Sometimes, the project manager might modify and use the RBS that was previously prepared by those charged with accounting for the organization's resources. For best results, the resource content of the RBS should be kept up to date, keeping costs current as well (see Figure 4–9).

Again, major efficiencies will arise from preparing the RBS only once, and then enhancing this single structure so that it becomes accurate, sophisticated, and appropriate. The enterprise RBS is essentially the same for all projects within the same organization, with the distinction that one project may use one portion of the RBS while another project might use a different portion of the RBS. Customization of the RBS simply involves carving out the needed portion for a particular project. Finally, it is exceptionally useful if other administrative units of the organization, such as human resources and accounting, conform to this structure, rather than the other way around.

Figure 4-9
Organizational Resource Breakdown Structure

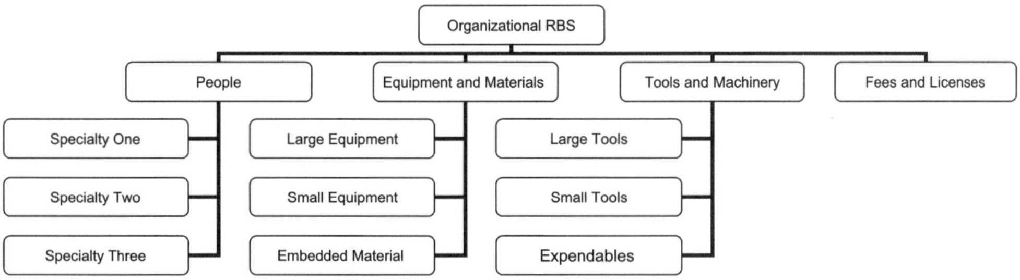

```
                           ┌──────────────────┐
                           │ Organizational RBS│
                           └──────────────────┘
        ┌──────────────┬──────────────────┬──────────────────┬──────────────┐
   ┌─────────┐  ┌──────────────────┐  ┌────────────────┐  ┌────────────────┐
   │ People  │  │Equipment and     │  │Tools and       │  │Fees and Licenses│
   └─────────┘  │Materials         │  │Machinery       │  └────────────────┘
                └──────────────────┘  └────────────────┘
┌──────────────┐  ┌──────────────────┐  ┌────────────────┐
│ Specialty One│  │ Large Equipment  │  │  Large Tools   │
└──────────────┘  └──────────────────┘  └────────────────┘
┌──────────────┐  ┌──────────────────┐  ┌────────────────┐
│ Specialty Two│  │ Small Equipment  │  │  Small Tools   │
└──────────────┘  └──────────────────┘  └────────────────┘
┌──────────────┐  ┌──────────────────┐  ┌────────────────┐
│Specialty Three│ │ Embedded Material│  │  Expendables   │
└──────────────┘  └──────────────────┘  └────────────────┘
```

PROJECT PORTFOLIO MANAGEMENT

Proper execution of projects is pivotal to overall organizational success and financial growth. There have been cases where large sums of money were spent on projects that did not produce a profitable product or service for the project sponsor. Therefore, there must be formalized tools for optimizing investment in the full suite of all projects. This formalized methodology must take into account the diversity of projects so that both the long- and short-term needs of the organization are met.

Even if the portfolio management process is not fully formalized, and therefore not consistently effective, it does help organizations become aware of their project expenditures and the benefits that they get from such expenditures. When there are many projects, and no formal selection process, project selection is subjective, ad hoc, or even political. Under these circumstances, different levels of an organization often subscribe to different and conflicting objectives.

Portfolio management is the process by which an enterprise focuses its limited resources toward new initiatives such as research and development, new products, or operational enhancements. Portfolio management is primarily known for evaluating and prioritizing prospective projects, but its functions also include accelerating, decelerating, or terminating ongoing projects. Naturally, an added level of sophistication would be to regard the portfolio management process as an ongoing activity rather than an evaluation that is conducted at specific points and largely forgotten between those two evaluation points. Formalized portfolio management is most successful in organizations that have reached or surpassed Level 3 of a staged maturity model, in which case all projects are planned and implemented with nearly the same procedures and competence.

The purpose of a portfolio management system is to identify projects that, more than other projects, best serve the business goals of the organization. The organizational entity that conducts portfolio management must monitor the progress of these projects in light of an evolving corporate strategy, individual project performance, and overall enterprise resource demands. Sometimes, the results of the formalized portfolio management system will point to postponing, or even decommissioning, some projects that address only low-priority business objectives.

Accurate, up-to-date data regarding cost, schedule, deliverables, and resources must be available when using the project portfolio management system to evaluate a project midstream in its life cycle. Only then can the portfolio management system provide the organization a current, accurate picture of where project resources are committed. Such knowledge enables quick reaction to external market conditions and redirection of valuable enterprise resources to those projects that achieve the most favorable competitive position.

An ideal portfolio contains a balanced group of projects that is fully aligned with the current organizational strategy. The details of the system must be customized to the circumstances and environment of each organization.

Once the portfolio management system is implemented, the organization might find that there is a significant difference between the desired levels of investment and the actual use of resources on a project-by-project basis. In turn, this knowledge might trigger informed realignment of enterprise resources. The literature shows that if the portfolio management structure is systematic and fully formalized, it benefits the entire organization significantly (Cooper, Scott, and Kleinschmidt 2001).

Ideally, a portfolio management system should be in continuous touch with the strategic direction of the organization, as this direction shapes the selection criteria and continuation conditions for projects. In turn, project attributes influence the portfolio's project mix, as updated estimates of cost and duration are compared to original values. When cost and duration values differ from the preliminary amounts used in project selection, a conscious decision must be made as to whether or not to continue that project.

The project portfolio management system puts the enterprise in an excellent position to compile data on the full complement of enterprise projects in a consistent fashion. More important, the process of project prioritization is repeatable and unbiased if decisions are based on quantified attributes of the project and quantified needs of the organization. The purpose of a formalized portfolio management system is to make explicit what is implicit in many current systems, so that enhancements can be made for the ultimate benefit of the organization.

Portfolio data include details of project objectives, cost, duration, risks, accomplishments, resource demands, and success factors. The availability of these data, together with a rating methodology, makes project selection and continuation decisions a straightforward process. Further, a portfolio management system provides communication tools for letting project personnel throughout the organization know project priority, so that they do not arbitrarily decide which projects are more important.

If the portfolio management function is treated as an ongoing process, then the organization will always have a dynamically prioritized list of projects. The portfolio management function will identify which projects need to be added to the pipeline, which need to be ejected from the pipeline, and which should continue in the pipeline.

Under portfolio management, a project undergoes initial scrutiny in light of current organizational objectives when it is conceived and conceptually planned (see Figure 4–10). After being selected for implementation, it is evaluated periodically in light of prevailing organizational objectives (see Figure 4–11). The midstream evaluation is significant and necessary because, during the intervening period, both the forecasted values of the cost and duration of the project might have changed, as well as the organization's objectives and strategies (see Figure 4–12). This monitoring process determines whether a project should continue to receive resources.

The categorical proportion of projects in the pipeline represents the organization's direction at that point in time, because the categorical mix will change dynamically (see Figure 4–13). When an organization regularly reviews projects in its portfolio, its suite of projects continually aligns with its mission. If an organization's mission is modified annually, so are the pipeline characteristics (see Figure 4–14).

A formalized portfolio management system affords the organization the capability to make conscious choices in selecting projects for implementation. Naturally, if projects were periodically tested for relevance to the organization's strategic direction, the same system would be used to revisit the conscious decision of expenditures of funds for that specific objective.

Figure 4-10
Portfolio Management: Sequence of Activities

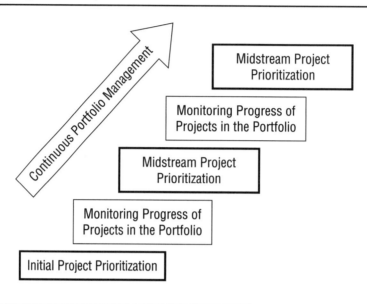

The straightforward, and slightly oversimplified, solution for a portfolio management system would be to proceed with a project of high return, low cost, and low risk, while postponing projects with low return, high cost, and high risk. In some cases, the enterprise might be willing to invest a small portion of project funds in projects that are highly risky and costly but offer substantial payoff if they are successful.

Figure 4-11
Initial Project Selection

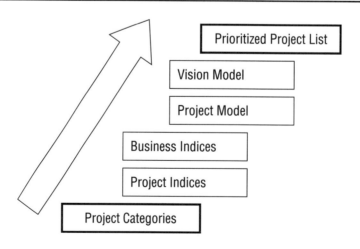

Figure 4-12
Midstream Project Evaluation

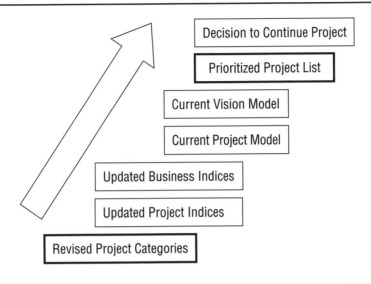

Ultimately, if there is a formal procedure in place, the portfolio management methodology can be enhanced to suit the needs of the organization by delivering a large amount of usable products for a minimal expenditure (see Figure 4–15). It is far more logical and relevant to characterize a project not only by its cost, return, and risk, but also by its impact on competitiveness, resource profile, and other more comprehensive organizational issues.

One of the better known portfolio management models is the stage-gate model proposed by Cooper, Scott, and Kleinschmitt (2001). In it, the project is broken down into several review phases called stages; the milestone between two successive phases is called a gate. The key feature of this process is that the validity of the project is revisited at every milestone, hence

Figure 4-13
Generic Project Categories

- Risk
  - High Risk, High Reward
  - High Risk, Low Reward
  - Low Risk, High Reward
  - Low Risk, Low Reward
- Urgency of Deliverable
  - Operational Necessity
  - Long-Term Payoff

Figure 4-14
Project Categories

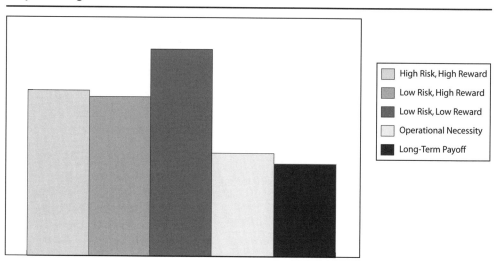

Figure 4-15
Project Categorization

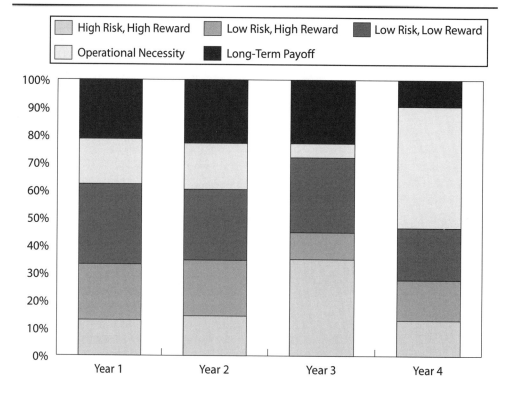

the name stage-gate. Probably the most valuable facet of this approach is the identification of the milestones at which the validity of the project needs to be affirmed for it to go forward.

Naturally, the number and texture of project phases would be different in different industries, maybe even in different projects. Accordingly, the nature of the inter-phase tests conducted at the gates is industry-specific and project-specific.

A detailed, formalized project portfolio management system determines the collection of projects that will have the most positive impact on the entire enterprise. With increasing use of the management-by-projects concept, an ongoing project portfolio management process ensures that the composite group of selected projects is totally supportive of the organization's financial portfolio.

The portfolio management process, in turn, provides motivation to project managers to enhance project information so that better decisions can be made. For example, the system could use sophisticated analogous or parametric models to estimate cost duration from project size. Using a sophisticated, and possibly complex, portfolio management model and having formal procedures to implement the model signal an organization's sophistication. In other words, just having a model does not indicate sophistication, nor does a regular review cycle.

The portfolio management system should not be simply a tracking system, or just a facilitating system, such as any of the abbreviated varieties of the Project Management Office. Rather, it should be an integrated decision-making tool. Then, the portfolio management system can use the progress of the project, combined with its budgeted scope-cost-duration attributes in light of current strategic objectives, to determine whether the project should go forward. In some situations, a project that is reasonably well run might be terminated simply because the deliverable no longer commands a top-priority position among other deliverables.

Portfolio Management Models

Given that the portfolio management system handles very large sums of corporate funds, it needs to be comprehensive. Even though variations of the same model might be used to prioritize different groups of projects, a collective portfolio should contain all the projects undertaken by the organization. In addition, the portfolio evaluation system should be sophisticated enough to recognize duplicate projects so that a decision can be made to combine them. Independent of how data on project attributes are created and ranked, best results can be achieved if the project is ranked using a consistent, formalized process as frequently as possible throughout the life of the project.

The current portfolio management models, which tend to be qualitative and judgment based, are not mathematically complex, although many are regarded as effective and satisfactory by their respective enterprises. The WBS-like model described here represents an initial attempt at introducing formality and directness into the process. Using this structure for the characterization and calculation of an indicator for project scoring, the first level will have elements for project and organizational attributes (see Figure 4–16). The relative weight placed on each element will depend on organizational objectives, strategic goals, and corporate environments.

Figure 4–17 provides a first approximation of these values. The total possible number of points assigned to the project is 500. The reason for this particular distribution is to arrive at a scale of 1 to 5 for the viability of the project, somewhat akin to the staged project management maturity ratings assigned to organizations.

As for distribution of funds among project categories, formality and openness to the process are enhanced if the organization regularly documents the proportion of funding among project types within the organization. Clearly, the balance between the various categories of projects remains a subjective issue. However, the proportion of funding allotted will speak volumes about the strategic orientation of the company. With publicized

---

Figure 4-16
Project Scoring Model

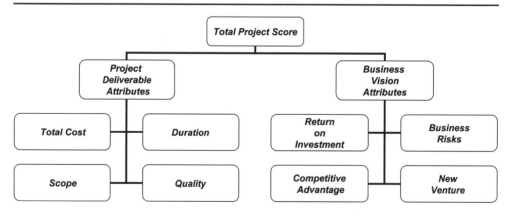

Figure 4-17
Sample Project Scoring Model

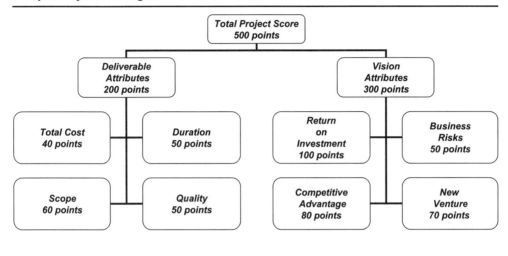

information, it is possible to compare the organization to itself over time, as well as to other companies in the same industry.

Figure 4–18 shows a typical proportioning of funds. Even though the percentages assigned may seem arbitrary, they implicitly signal the importance the organization places on different recipients of project funds.

Having developed this funding allocation scheme, and having developed a project-scoring model, the task of prioritizing projects becomes logical, straightforward, and formalized. Figure 4–19 depicts funding categories with the projects they currently support. This structure illustrates two realities of project funding. First, at any given point, there are limited amounts of funds available for each project category. Second, within each category, funds are dispensed to projects highest on the list until funds are depleted. Accordingly, all projects below the point of funding would either be cancelled or deferred until the next review cycle. Naturally, the funding

Figure 4-18
Sample Project Funding Distribution

• Information Systems	15%
• New Facilities	25%
• Applied Research	30%
• New Products	30%

Figure 4-19
Sample Project Ranking (Grouped by Categories)

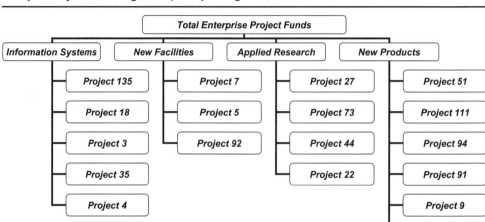

proportion can change at every review point, as can the order in which projects in each category are funded.

When managing a project portfolio through the use of models and indices, one metric must be focused on balancing the different types of projects, such as short term, long term, low risk, high risk, etc. With the use of this categorization index, all similar projects would be funded from a distinct amount of funds that is separate for each category.

The use of a category index infuses a certain amount of formality into the funding process, although sometimes organizations choose to allocate an arbitrary amount of funds to a particular group of projects. For example, a deliberate decision can be made to allocate funds to very high-risk projects that have high returns if they are successful. Further, project diversification is often a primary goal of a portfolio management system. Therefore, the system ensures that each desired category of projects has at least one project in the implementation pool.

Portfolio Management Indices

Each project review model, in any of the funding categories, will comprise several indices that characterize the project to the satisfaction of the organization. The indices of a portfolio management model can be divided into two distinct categories: (1) those that deal with the attributes and goals of the sponsoring organization, and (2) those that deal with the features of the projects that are intended to meet the identified goals of the organization. When such a model is used to evaluate a project, the attractiveness of the project is dependent on how well the project fares in both categories

Indices that characterize the organization include those focusing on business objectives strategy, profitability strategy, market conditions, interest rates, and general economic growth. The organization-related indices can be either quantitative or qualitative (see Figure 4–20).

Figure 4-20
Project Selection: Organization Indices

* Quantitative
  * Benefit-Cost Ratio
  * Payback Period
  * Average Rate of Return
  * Net Present Value
  (These indices are usually financial)

* Qualitative
  * High-Level Mandate
  * Operational Necessity
  * Competitive Necessity
  * Product Line Extension
  * Market Share
  (These indices are usually strategic)

Quantitative indices are usually finance-based, have a definite formula, and are relatively easy to determine (see Figure 4–21). Qualitative indices are usually rooted in strategy, competitiveness, or marketability. Qualitative organizational indices tend to be more experience-based and subjective. Indices that characterize the project deal with the performance, or predicted performance, of individual projects, specifically cost, schedule, and deliverable (see Figure 4–22).

The project-related indices sometimes describe the variances between planned and actual values of the scope-cost-schedule attributes of the project (see Figure 4–23). Such variances are crucial pieces of information during the midstream evaluation of projects when the decision has to be made whether to continue the project or abandon it.

Figure 4-21
Organizational Indices: Financial

* Total expected value of the portfolio
* Discounted cash flow of income from the deliverable
* Internal rate of return
* Net present value of earnings resulting from the project
* Expected commercialization value of the deliverable
* Time to break even
* Total cost as a percentage of the total available funds

Figure 4-22
Organizational Indices: Strategic

- Probability of success of the deliverable
- Validity of the project vision
- Utility of the project deliverable
- Strategic importance
- Attractiveness of the deliverable
- Impact of the deliverable on enterprise
- Benefits of the deliverable to the enterprise
- Duration of project as compared to the urgency of the need for the deliverable

Figure 4-23
Project Selection Project Indices

- Delivery date in relation to needed date
- Resource availability
- Conceptual estimate of cost and duration
- Updated estimate of cost and duration
- Original scope and quality
- Updated scope and quality
- Probability of project success
- Variances in the deliverable
  - Scope
  - Quality
  - Cost
  - Duration

Organizational metrics quantify the attributes of the environment within which projects must operate. In a way, organizational metrics measure the friendliness of the enterprise toward projects. Organizational metrics include, first and foremost, project portfolio models; however, they also include models and indices that quantify an organization's project management maturity and the effectiveness of its PMO.

INSTRUMENT 4–A

Continuous Improvement in Processes

By acting on the processes used to achieve results in project management, the organization's performance will continue to improve. However, the organization's culture must change to support these improved practices.

Use the following checklist to determine the current state of the organization.

	Yes	No
✓ Does the organization have documented project management processes?	_____	_____
✓ If the processes are documented, is there evidence that they are being followed?	_____	_____
✓ Has a Process Improvement Plan been prepared as a subsidiary plan to the overall Project Management Plan?	_____	_____
✓ Is process improvement a topic at project reviews?	_____	_____
✓ Are reward and recognition linked to process improvement?	_____	_____
✓ Is process improvement included as part of individual development plans?	_____	_____
✓ Is training conducted on the organization's standard project management processes?	_____	_____
✓ Are historical data used to improve estimates?	_____	_____
✓ Are inspections and risk data used to detect trends?	_____	_____
✓ Are actual values of cost, resource use, and duration tracked at the same level of precision as estimates?	_____	_____
✓ Does the project management process actually serve the projects?	_____	_____
✓ Is assistance available to help project teams adopt and use the project management processes and tailor them to the requirements of the specific project?	_____	_____

Consider the following questions to help determine which improvement suggestions will have the greatest impact on the organization:

What are the specific business goals and objectives that will be addressed?

How will the improvement project impact ongoing projects and other work?

Are there any external factors to consider?

How much effort will be required to formalize the process improvement and to implement it?

How much time is needed?

Will any funding be needed?

What training will be needed in the use of the new process?

Who will conduct the training?

What other concurrent projects must be considered?

Will any existing systems require change as a result of the process improvement?

How will the implementation be managed?

Will a pilot program be used before full-scale implementation throughout the organization?

Are there any specific barriers that must be overcome in the implementation process?

How will the new process be evaluated to assess its effectiveness?

INSTRUMENT 4–B

Project Management Style

This instrument assesses the project management environment of an organization. The premise is that the behavior of the people in an organization indicates the preferences of upper management.

The statements below constitute the anchors (i.e., numbers 1 and 10, respectively) of a 1 to 10 rating scale. Assess organizational attributes within these extremes, assigning a rating between 1 and 10, inclusive.

Statement	Rating

A. People assigned to my projects seem to prefer to
   1   Work on ongoing operations in the organization
  10 Work on projects	

B. People on my project team
   1   Need direction concerning their assigned tasks
  10 Work independently and collaboratively on their assigned tasks	

C. People on my project teams
   1   Want to avoid responsibility
  10 Enjoy having responsibility for specific tasks	

D. People feel that achievement in work is
   1   Irrelevant
  10 Highly valued by project professionals	

E. Most people on projects are
   1   Not creative
  10 Highly creative	

F. The possibility of additional money is
   1   The only reason for working on projects in our organization
  10 Just one benefit of project work in our organization	

G. In terms of improving the quality of life in the organization, people
   1   Lack the desire to do so
  10 Strive to continually make improvements	

H. Objectives and goals are
   1   Not desired by members of my project team
  10 Viewed as an aid toward the effectiveness of projects	

Statement	Rating

I. The people in this organization are rewarded based on
   1   The financial health of their parent functional division
   10 The success of their assigned projects	

J. In this organization, Project Managers make daily project decisions based on
   1   The priorities of the hosting division
   10 The detailed and predefined project priorities	

INSTRUMENT 4–C

Organizational Project Management Attributes Checklist

This instrument helps quantify the organization's sophistication in managing projects. By repeating the survey on a regular basis, and by comparing those results with the baseline, one can determine the extent to which the organization has matured since the previous assessment.

PROJECT INTEGRATION MANAGEMENT

1. What is your view of project management in this organization?
2. Is a project charter prepared? If yes, who issues it and what are its contents?
3. What is included in your Project Management Plan?
4. Who participated in the development of the Project Management Plan?
5. Who reviews and signs off on the Project Management Plan?
6. Who receives copies of the plan?
7. How is the Project Management Plan used as the project proceeds?
8. How often is the Project Management Plan updated?
9. If the Project Management Plan is updated, who is notified?
10. Who is your project sponsor?
11. Does the organization have a standard project life cycle? If yes, please describe it.
12. Does the organization have a project management methodology? If yes, please describe it. If no, what do you feel should be part of this methodology?
13. Is there a project management information system?
14. Is standard project management software used across the organization on projects?
15. What type of information is collected on project status?
16. What is involved in project reviews?
17. Is earned value used to measure and report project progress?
18. Are lessons learned documented and maintained so they can be used by future projects?
19. Should this organization establish a Project Management Office (PMO)? If yes, what functions should the PMO perform?
20. Is a project closeout plan prepared?

PROJECT SCOPE MANAGEMENT

1. Is a scope statement prepared?
2. Is a Scope Management Plan prepared?
3. Is a Work Breakdown Structure (WBS) prepared? If yes, how often is it updated?

4. Are items in the WBS assigned to particular individuals or organizational units?
5. Is a WBS Dictionary prepared? If yes, how often is it updated?
6. Is a scope baseline prepared?
7. Are inspections conducted?
8. Is a process in place for formal customer signoff on deliverables?
9. How is scope change handled?
10. Is scope creep common?
11. Are Change Control Boards used?
12. Is formal configuration management used?
13. Is configuration management software used?
14. Are lessons learned documented?
15. At the end of the project, is official customer confirmation obtained specifying that all requirements have been met satisfactorily?

PROJECT TIME MANAGEMENT

1. Is an activity list prepared?
2. Is a project schedule prepared? If yes:
    a. Were schedule risks identified?
    b. Were dependencies identified between activities?
    c. Has the critical path been identified? If yes, were activities on the path tracked regularly?
    d. Are there a project calendar and a resource calendar?
    e. Does the schedule include key events and/or major milestones identified by the customer?
3. Is a Schedule Management Plan prepared?
4. How are schedule changes handled?
5. How often is the schedule revised and reissued?
6. Is earned value used to measure and monitor schedule performance?
7. Do formalized procedures exist for compressing the network to achieve a lower duration?
8. Do formalized guidelines exist for expanding the network in response to a shortage in resources?
9. Is there an organizational standard for the software used as the scheduling tool?
10. Are there organizational policies and tools to handle multi-project resource planning and monitoring?

PROJECT COST MANAGEMENT

1. How are project cost estimates prepared?
2. How is the cost estimate correlated to the organization's accounting system?
3. How is the project budget prepared?
4. How are changes to the budget handled?
5. Is a Cost Management Plan prepared?
6. Is a cost baseline used?
7. What comprises the cost control system?
8. How often are budget updates required?
9. Is earned value used to measure and forecast project cost performance?
10. What type of cost tracking software is used?

PROJECT QUALITY MANAGEMENT

1. Are quality audits and inspections conducted on a regular basis?
2. How is the overall quality of projects evaluated?
3. Does the organization have a quality policy?
4. Does the project have a quality policy?
5. Is a Quality Management Plan prepared?
6. Are data collected on the cost of quality?
7. How is customer satisfaction assessed?
8. What types of data on quality performance are collected?
9. Is a Process Improvement Plan prepared?
10. Does the organization participate in benchmarking activities?

PROJECT HUMAN RESOURCE MANAGEMENT

1. How long have you been a Project Manager?
2. What are your responsibilities as a Project Manager?
3. What types of project management training have you received?
4. What types of project management training do you feel would be useful to you in your job as a Project Manager?
5. How were you selected to be a Project Manager?
6. How were your team members selected?
7. Are there any incentives to completing projects on time, within budget, and according to scope? If no, what types of incentives would you recommend?
8. Is a Responsibility Assignment Matrix prepared?
9. Is a Staffing Management Plan prepared?
10. Is a project team directory compiled?
11. Is a Resource Breakdown Structure prepared?
12. What types of team-building activities are conducted?
13. Do you provide input into each team member's performance appraisal?
14. Is it often necessary to escalate conflicts to higher level managers for resolution?
15. Is a team charter prepared?

PROJECT COMMUNICATIONS MANAGEMENT

1. Is a stakeholder analysis conducted?
2. Is a Communications Management Plan prepared?
3. Are issue logs used for tracking stakeholder concerns?
4. Are final project reviews held? If yes, is there a standard process for these reviews?
5. Are lessons learned documented? If yes, how are they used?
6. Are forecasts of project performance prepared?
7. Are time reporting systems established?
8. Are cost reporting systems established?
9. Are regular status review meetings held?
10. Is feedback from stakeholders routinely solicited?

PROJECT RISK MANAGEMENT

1. Is a Risk Management Plan prepared? If yes:
   a. Who was involved in preparing the plan?
   b. Is this organization risk averse, risk neutral, or risk seeking/proactive?

2. How are risks identified on projects?
3. What risk identification methods are used?
4. Do the identified risks map to the WBS?
5. Are risks organized into categories? If yes, what categories are used?
6. What types of risk analyses are performed?
7. In preparing risk responses:
   a. How are risk owners identified?
   b. Is there a standard contingency reserve?
   c. Is there a risk budget?
   d. What metrics are used to measure the effectiveness of the risk response strategy?
8. Are risk reviews held?
9. What types of data are collected to monitor and control risks?
10. How is earned value used in project risk management?
11. How often are workarounds or corrective actions needed because of risks?
12. Are lessons learned documented concerning risk management?
13. Is a risk repository used?
14. Are variance and trend analyses conducted?
15. Are fallback plans prepared?

PROJECT PROCUREMENT MANAGEMENT

1. Is a make-or-buy analysis conducted?
2. Is a Procurement Management Plan prepared?
3. What are your responsibilities in procurement management activities versus those performed by the contracting unit?
4. Are contract administration activities assigned to team members?
5. Is there a contract change control system?
6. What type of information is collected to assess supplier/vendor performance?
7. Is formal notification provided to suppliers when their work has been completed satisfactorily?
8. Does the organization regularly work with the same suppliers on its projects?
9. Does the organization have a list of approved suppliers/vendors?
10. Is a standard checklist followed for contract closeout?

Maturity Assessment
(abbreviated form)

This instrument can provide a preliminary determination of the organization's maturity level. If the responses to more than 75% of the statements corresponding to each level are affirmative, then the organization is likely at that maturity level.

If these statements describe your project management environment, the organization is at Level Zero:

- No procedures
- No policies
- No formal planning
- No formal monitoring
- No formal collection of project history
- Projects consistently miss targets for cost
- Projects consistently miss targets for duration
- Projects consistently miss targets for scope
- Projects consistently miss targets for quality

If these statements describe your project management environment, the organization is at the Initial Level:

- Inconsistent procedures and results
- Sporadic team support
- Inconsistent familiarity with other team members' areas of expertise
- Lack of project management training
- Little interaction among stakeholders
- Lack of confidence in teamwork
- Inappropriate conflict management policies
- Disorganized staffing decisions
- No formalized project purpose
- Limited attention to planning
- Limited use of the Work Breakdown Structure

If these statements describe your project management environment, the organization is at the Developed Level:

- Organizational support for projects
- Formalized project charter

- Clear definition of roles and responsibilities
- Formalized project Scope Management Plan
- Formalized project Scope Statement
- Formalized team formation
- Formalized Project Management Plan
- Formalized project Communications Management Plan
- Well-defined performance criteria
- Some progress monitoring and data clearinghousing

If these statements describe your project management environment, the organization is at the Enhanced Level:

- Projects linked to organizational strategic goals
- Formalized project management methodology used
- Common purpose for project teams
- Standard project templates
- Streamlined project team formation
- A visible, participatory project team culture
- Formalized individual and team performance evaluation
- Formalized project progress monitoring policies
- Routine collection and use of historical data

If these statements describe your project management environment, the organization is at the Advanced Level:

- Organizational recognition of the importance of projects
- Organizational support of project teams
- Project teams involved in policy issues
- Open communication and a visible atmosphere of trust
- Quantitative metrics for project evaluation
- Formalized mentoring program
- Collaborative leadership
- Team effectiveness metrics
- Team and individual rewards and recognition

If these statements describe your project management environment, the organization is at the Leader Level:

- Projects regarded as necessary for organizational transformation and innovation
- Teams considered a strategic resource
- Continuous improvement of templates and processes
- Project teams deployed appropriately
- Risks viewed as opportunities
- Professional responsibility emphasized
- Team environment conducive to professional creativity
- Formalized improvements in project performance
- Experiences provide the foundation for continuous improvement

INSTRUMENT 4–E

Organizational Metrics Categories

EXAMPLES OF PERFORMANCE METRICS

- Completeness of requirements
- Accuracy of the cost estimate
- Extent of rework
- Number of key milestones completed
- Number of key milestones missed
- Use of the Work Breakdown Structure (WBS) to develop project plans
- Use of the team charter to manage conflicts
- Resource utilization versus the plan
- Expected results and actual results in testing
- Effectiveness of risk response strategies in mitigating risks
- Vendor progress in meeting schedule, cost, and performance
- Extent of requests for information outside of regular communications

EXAMPLES OF STABILITY METRICS

- Effectiveness of scope, schedule, and cost-tracking processes
- Value of cost tools and techniques in managing projects
- Value of scheduling tools and techniques in managing projects
- Effectiveness of contract change management system
- Revisions to subsidiary plans of the overall Project Management Plan in
  - Procurement management
  - Cost management
  - Quality management
  - Schedule management
  - Scope management

EXAMPLES OF COMPLIANCE METRICS

- Product conformance with requirements
- Effort required to use the standard project management information system
- Timeliness of project information
- Customer acceptance of product deliverables
- Extent of tools and templates available to the team

- Extent of changes to the cost baseline
- Number of workarounds required
- Number of conflicts requiring escalation outside the project team
- Applicability of the methodology for the range of projects under way by the organization

EXAMPLES OF CAPABILITY METRICS

- Use of knowledge, skills, and competency profiles
- Participation in project management career path
- Participation in mentoring programs
- Extent of improvement of project predictability
- Extent to which each team member is an active participant on the team
- Success of projects undertaken by the team
- Status of the team's best practices in project management
- Use of models for schedule, cost, and performance
- Capability and ease of use of the team's integrated systems

EXAMPLES OF IMPROVEMENT METRICS

- Involvement of individual team members in performance improvement initiatives
- Impact of each improvement proposal in terms of increasing capability in one of the project management competencies
- Effect of technology in terms of performance improvement
- Optimization of the motivations and viewpoints of the client and the project team
- Benchmarking data within the industry and even outside of the industry

INSTRUMENT 4–F

Effectiveness of the Project Management Office

This instrument can help determine the extent to which the organization benefits from its existing Project Management Office (PMO). The effectiveness of the PMO is a function of both its sophistication and the organization it supports.

At the broadest level, the average score for all statements provides a score (between 1 and 5) for the effectiveness of the organization's PMO. The resulting score represents a first approximation of organizational maturity, which also is measured on a scale of 1 to 5 in staged maturity models.

1—Strongly Disagree/Not Available
2—Disagree
3—Neutral/No Opinion
4—Slightly Agree
5—Definitely Agree

Statement	1	2	3	4	5
1. PMO staff members have the expertise to fill gaps in terms of needed team resources on the project.					
2. PMO staff members have the expertise to serve as mentors for new team members or new project managers.					
3. PMO staff members can serve as consultants and provide occasional validation and assistance.					
4. PMO staff members set objectives for project management improvements in the organization.					
5. PMO staff members collect and maintain project archives for use in assessing lessons learned.					
6. PMO staff members maintain a standard data repository that is user-friendly and cross-referenced.					
7. PMO staff members set guidelines for organizationwide competencies in project management.					
8. PMO staff members set standards for project management in the organization.					

Statement	1	2	3	4	5
9. PMO staff members audit projects periodically to ensure that a common methodology is followed in project management, focusing on using these results to improve standard methods.					
10. PMO staff members operate and maintain a standard set of tools for project management in the following areas:					
a. Project planning					
b. Work Breakdown Structure development					
c. Configuration management					
d. Schedule development and tracking and monitoring					
e. Requirements management					
f. Resource utilization					
g. Cost estimating					
h. Cost budgeting and cost tracking					
i. Risk management					
j. Earned value management					
k. Performance measurement					
l. Status reporting					
m. Project reviews					
n. Quality management					
o. Project closeout					
11. PMO staff members support project team members in the use of standard project management software.					
12. PMO staff members provide assistance in the following areas at the beginning of the project:					
a. Designing the project management information system					
b. Defining the control systems					
c. Setting up the project workbook					
d. Preparing the project charter					
e. Preparing the preliminary and final scope statement					
f. Facilitating the project kickoff meetings					
g. Conducting a life-cycle cost analysis					

Statement	1	2	3	4	5
13. PMO staff members provide support in project risk management in areas including:					
a. Assisting the team in preparing a Risk Management Plan					
b. Identifying, categorizing, and analyzing potential risks based on risks in previous projects					
c. Conducting interviews with people on the project to obtain their perspectives on risks					
d. Facilitating a Delphi analysis for risk identification					
e. Assisting the team in conducting risk probability and impact analysis					
f. Assisting the team in using project simulation techniques for risk analysis					
g. Assisting the team in preparing risk response plans					
h. Tracking and monitoring potential risks					
i. Conducting risk audits					
j. Conducting risk reviews					
k. Establishing a repository of risk management data for use throughout the organization					
14. PMO staff members provide assistance to the project team in establishing and maintaining the project's war room (on a co-located project) or electronic team room (on a virtual project).					
15. PMO staff members establish and manage an integrated change control process.					
16. PMO staff members provide assistance in project control, including items such as schedule maintenance, budget tracking, resource tracking, and documentation management.					
17. PMO staff members publish a newsletter to project stakeholders.					
18. PMO staff members facilitate project reviews to assess the status and report the progress of the project.					
19. PMO staff members identify trends and commonalities in issues across projects.					
20. PMO staff members manage the project management training for the organization.					

Statement	1	2	3	4	5
21. PMO staff members maintain a portfolio of customized estimating models, including:					
a. Ratio models					
b. Analogous models					
c. Power series models					
22. PMO staff members maintain organization-specific data on:					
a. Range estimates					
b. Learning curves					
c. Experience curves					
d. External and internal risks					
23. PMO staff members perform estimating to determine:					
a. The financial size of the project					
b. The effort required in terms of resources					
c. The schedule					
d. The cash flow to complete the project					
24. PMO staff members develop a set of common criteria for use in project selection.					
25. PMO staff members establish an integrated management policy for multi-project resource use through a common project information system for all projects.					
26. PMO staff members establish a project team–based reward and recognition system.					
27. PMO staff members maintain an awareness of the latest developments in project management and represent the organization at project management forums and meetings.					
28. PMO staff members formally measure and track customer satisfaction on projects.					
29. PMO staff members routinely update project selection models in line with the latest organizational strategic direction.					
30. PMO staff members routinely update the models by which the success of projects is measured.					

Post-Delivery Project Audit Checklist

Use this instrument to assess the level of sophistication of project management activities. Depending on when the audit is performed, some questions might not be applicable. Record the percentage of questions in each category that were answered in the positive or the affirmative. Comparing scores for each category with the organizational average provides an indication of improvement over the life of the project.

INITIATING ACTIVITIES

✓ Determine whether the project charter was helpful in resolving any conflicts concerning the Project Manager's authority and responsibilities.
✓ Determine the effectiveness of the statement of work in developing the charter.
✓ Assess whether the organizational, environmental, external assumptions, and constraints identified in the charter were applicable.
✓ Determine whether the Project Manager had the needed authority, as expressed in the charter, given the nature of the project.
✓ Assess the various environmental factors and systems that surrounded and influenced the project as the charter was developed.
✓ Determine whether the project was linked to the organization's strategic plan.
✓ Assess the various organizational processes and procedures that were used in developing the project charter.
✓ Determine the usefulness of the project management methodology in developing the charter and the preliminary scope statement.
✓ Assess the project's initial estimate of its financial contribution.
✓ Determine the usefulness of the preliminary scope statement in defining the project; its characteristics, boundaries, associated products, and services; and methods of acceptance and scope control.

PLANNING ACTIVITIES

✓ Determine whether a scope statement was prepared.
✓ Determine whether the Project Management Plan covers the entire project life cycle and follows the project management methodology.
✓ Assess the usefulness of the project management methodology throughout the project planning process.
✓ Determine whether a performance measurement baseline was prepared.

✓ Assess the level of involvement of the project team, clients, and other stakeholders in developing the Project Management Plan.

✓ Determine whether external factors, constraints, or assumptions were identified correctly.

✓ Assess the stability of the requirements and whether they were defined sufficiently at the beginning of the project.

✓ Determine the extent of use of the Work Breakdown Structure (WBS) as a framework for planning the project.

✓ Assess the usefulness of the project's WBS to serve as a template for future projects.

✓ Determine whether a scope or technical baseline was established.

✓ Assess the usefulness of the Scope Management Plan.

✓ Determine whether an activity list was prepared and whether it can serve as a template for future projects.

✓ Determine whether the project team established too many discretionary dependencies that limited schedule options.

✓ Assess the interface between risk management and schedule preparation.

✓ Determine whether a schedule was prepared.

✓ Determine whether a schedule baseline was prepared.

✓ Assess the usefulness of the Schedule Management Plan.

✓ Assess the accuracy of resources in terms of actual resource requirements.

✓ Assess the accuracy of the cost estimate that was prepared.

✓ Determine whether a cost baseline was established.

✓ Assess the usefulness of the Cost Management Plan.

✓ Determine whether changes were needed to the organization's quality policy to meet the needs of the project.

✓ Determine whether a quality baseline was established.

✓ Determine whether a Process Improvement Plan was prepared.

✓ Determine whether a Quality Management Plan was prepared.

✓ Assess the usefulness of quality system.

✓ Determine whether the cost of quality was considered.

✓ Determine whether a Resource Assignment Matrix was prepared.

✓ Assess the usefulness of the Resource Breakdown Structure.

✓ Assess the usefulness of the Staffing Management Plan.

✓ Determine whether qualified staff members were available for the project at the required times.

✓ Assess whether any stakeholders exerted negative influence over the project.

✓ Assess the usefulness of the Stakeholder Management Plan.

✓ Assess the usefulness of the Communications Management Plan.

✓ Assess the level of commitment to project risk management.

✓ Assess the usefulness of the Risk Management Plan.

✓ Determine whether the risk classification system that was used can serve as a template for other projects.

✓ Evaluate the usefulness of risk identification approaches for future projects.

✓ Determine whether the organization's risk repository was used.

✓ Determine whether a make-or-buy analysis was conducted.

✓ Assess the usefulness of the Procurement Management Plan.

✓ Determine whether the project team actively worked with the procurement department to provide input before any solicitations were issued and during the source selection process.

EXECUTING ACTIVITIES

✓ Determine whether client expectations were solicited, included, met, or exceeded.
✓ Determine whether the client was informed of progress, changes, and delays.
✓ Evaluate recommendations from audits in terms of quality and project improvements.
✓ Determine the usefulness of client satisfaction surveys to identify needed process improvements.
✓ Determine if the project team was a high-performing team that could work well together on a future project.
✓ Assess whether the Project Manager had input into team member performance evaluations.
✓ Determine whether a team-based performance evaluation system was used.
✓ Determine the usefulness of any training conducted in terms of improvements of both individual and team skills.
✓ Determine potential improvements in team development.
✓ Determine the usefulness of the team charter.
✓ Evaluate the usefulness of the project's information distribution system.
✓ Determine whether qualified lists of approved vendors were used for project purchases.
✓ Determine how changes were authorized to the project's scope.

MONITORING AND CONTROLLING ACTIVITIES

✓ Assess the causes of major scope, time, and cost deviations.
✓ Determine whether earned value management was used.
✓ Assess whether formal client acceptance of deliverables was obtained, based on defined acceptance criteria.
✓ Assess the extent of scope changes during the project.
✓ Determine the extent of any schedule delays.
✓ Assess schedule updates that resulted from scope change.
✓ Determine the extent of any schedule corrective actions.
✓ Assess budget updates that resulted from scope changes.
✓ Evaluate the severity of cost variances.
✓ Determine what was required to bring expected performance in line with the Project Management Plan.
✓ Assess the reasons key corrective actions were selected.
✓ Assess client feedback throughout the project in terms of meeting quality standards.
✓ Ascertain the usefulness of the project review process.
✓ Evaluate the use of earned value analysis and trend analysis to predict future project status and progress.
✓ Evaluate the usefulness of the reports that were prepared to facilitate forecasting.
✓ Ascertain the usefulness of a project risk audit to examine the project risk management process.
✓ Determine whether the risk ranking was used to make decisions concerning the project at project review meetings and to assess trends in terms of the effect of risk on project objectives.
✓ Assess the usefulness of contingency plans in reducing the cost of actions, if risks occurred.
✓ Assess the number of workarounds that occurred, as a measure of the effectiveness of risk responses.
✓ Assess the effectiveness of the contract change control system.

CLOSING ACTIVITIES

✓ Assess whether the client provided formal acceptance of project deliverables.
✓ Assess whether suppliers received formal notification when contracts were completed.
✓ Determine whether records management policies were followed.
✓ Assess whether the employee skills database was updated.
✓ Determine whether lessons learned were collected throughout the project and made part of the organization's knowledge repository.
✓ Assess whether a closeout checklist was used.

INSTRUMENT 4–H

Assessing the Usefulness of Templates/Processes

The overall level of utility of using templates and processes is the average of the scores for the questions below. This index constitutes a baseline upon which to improve the success of future projects based on team feedback regarding performance on the current project.

1—Not Applicable/Not Done
2—Rarely
3—Sometimes
4—Often
5—Always

Question	1	2	3	4	5
1. Was a standard process followed for project selection?					
2. Was a standard methodology used to develop a proposal for the project?					
3. Was a standard template followed to develop the scope statement?					
4. Was a standard template followed to develop the Project Management Plan?					
5. Was a standard template used to develop the following subsidiary management plans:					
a. Scope Management Plan?					
b. Schedule Management Plan?					
c. Cost Management Plan?					
d. Quality Management Plan?					
e. Process Improvement Plan?					
f. Staffing Management Plan?					
g. Communications Management Plan?					
h. Risk Management Plan?					
i. Procurement Management Plan?					
j. Contract Management Plan?					

Question	1	2	3	4	5
6. Was a standard template used to develop the Work Breakdown Structure for the project?					
7. Was a standard template used to prepare the project charter?					
8. Was a standard template used to develop an activity list?					
9. Was a standard template used to assign project roles and responsibilities at the work package level?					
10. Were standard checklists used as a basis for risk identification?					
11. Was a standard system used to track action items and issues until their resolution on the project? Did the system include:					
a. How to document an issue?					
b. How to evaluate an issue?					
c. How to state the action items necessary to resolve the issue?					
d. How to communicate to others regarding the issue?					
e. How to formally close the issue?					
12. Was a standard process followed to collect data for use in project monitoring and control?					
13. Was a standard format used to prepare project status reports?					
14. Was the organization's standard project management methodology followed?					
15. Was a standard approach used to conduct project reviews during the course of the project?					
16. Was a standard format used to assign resources to projects?					
17. Was a standard classification system used for project changes that defines (1) which changes need approval and from whom, and (2) which changes the Project Manager can implement immediately?					
18. Was a standard process followed for scope change control? Did this process include standard forms to:					
a. Request a change?					
b. Analyze the impact of the change?					
c. Communicate the change to project participants?					
d. Authorize implementation of the change once it is approved?					
19. Was a standard process followed to set up and operate a Change Control Board?					

Question	1	2	3	4	5
20. Was a standard process followed for schedule control?					
21. Was a standard process followed for cost control?					
22. Was a standard process followed for records management?					
23. Was a standard format followed to report staff time charged to the project?					
24. Was a standard process followed for project reviews? Did this process include:					
a. Meeting agenda?					
b. Detailed description of roles?					
c. Clear definition of responsibilities?					
d. Issue identification?					
e. Action item tracking?					
f. Preparation and distribution of minutes?					
25. Was a standard process followed to obtain customer signoff on each deliverable?					
26. Was a standard process followed to obtain the customer's final acceptance on the project?					
27. Was a standard checklist of items completed during project closeout?					
28. Was a consistent procedure followed in clearinghousing project data for the benefit of future projects?					
29. Was a standard template used to disseminate this project's lessons learned to other project teams?					
30. Was a standard process used to evaluate, identify, and reward the project's best performers?					

Documenting Lessons Learned

This instrument helps determine the extent to which the organization encourages project team members to collect and use lessons learned. Ultimately, this instrument can be used to develop a baseline for continuous improvements in the project management environment.

At the broadest level, the average score for all questions provides a score (between 1 and 5) for utilizing organizational experience. This is an initial approximation of organizational maturity, which also is measured on a scale of 1 to 5. Summarizing the scores for all the questions in each knowledge area (scope, cost, quality, etc.) provides the next level of detail. Summarizing the scores for each of the three categories of each of the knowledge areas (i.e., process, compliance, and efficiency) provides the final level of sophistication in analyzing these data.

1—Strongly Disagree
2—Disagree
3—Neutral
4—Agree
5—Strongly Agree

	1	2	3	4	5
MANAGEMENT OF THINGS ISSUES					
Scope					
Process					
1. We used the project charter as the governing document in assigning organizational resources to the project.					
2. We documented all project constraints and assumptions as part of the scope statement.					
3. We developed a Work Breakdown Structure (WBS) so that the work package level was easily assignable to a single individual or organizational unit to complete.					
4. We received formal documentation that the client or sponsor accepted the product and each major deliverable.					
5. We documented lessons learned from scope changes.					

	1	2	3	4	5
Compliance					
1. We followed the preliminary scope statement in finalizing the project scope statement.					
2. We used standard methods to translate project objectives into tangible deliverables and requirements.					
3. We used a standard format for the Scope Management Plan (SMP).					
4. We used a standard template to develop the WBS.					
5. We used a standard system for scope control.					
Efficiency					
1. Our SMP was sufficiently detailed in terms of the scope changes experienced and in classifying these changes for future use.					
2. In preparing our WBS, it was necessary to modify the project scope statement.					
3. Throughout the project, we conducted sufficient inspections, reviews, or audits in order to ensure that project results conformed to requirements.					
4. We needed to adjust cost, time, quality, and other project objectives because of scope changes.					
5. Because of the nature of scope changes, it was necessary to adjust the technical baseline to reflect the approved changes.					
Quality					
Process					
1. We used the organization's quality policy for the project's quality policy.					
2. We documented our approach to quality assurance, quality control, and quality improvements in the project Quality Management Plan (QMP).					
3. We identified quality improvement initiatives that led to additional benefits for stakeholders through the use of quality audits.					
4. We performed quality assurance throughout the project.					
5. We performed quality control throughout the project.					

	1	2	3	4	5
Compliance					
1. We used a standard format for the QMP.					
2. We used standard checklists as part of quality control initiatives.					
3. We used a quality audit as a tool to identify lessons learned on the project.					
4. We prepared change requests and followed scope change control procedures when implementing quality improvements or adjusting processes.					
5. We ensured that completed checklists became part of the project's records.					
Efficiency					
1. We required minimal investments in product quality improvements in terms of defect prevention and appraisal, so no additional support outside the project's allocated budget was required.					
2. We met quality requirements, as there was little need for rework during the project.					
3. We did not identify requirements for further activities in other areas after completing quality planning initiatives.					
4. Through our quality control efforts, the majority of the items on the project were accepted.					
5. The total cost of our project quality efforts was less than anticipated as part of the budget.					
Contract					
Process					
1. We performed a make-or-buy analysis as the basis for contract requirements on the project.					
2. We documented the types of contracts to be used on the project in the Procurement Management Plan.					
3. We set up a system to coordinate all procurement activities with scheduling, cost, and performance reporting.					
4. The project team worked with members of the contracts/procurement department to determine specific roles and responsibilities.					
5. We provided each contractor a formal written notice when its contract was completed.					

	1	2	3	4	5
Compliance					
1. We used a standard format for the Procurement Management Plan.					
2. We selected the types of contracts to use based on documented procedures.					
3. We used standard forms for the majority of contract planning initiatives.					
4. We ensured that required contract reviews were completed, and approvals were received, before awarding a contract.					
5. We ensured that all work was completed correctly and satisfactorily, and documentation was complete, before closing a contract.					
Efficiency					
1. We had no difficulty coordinating the efforts of multiple providers on the project because of the Procurement Management Plan.					
2. We structured procurement documents so that prospective sellers had few, if any, questions but were still able to propose better ways to satisfy requirements.					
3. We employed final contract language that showed all agreements reached during the negotiations process.					
4. We used evaluation criteria and weighting/screening systems that enabled timely decisions in terms of ultimate contract awards.					
5. We experienced minimal change requests involving either the terms of the contract or the requirements, and no contested changes occurred.					
Cost					
Process					
1. We coordinated activity resource estimating with cost estimating.					
2. We considered the effect of both the cost of the resources needed to complete the project activities and the cost of using the project's product.					
3. We estimated and budgeted controllable and uncontrollable costs separately.					
4. We assigned each cost estimate to the correct accounting category in the chart of accounts.					

	1	2	3	4	5
5. We estimated costs for all resources to be charged to the project and provided documentation as to the basis of the estimate.					
Compliance					
1. We used a standard format to develop our Cost Management Plan (CMP).					
2. We established a cost baseline to measure and monitor project cost performance.					
3. We used a standard system for cost control.					
4. We used standard tools and techniques to develop cost estimates for all project resources.					
5. We used standard tools and techniques to track planned costs versus actual costs and to forecast the effects of cost changes.					
Efficiency					
1. We used life-cycle costing, along with value engineering techniques, to reduce cost and time estimates and to improve quality and performance on the project.					
2. We did not need to adjust any other aspects of the project plan based on revisions to cost estimates.					
3. We did not need to update our budget based on revised cost estimates.					
4. We formulated effective responses to cost variances that did not cause quality or schedule problems or produce an unacceptable level of risk later in the project.					
5. We prepared a cost estimate at completion early in the project, which turned out to be an accurate forecast of total project costs.					
Schedule					
Process					
1. We prepared an activity list that was organized as an extension to the WBS.					
2. We did not need to establish discretionary dependencies early in the project.					
3. We considered both elapsed time and calendar time in developing estimates of activity duration.					
4. We considered resource capabilities as well as identified risks in preparing estimates of activity duration.					

	1	2	3	4	5
5. We used both project and resource calendars in developing the project schedule.					
Compliance					
1. We used a standard format to develop our Schedule Management Plan.					
2. We used standard project management software to develop the project schedule and track and monitor schedule variances.					
3. We used a standard system for schedule control.					
4. We established a schedule baseline to measure and monitor schedule performance.					
5. We used a standard template to expedite the preparation of the activity list and project network diagram.					
Efficiency					
1. We established a coding structure for each activity to allow sorting of different attributes assigned to each activity in developing the project schedule.					
2. Because of the completeness of the WBS, refinements were not required when developing the activity list.					
3. We were able to shorten the project schedule without having to change project scope.					
4. Our schedule updates did not require changes to other aspects of the Project Management Plan.					
5. We used new schedule targets as the normal method of schedule revisions.					
Integration					
Process					
1. We used the Project Management Plan to guide project execution and to provide a baseline for progress measurement and control.					
2. We followed change control system procedures before changing any project documents.					
3. We used performance measurement techniques to assess whether variances from the Project Management Plan required corrective action.					
4. We held regularly scheduled status meetings, either face-to-face or virtual, to exchange project information.					

	1	2	3	4	5
5. We consulted with our stakeholders in the development of the Project Management Plan.					
Compliance					
1. We followed a standard project planning methodology as we developed the Project Management Plan.					
2. We used the organization's established project management information system for the project.					
3. We used standard formats to prepare the project charter and preliminary scope statements.					
4. We used a standard work authorization system before work began on a specific activity or work package.					
5. We used a standard integrated change control system.					
Efficiency					
1. Our performance measurement baseline did not change during the project.					
2. Our assumptions concerning the project did not require change as the project ensued.					
3. We did not require extensive corrective action to bring expected future performance in line with the Project Management Plan.					
4. Our change control system enabled automatic approval of defined categories of changes.					
5. We did not need to reissue the Project Management Plan to stakeholders.					
Reporting					
Process					
1. We used the stakeholder analysis to determine specific reporting requirements.					
2. We distributed project information as detailed in the Communications Management Plan.					
3. We received official confirmation from the customer that all project requirements were met before closing the project.					
4. We documented project results to formalize project acceptance.					
5. We used other techniques, such as variance analysis, trend analysis, and earned value, in conjunction with performance reviews to assess performance.					

	1	2	3	4	5
Compliance					
1. We used a standard format to prepare the Communications Management Plan.					
2. We used a standard format for project status and progress reports.					
3. We followed a standard format for project reviews.					
4. We used established baselines to assess performance for purposes of reporting.					
5. We followed a standard approach to archive project records.					
Efficiency					
1. We set up various methods to facilitate information sharing among our team during the project.					
2. We did not need to prepare additional reports other than those anticipated in the Communications Management Plan.					
3. We did not need to request changes to various aspects of the project based on analysis of project status and progress reports.					
4. We were able to use the schedule performance index (SPI) and the cost performance index (CPI) to accurately forecast cost and schedule performance by the time the project was 15% to 20% complete.					
5. We documented results at the end of each phase of the project to ensure that important and useful information was not forgotten.					
Risk					
Process					
1. We updated checklists used for risk identification throughout the process.					
2. We involved our stakeholders in the development of our Risk Management Plan.					
3. We established roles and responsibilities for each action in the Risk Management Plan.					
4. We viewed risk identification as an ongoing, iterative activity during the project.					
5. We tested assumptions made while analyzing potential risks to the project.					

	1	2	3	4	5
Compliance					
1. We followed a standard process to develop our Risk Management Plan.					
2. We used standard tools and techniques for risk identification and analysis.					
3. We followed a standard process to develop risk response plans.					
4. We used a standard amount for contingency allowances, should identified risks occur.					
5. We used a standard risk repository for data on risk management activities.					
Efficiency					
1. Our risk identification was detailed, and with our response plans, workarounds were not required.					
2. We did not need to update the Project Management Plan to respond to specific risks.					
3. During risk monitoring, our project assumptions remained valid.					
4. We did not have to perform additional risk response planning during the project to control new risks.					
5. We did not have any residual or secondary risks based on the response planning process.					
PEOPLE ISSUES					
Team					
Process					
1. Team members signed a team charter to indicate their commitment to it throughout the project.					
2. Team members collectively planned the project work and established standards for decision making.					
3. Team members regularly reviewed team progress against commitments.					
4. Team members established objective performance criteria for use in both team and individual performance evaluations.					
5. Team members worked to promote collaborative leadership.					

	1	2	3	4	5
Compliance					
1. We followed a standard format to develop a team charter.					
2. We followed a standard format to prepare a Responsibility Assignment Matrix.					
3. We followed a standard format to prepare a team directory with information that could be accessed by any team member at any time.					
4. We followed a standard format to establish a team-based reward and recognition system.					
5. We followed a standard process to assign people to the project team and to reassign them when their work was completed.					
Efficiency					
1. The team did not need to escalate conflicts and problems to higher level managers for resolution.					
2. Duplication of work was not an issue because team members had confidence in the ability of others on the team to complete their assigned tasks on time.					
3. Team meetings were considered productive and useful ways to spend time.					
4. Because information was shared among the team members, people on the team were able to discuss different perspectives on issues and seek innovative ways to accomplish the project's objectives.					
5. There were no interpersonal or other issues that prevented the team from working together effectively.					
Client					
Process					
1. Members of the client's organization were considered active participants throughout the project.					
2. Members of the client's organization and the project team engaged in joint planning, which minimized misunderstandings regarding expectations as to the project's scope.					
3. The project team emphasized and facilitated proactive collaboration with clients.					
4. The team worked to build client confidence in the company.					
5. The team worked to position itself with the client, both vertically and horizontally, in the organization.					

	1	2	3	4	5
Compliance					
1. The team worked to ensure that it followed the client's applicable standards throughout the project.					
2. The team addressed project progress with the client through formal project reviews that were held on a regularly scheduled basis.					
3. We followed a standard approach to foster client collaboration with the project team.					
4. The team followed principles of customer relationship management throughout the project.					
5. The team followed a methodology that incorporated innovations into its processes and tools to assist in achieving a customer-oriented solution.					
Efficiency					
1. The client's requirements did not change significantly during the course of the project because of the close working relationship between the client and the team during requirements definition.					
2. The client did not need extensive training in product use once it was delivered.					
3. Client dissatisfaction was minimal because the team worked to uncover and correct problem areas.					
4. The team obtained client feedback as deliverables were completed to minimize the need for rework and to support formal project acceptance.					
5. The team provided members of the client's organization with online access to the project management information system.					
Vendor					
Process					
1. Members of vendors' organizations were considered active project participants.					
2. The project team established a clear definition of roles and responsibilities of vendors.					
3. The project team documented commitments of both parties with vendors after contract award.					
4. The project team updated vendor records to reflect final results.					

	1	2	3	4	5
5. The team ensured that vendors were paid promptly upon submission of invoices in accordance with contract terms and conditions.					
Compliance					
1. A standard process was followed for issue resolution, including escalation of problems.					
2. Standard payment terms were defined that showed a specific link between vendor progress and compensation paid.					
3. Standard evaluation criteria were used in progress reviews.					
4. The team addressed project progress with vendors through formal project reviews.					
5. The team followed a standard approach to foster vendor collaboration with the project team.					
Efficiency					
1. The project team established mutual goals and objectives with vendors to promote clarity and to avoid the need for later scope changes.					
2. The project team shared risks with vendors.					
3. The project team established a partnering relationship with vendors to minimize possible issues and contested changes.					
4. The team provided online access to the project management information system to members of vendors' organizations.					
5. The project team used procurement audits as a way to identify lessons learned, both successes and failures.					
Communication					
Process					
1. Team members encouraged the expression of diverse points of view when communicating with others on the team.					
2. Team members demonstrated professional skills, behaviors, and attitudes in communicating with others.					
3. Team members valued feedback received from others in terms of working relationships.					
4. Team members worked to make it easy for others to disclose information, share ideas, and openly discuss problems and concerns.					
5. Team members involved others in problem solving and issue resolution.					

	1	2	3	4	5
Compliance					
1. Team members followed processes established for interpersonal communication within the team and with other stakeholders.					
2. Team members shared information appropriately within the professional community.					
3. Team members ensured that project confidentiality requirements were maintained.					
4. Team members prepared for project meetings, did not dominate meetings, and followed established guidelines to ensure that meetings were productive.					
5. Team members ensured that intellectual property issues were not compromised.					
Efficiency					
1. Team members recognized the most important information and communicated it to others effectively, concisely, and clearly.					
2. Team members recognized when to use formal communication channels with project stakeholders and when informal communication channels were preferred.					
3. Team members strived to display openness and flexibility in communications dealing with alternatives and problem solving.					
4. Team members focused on issues and not personalities.					
5. Team members requested information from others to complete assigned tasks efficiently.					

INSTRUMENT 4–J

Customer Satisfaction

Use this index as a baseline upon which to improve the success of future projects based on customer feedback. The overall customer satisfaction index is the average of the scores for each question below.

1—Never
2—Rarely
3—Sometimes
4—Often
5—Always

Question	1	2	3	4	5
1. Did the project's product or delivered service meet customer requirements?					
2. Was the project delivered as expected on time?					
3. Were intermediate milestone dates met as planned?					
4. Were there changes in scope that resulted in a change in the delivery date?					
5. Were there changes in scope that resulted in a change in the price?					
6. Were there changes in scope that resulted in a change in product quality?					
7. Were regular reports regarding the progress of the project prepared and distributed?					
8. Was it possible to request additional information concerning the project at any time?					
9. Were customer project reviews held on a regular basis during the project?					
10. To what extent will the end price of the project affect decisions to work with this supplier in the future?					
11. Was it easy to contact the Project Manager or another member of the project team when questions arose?					
12. Throughout the project, did the project team regularly request feedback on its progress?					

Question	1	2	3	4	5
13. Did a collaborative environment exist with the project team?					
14. Did the project team consistently act in a manner that demonstrated professional responsibility in their activities?					
15. Did the project team generally express a forward-looking view in terms of managing project resources while anticipating uncertainties?					
16. Did the atmosphere on the team encouarage a free-flowing exchange of information during the project?					
17. Was there a shared vision concerning the project based on a common purpose, mutual ownership, and collective commitment?					
18. Was there a common understanding of the priorities of the work to be done?					
19. Was identifying and managing project risks a joint responsibility?					
20. Was customer satisfaction the project team's ultimate goal?					
21. Did the project team espouse the customer's definition of quality?					
22. Did members of the project team continuously work to translate customer needs and expectations into a verifiable set of requirements that served as the basis for the project's scope?					
23. Did a customer representative serve on the project's Change Control Board?					
24. Were changes that affected the end product of the project communicated?					
25. Was any unsolicited customer feedback used by the project team for process improvements?					
26. Did the project team focus primarily on meeting the customer's specific requirements as a measure of its success?					
27. Did the project team focus on controlling requirements as the first step toward schedule and cost control?					
28. Was there a mutual understanding of the project's requirements?					
29. Did the project team work to provide a sense of confidence about its company?					
30. In working with the project team, did team members suggest other ideas that might help in meeting emerging needs outside the immediate project?					

CHAPTER 5

Implementing a Metrics Program

The goals of a metrics system can vary in urgency, as determined by the strategic objectives of the organization (see Figure 5–1). The sophistication of the metrics system—and its funding—likewise can vary depending on whether the organization's overall goals are to improve project-by-project performance, divisional project performance, enterprise project performance, or enterprise project management maturity. (Rad and Levin 2002)

If the goals are division-specific, then the organization might highlight the current maturity rating of the division together with the desired rating. Improvement objectives would then be stated either as an incremental advancement or as a collective achievement goal. Thus, the goal might be, independent of current status, to improve performance in all project management process areas by one maturity level following a staged model. Alternatively, the goal might be to attain a certain level (e.g., Level 4) in project performance on all projects. If the metrics goals are project-specific, then the goals might be tied either to project success ratings or to overruns in cost and schedule.

Because so many aspects of a project can be measured, the opportunities can be overwhelming. In some organizations, measuring the values of the indices of the model can become an end unto itself. To avoid this, metrics procedures should not be "check-the-box" processes, because such simplistic reports usually exist to satisfy a perfunctory scheduled review or audit. Rather, a metrics system should be regarded as a tool to show a sustained organizational benefit achieved primarily because of a project management culture.

Metrics needs to be viewed not as one-time exercises, but as continuing initiatives toward enhanced productivity and effectiveness. Thus, the focus of using a metrics system is not to provide a quick fix for projects in trouble, but to establish the pathway for a journey to excellence.

To that end, sometimes it might be necessary to reexamine current metrics with specific applicability to projects. For example, indices such as

Figure 5-1
Goals of a Metrics System

Funding and Commitment

Set Corporate Standards

Achieve Higher Corporate Profits

Communicate the Importance of Project Management throughout the Organization

Have Competent, Productive Project Teams

Implement Standard Project Management Approaches

Finish this Project on Time/within Budget According to Specifications

Minimize Risks and Maximize Opportunities

profitability usually come too late for mid-course corrections and remedial actions. Therefore, financial and non-financial information should be integrated in a usable way. In planning a metrics program, it is important to identify the most important project and process management issues, select and define the corresponding metrics, and integrate these metrics incrementally into existing processes.

Sometimes metrics might be collected only to fulfill a corporate requirement to report on information on certain arbitrarily targeted dates or to meet a specific contractual reporting requirement. If the metrics system is not designed and implemented properly, the organization might not collect any data, might collect data but use only the portion that can be gleaned, or might collect data for a lot of metrics that have no valuable use. Each of these circumstances should be avoided.

Metrics must be well defined, and guidelines for their use must be fully accepted by those who will use them. The project management metrics program should be designed and implemented in such a way that project personnel will come to regard metrics as the basis for actions that support project management excellence and overall organizational improvements. Data provided by the metrics system can become the basis for informed analysis only when there is agreement on what is happening and what should be happening in projects.

With the help of a well-planned metrics system, project team members will come to recognize both the long-term benefits of metrics and the obstacles that could exist during the implementation of a metrics program. To facilitate successful implementation of a metrics system, communication about metrics initiatives must be direct, consistent, and widespread. The utility of a metrics system must be visibly communicated throughout the organization to establish commitment to sustaining the program. Whoever is responsible for the program should have strong communications skills and be able to balance the metrics program's needs with the participants' readiness to accept and embrace change.

Each person's involvement in the metrics program should be known and communicated. Every effort should be made to ensure that program implementation is not an organizational secret, as that status will breed notions of conspiracy, especially if the organization is undergoing downsizing, outsourcing, or reorganization.

Project professionals who have achieved project management certification will recognize the value of a well-crafted project management metrics system. However, there might be cases where some project personnel or other project stakeholders do not fully embrace the value of metrics. Ongoing training may be necessary to keep the metrics program in focus and on track.

Implementing a metrics program generally requires a cultural change within the organization to help project professionals overcome inherent resistance to monitoring project performance and to widespread reporting of organizational results. In such cases, the initial purpose of a metrics system might be simply to provide project professionals the tools to communicate the benefits of project management to senior executives and operational personnel. Moreover, time must be set aside for stakeholder meetings to discuss the added value that a metrics system brings to the organization. A number of briefings and workshops may be required before people throughout the organization recognize the purpose of the metrics system.

METRICS PROGRAM DESIGN

Implementation of a formalized metrics system must be treated just like any other project, perhaps even more so, to highlight the advantages of effective planning and monitoring. Thus, the steps associated with a project management process must be followed in implementing a metrics program. The metrics system design must include a detailed implementation plan with procedures and policies for using the results derived from the system. Moreover, the data from the metrics system must be fully incorporated into existing policies and procedures. (Instrument 5–A)

Clever data presentation and intricate analysis methods should not be the goal; often, they are not worth the effort (Lucero and Hall 2001). Rather, the primary objective should be to allow managers to derive information as early as possible. Thus, the results of the data collection process should be reported as soon as practicable, because data that are reported too late are essentially useless.

As part of planning the metrics system, the success criteria for the metrics system, and for project management, must be developed. In tangible terms, the metrics system's impact on the following must be identified: individual projects, programs, the project portfolio, morale improvement, and operational benefits.

Since a metrics system is a collection of relatively simple pieces of data from several facets of a project, care must be taken to ensure that the constituent indices and models of the system are directly related to the project attribute they are intended to characterize. To add utility to the indices, they could be packaged within a predictive model.

Predictive models can be mathematical or graphical in nature, depending on the organization. When considering complex environmental issues, models are far more likely to predict realistic project outcomes than any single metric. For example, the amount of money spent is only one facet of a project's progress. The resources used, the cost of those resources, and the number of deliverables completed provide a better picture of a project's progress. All models, even very sophisticated ones, are only partial representations of the reality they attempt to portray.

Quantitative data collected from the attributes of things or even people are usually assumed to be accurate and unbiased because they are expressed as precise numbers. However, many seemingly objective data are influenced by someone's subjective judgment. Designers of metrics systems should be mindful that project professionals will collect many data items that reflect some degree of subjective judgment. Parenthetically, it is hoped that this subjective judgment is fully in line with the guidelines of professional responsibility.

Consider the example where data on the number of design units that have passed an integration test are presumed to be precise numbers determined by the technical characteristics of the software under test. However, the number of tests conducted depends primarily on a team member's interpretation of the criteria used for the test. Changes to the integration test criteria could come from the team member's interpretation of the level of assembly, the size of the software components that are integrated for each test case, the number of inputs or conditions required for each test case, and the level of conditional stress during the test (such as concurrent tasking, shared memory availability, and process utilization) (Lucero and Hall 2001). Furthermore, qualitative indices will be affected not only by these issues, but also by the fact that their measurement is far more dependent on the judgment, viewpoint, and expertise of the examiner.

Planning for metrics systems, and using their specific metrics, require a determination, in realistic terms, of the status of the organization's environment. To characterize the organization's attitude toward change, a determination must be made as to whether the culture is project oriented or specialty driven. The key features of current practices will form the foundation and logic for how projects are selected, how they are managed, and the specific methodologies that will be used.

Current corporate practices also must be detailed in order to determine the extent to which there is tolerance for inaccurate project data and project overruns. Top management can provide insight into the current corporate and business functions of business units and the duties of personnel within those units. In addition, key knowledge areas must be identified, primarily because the operation of the metrics system, and its constituent indices, must match the company's strategic project management needs. Likewise, it is essential to involve the Project Management Office (PMO) in the process from the very beginning of the implementation phases, even if the metrics are not fully a part of the PMO's function.

Metrics should inspire confidence by virtue of repeatable accuracy and being rooted in valid assumptions, concepts, and calculations. Since the utility of each metric extends beyond the boundaries of a given project, collection and reporting of data should be part of the organization's policies.

When designing a metrics system, the goal should be to cover not only the project deliverables but also the entire enterprise. Collecting quantitative planning and progress data should not be limited to large projects; it should apply to all projects regardless of size and complexity. Naturally, the set of indices and models comprising the metrics system will vary somewhat depending on the size and nature of the project.

It is advisable to develop common definitions for key project activities and milestones. Such uniformity facilitates the development of a sophisticated Work Breakdown Structure (WBS) (based on templates from past projects), a typical WBS Dictionary, an organizational Resource Breakdown Structure (RBS), and a set of standard report templates. High-level summary reports and cross-functional reports must include detailed data on conflicts between projects arising from overallocation of resources.

If formalized metrics are not used consistently throughout the organization, they will not be employed beyond the span of the project for which they were developed. Metrics, when using standard and consistent scales organizationwide, are powerful tools for informing stakeholders of progress in meeting project objectives. They gain further utility when used to compare like items across multiple projects, as they form a logical basis for suggesting needed changes in ongoing efforts. Unfortunately, in organizations that have not reached Level 2 or Level 3 of a staged maturity scale, it is the project manager who establishes the methods for monitoring project status, and the luxury of comparing data across projects is not available.

Goldratt (1990) notes, "Tell me how you measure me, and I will tell you how I will behave. If you measure me in an illogical way, do not complain about illogical behavior" (26). This statement implies that the way measurements are taken may cause people in the organization, or the organization as a whole, to behave in a given manner. Goldratt further warns: "Change my measurements to new ones that I don't fully comprehend and then nobody knows how I will behave, not even me" (88). Thus, as organizational processes for the new suite of metrics are being developed, earlier data collection processes must be reviewed in light of their verified utility to projects.

It is useful to identify key pieces of information that are not included in the current system in order to devise means of incorporating them into future versions. Finally, it is helpful if the implementation team validates and improves planned processes before collecting metrics data. Even then, it might be two years or more until the capture and analysis of data yield useful results.

ATTRIBUTES OF MODELS AND INDICES

The main purpose of using a single metric, or a suite of metrics as part of a comprehensive model, must be decided before collecting the related data. Definitions of each index, and eventually of each model, should begin with a precise description of the project management issue that is to be measured. The direct or indirect linkage among the metric, the project goals, and the organizational goals must be highlighted (see Figure 5–2).

The thresholds of the metric that define normalcy (i.e., the range of data that includes normal behavior) should be clearly defined. Beyond that,

Figure 5-2
Characteristics of a Metric

- The attribute to be measured
- The measurement process
- The measurement frequency
- Significance of the metric
  - To this project
  - To the enterprise
  - To future projects
- Thresholds
  - Contingency plan if the threshold is reached

one threshold should define a point considered excessive, where remedial measures must be put in place to bring the project back on course. Another threshold should define exemplary performance, attainment of which should be noted, applauded, and replicated across the organization.

Celebratory thresholds include early delivery, notable cost underrun, or unusual technical quality of the deliverable. On the other hand, danger thresholds should signal an unacceptable cost overrun, late delivery, and a seriously defective project product. Finally, each time a new metric is introduced, the following information should be detailed and explained fully: data collection process, data collection frequency, results dissemination process, and corresponding feedback policies.

In addition to a list of values that describe normal performance, exceptional performance, and unacceptable performance, the definition of each index must include a corresponding plan of action for cases where the threshold of tolerance for that index has been breached. For example, it might be specified that cost performance will be rated as superb if there is an underrun of 10% or more. Such performance should be applauded, with proper recognition to the project manager and team members.

On the other hand, cost performance might be rated as unacceptable if there is an overrun of 150% or more. When this threshold is breached, organizational project recovery measures must be put in place to bring the project back on a stable track. To extend this concept further, it is important to determine how many current projects map onto this range of acceptability and how many should map onto this range once the metrics system is fully in place.

Project managers should know which index has the most impact on their project's performance monitoring. Some attributes that are easy to measure might not be particularly important. Attributes that are more difficult to measure might be more important. Therefore, metrics should be assigned a priority ranking, and all metrics should not be treated equally.

It is useful if individual metrics, or the metrics system as a whole, have predictive capabilities. Thus, the metrics system can become a predictive tool and an early warning system for the project's mal-performance, and for those cases where there is a mismatch between the deliverable and market needs.

At a minimum, the index should have the capability to measure a specific performance attribute. The metric also should have features that can be integrated with other metrics in order to synthesize overall project performance or even overall enterprise performance. The following issues should be considered:

- *Clarity:* Can everyone understand what is being measured, how data are collected, and how the results should be interpreted?

- *Repeatability:* Can someone else perform the same measurement and get the same result?

- *Traceability:* Are the origins of the data identified in terms of sequence, activity, status, environment, and tools used?

- *Precision:* To what degree of accuracy does the metric express the item being measured?

Furthermore, a metric system should respond to the following questions for each index:

- What is the attribute or subject of the metric?

- Is the right attribute being measured?

- How often is the measurement performed?

- What are the thresholds of the metric?

- Who are the people who need to be informed of a specific metric's values?

- How can we motivate the team with this metric?

SCHEDULE OF IMPLEMENTATION

The metrics system should be designed specifically with an eye toward the collection of data for project and enterprise success factors. The project metrics program might choose to begin its implementation with a focus on things attributes of only one project. Then, building on the success of this mini-implementation, data collection and reporting can be extended to people attributes of the project, and eventually to things-people attributes of more than one project (see Figure 5–3).

Ultimately, the metrics program can be expanded to include attributes of the enterprise that encompass all projects. Further, by conducting periodic assessments, the metrics system can benchmark the organization's current maturity level to the target maturity level and to industry standards of best practices. These interim assessments will chart a course for the full sophistication of the organization by identifying areas that are in need of improvement and by demonstrating the effectiveness of the metrics system in achieving the ultimate goal.

During the early stages of metrics system implementation, specific expectations must be defined for the organization concerning metrics and how they will be used. The plan must specify incremental progress milestones, such as first visible impact, intermediate significant achievements, and completion target. To reap the full benefits of successful implementation

---

Figure 5-3
Metrics Suite

People

Competency
- Teamwork
- Motivation
- Morale
- Utilization
- Knowledge Management

Enterprise

Project Category
- Strategic Alignment
- Financial Measures
- Client Impact
- Potential Revenues
- Potential Benefits
- Operational Impact
- Growth Impact
- Market Risk

Things
- Cost
- Delivery Date
- Project Risk
- Deliverable Attributes
- Deliverable Quality

of a metrics system, it is often useful to implement the system in stages, because even with sizeable investments, it will take several years before sustained improvements are observable in the organization's project performance.

The overall process includes the following steps:

- *Step 1: Establish the Vision and Strategy.* The metrics system can be an add-on to existing methods of project management monitoring and forecasting in an organization, or it can be new and revised indices for organizational business attributes and project management. To define the metrics system strategy, the organization's key factors for success, competitors' programs and priorities, the organization's strengths and weaknesses in light of the competition, and likely external changes must be assessed.

- *Step 2: Prepare an Execution Plan.* This plan should include a transition plan for the metrics system. The plan should detail organizational interfaces because barriers between organizational units need to be eliminated to facilitate knowledge management. The plan should guide the implementation of the metrics system, eliminate or reduce uncertainty in roles and responsibilities, document assumptions and constraints, provide a basis for monitoring and controlling the metrics system implementation, and facilitate communication with stakeholders.

- *Step 3: Implement the System.* The metrics system's initial focus should be on areas involving the greatest impediments to improved project results. Since project management processes and practices will need to be modified, staff from all stakeholder organizations should actively participate in the implementation. Greater project personnel involvement will foster greater commitment, increased sharing of lessons learned, improved coordination, and early warning of problems. The implementation team must conduct reviews of the metrics system's effectiveness in the light of continuous improvement initiatives. Then, the implementation team must communicate the results and progress to all stakeholders.

When implementing a new metrics system, or simply compiling and formalizing an existing one, it is important to strike a balance between the organizational culture and the best practices of project management. Metrics can serve as a facilitator of continuous improvement efforts because they provide an unbiased indication of the current status and a clear description of the desired future. (Instrument 5-B)

Metrics Collection Checklist

Use this instrument to document the rationale for selecting a metric. This instrument should be reviewed and enhanced regularly, as should the corresponding records of each metric.

✓ What is the purpose of the metric?
✓ What best describes the metric?
✓ Where should the metric be used?
✓ Where should the metric not be used?
✓ Who will collect the data?
✓ Who will verify the data?
✓ How should the data be collected?
✓ How often should the data be collected?
✓ How should the data be analyzed?
✓ Who should analyze the data?
✓ What is considered a normal value?
✓ What is the lower threshold?
✓ What is the upper threshold?

INSTRUMENT 5–B

Metrics Implementation Checklist

Use this instrument as a permanent record for the selection and use of a given metric. This form should be reviewed regularly to identify enhancement opportunities.

✓ State the purpose of each metric.
✓ Describe the benefits of collecting each metric to the enterprise.
✓ Determine whether there are any special considerations relevant to the metric.
✓ Determine whether the metric is required to be collected on every project, or whether the Project Manager has flexibility in terms of collecting and reporting the needed data.
✓ Determine who is responsible for collecting the required data.
✓ Determine whether those responsible for data collection will require any special training.
✓ State the time in which the metric is to be collected.
✓ Describe the analysis process associated with the metric.
✓ Describe how results from the metric's data collection are to be used.
✓ Determine how the results will be integrated with the other metrics in the system.
✓ Determine the ease of interpreting the results of each metric.
✓ Determine the usefulness of the results of each metric.
✓ Assess the cost of implementing each metric in the system.
✓ Determine if different metrics are needed for different phases of the project life cycle.

References

Alarcon, L.F., and D.B. Ashley. 1992. *Project performance modeling: A methodology for evaluating project execution strategies*. Source document 80. Austin: The University of Texas at Austin, The Construction Industry Institute.

Arttto, K.A., P.H. Dietrich, and T. Ikonen. 2002. Industry models of project portfolio management and their development. *Proceedings of PMI research conference 2002*. Newtown Square: Project Management Institute.

Augustine, T., and C. Schroeder. 1999. An effective metrics process model. *CrossTalk* 12, no. 6 (June): 4–7.

Baker, N.R. 1974. R&D project selection models: An assessment. *IEEE Transactions on Engineering Management* 21: 165–171.

Bard, J.F., R. Balachandra, and P.E. Kaufmann. 1988. An interactive approach to R&D selection and termination. *IEEE Transactions on Engineering Management* 35: 139–146

Boyatzis, R.E. 1982. *The competent manager: A model for effective performance*. New York: John Wiley & Sons.

Cleland, D., and L. Ireland. 2002. *Project management: Strategic design and implementation*. 4th ed. New York: McGraw-Hill Construction Division.

Cooper, R.G., E.J. Scott, and E.J. Kleinschmidt. 2001. *Portfolio management for new products*. Cambridge: Perseus Publishing.

Crawford, J.K. 2002. *The strategic project office: A guide to improving organizational performance*. New York: Marcell Dekker.

Crawford, J.K., and J.S. Pennypacker. 2000. The value of project management. *Project Management Institute 2000 symposium proceedings*. Newtown Square: Project Management Institute.

Cunningham, J., G. Ryan, and V. David. 2002. Soft skills, hard numbers. *PM Network* 16, no. 6: 60–63.

Day, G.S. 1977. Diagnosing the product portfolio. *Journal of Marketing* 41, no. 2: 29–38.

Day, G.S. 1986. *Analysis for strategic marketing decisions*. St. Paul: West Publishing.

Dekkers, C.A. 1999. It is the people who count in measurement: The truth about measurement myths. *CrossTalk* 12, no. 6 (June): 12–14.

Dekkers, C.A. 2003. Combat resistance to software measurement by targeting management expectations. *CrossTalk* 16, no. 7 (July): 25–27.

Dixon, C. 2000. Curriculum helps organizations establish successful measurement systems. *News@SEI* 3, no. 1: 10–11.

Drucker, P. 2000. Knowledge work. *Executive Excellence* (April): 11–12.

Dye, L.D., and J.S. Pennypacker, eds. 1999. *Project portfolio management: Selecting and prioritizing projects for competitive advantage.* Havertown: Center for Business Practices.

Dymond, K.M. 1995. *A guide to the CMM.* Annapolis: Process Inc.

Edvinsson, L., and M.S. Malone. 1997. *Intellectual capital: Realizing your company's true value by finding its hidden roots.* New York: Harper Business.

Florac, W.A., R.E. Park, and A.D. Carleton. 1997. *Practical software measurement: Measuring for process management and improvement.* Pittsburgh: Software Engineering Institute.

Frame, J.D. 1999. *Project management competence: Building key skills for individuals, teams, and organizations.* San Francisco: Jossey-Bass Publishers.

Freeman, M., and P. Beale. 1992. Measuring project success. *Project Management Journal* 23, no. 1: 8–17.

Gates, M. 1976. Bidding model—A Monte Carlo experiment. *ASCE Journal of the Construction Division* 102, no. 4: 669–80.

Gates, M. 1978. Review of existing and advanced construction estimating techniques. *Proceeding of the 1978 conference on construction estimating and cost control methods.* New York: ASCE Construction Division.

Geaney, M.M., and J. Engel. 1996. Core competencies for project managers. *27th annual symposium.* Sylva, NC: Project Management Institute.

Goldenson, D.R., J. Jarzombek, and T. Rout. 2003. Measurement and analysis in capability maturity model integration models and software process improvement. *CrossTalk* 16, no. 7 (July): 20–23.

Goldratt, E. 1990. *The haystack syndrome.* Croton-on-Hudson: North River Press.

Grady, R.B. 1992. *Practical software metrics for project management and process management.* Englewood Cliffs: Prentice Hall.

Helping Siemens achieve higher project success rates. http://www.esi-intl.com/public/esiadvantage/siemens.asp. Site visited November 2002.

Jarzombek, J. 1999. The need for a measurement and analysis process: Focusing on guidance for process improvement. *CrossTalk* 12, no. 6 (June): 2.

Jones, C. 2003. Making measurement work. *CrossTalk* 16, no.1 (January): 15–19.

Kaplan, R.S., and D.P. Norton. 1992. The balanced scorecard—Measures that drive performance. *Harvard Business Review* (January–February): 71–79.

Knutson, J. 1999. From making sense to making cents: Measuring project management ROI—Part 1. *PM Network* (January): 25–27.

Levin, G. 1998. The changing nature of the project audit: No longer a "gotcha game." In *Proceedings of the 29th annual Project Management Institute 1998 seminars & symposium*. Sylva, NC: Project Management Institute.

Levin, G. 1999. Aspiring to peak performance: A personal improvement model for project management professionals. In *Proceedings of the 30th annual Project Management Institute 1999 seminars & symposium*. Sylva, NC: Project Management Institute.

Levin, G., G. Hill, P. DeFilippis, J. L. Ward, and P. Shaltry. D. Richards, ed. 1999. *Project framework: A project management maturity model*. Arlington: ESI International.

Lonnqvist, A., and P. Mettanen. 2002. Criteria of sound intellectual capital measures. In *Proceedings of the 2nd international workshop of performance measures: Performance measures for increased competitiveness*. IFIP WG5.7, pp. 147–157.

Lucero, D.S., and F. Hall. 2001. The best measurement tool is your telephone. *CrossTalk* 14, no. 3 (March): 15–18.

Lynch, R.L., and K. Cross. 1995. *Measure up! Yardsticks for continuous improvement*. 2d ed. Cambridge: Blackwell Publishers.

McClelland, D. 1961. *The achieving society*. New York: The Free Press.

McGregor, D. 1960. *The human side of enterprise*. New York: McGraw-Hill.

Miller, R., and G. Wurzburg. 1995. Investing in human capital. *OECD Observer* 193 (April–May): 16–20.

Natwick, G. 2003. Integrated metrics for CMMI and SW-CMM. *CrossTalk* 16, no. 5 (May): 4–7.

Neely, A. 1998. *Measuring business performance: Why, what and how?* London: Profile Books Ltd.

Neely, A., and C. Adams. 2001. Perspectives on performance: The performance prism. *Journal of Cost Management*, 15, Issue 1, p. 7–15.

Neely, A., J. Mills, M. Gregory, H. Richards, K. Platts, and M. Bourne. 1996. *Getting the measure of your business*. London: Findlay.

Neuendorf, S. 2002. *Project measurement*. Vienna, VA: Management Concepts.

O'Hara, S., and G. Levin. 2000. Using metrics to demonstrate the value of project management. In *Proceedings of the 31st annual Project Management Institute 2000 seminars & symposium*. Sylva, NC: Project Management Institute.

Okkonen, J. 2002. Performance measurement in a virtual environment. Paper presented at 2nd International Workshop of the IFIP, Hanover, June 6.

Okkonen, J., V. Pirttimaki, M. Hannula, and A. Lonnqvist. 2002. Triangle of business intelligence, performance measurement and knowledge measurement. Paper presented at the Annual Conference on Innovative Research in Management, Stockholm, Sweden, May 9–11, 2002.

Pennypacker, J.S., and K.P. Grant. 2003. Project management maturity: An industry benchmark. *Project Management Journal* 34, no.1: 4–11.

Perkins, T.K. 2001. The nine-step metrics program. *CrossTalk* 14, no. 2 (February): 16–18.

Peters, T. 1991. *Thriving on chaos: Handbook for a management revolution.* First Harper Perennial edition. New York: HarperCollins.

Phillips, J.J., T.W. Bothell, and G.L. Snead. 2002. *The project management scorecard: Measuring the success of project management.* Woburn: Butterworth Heinmann.

Project Management Institute. 2004. *A guide to the project management body of knowledge.* 3d ed. Newtown Square, PA: Project Management Institute.

Rad, P.F. 2002. *Project estimating and cost management.* Vienna, VA: Management Concepts.

Rad, P.F., and G. Levin. 2002. *Advanced project management office.* Boca Raton: CRC Press.

Rad, P.F., and G. Levin. 2003. *Achieving success through virtual teams.* Boca Raton: J. Ross Publishing.

Sanvido, V., F. Grobler, K. Parfitt, and M. Guvenis. 1992. Critical success factors for construction projects. *ASCE Journal of Construction Engineering and Management* 118, no. 1: 94–111.

Storeygard, R. 1995. Growing the professional project leader. Paper presented at Project Management Institute 26th Annual Seminar/Symposium, New Orleans, October 16–18. Sylva, NC: Project Management Institute.

Thamhain, H.J. 1996. Best practices for controlling technology-based projects. *Project Management Journal* (December): 37–48.

Ward, L. 2002. Executive session. *ESI Horizons* 4, no. 5: 2–4.

Wheelwright, S., and K. Clark. 1994. Revolutionizing product development. *Harvard Business Review* 72, 3, May–June 1994, 94–97.

Index